THE SONG OF SONGS

AND

LAMENTATIONS

THE SONG OF SONGS

AND

LAMENTATIONS

A Study, Modern Translation and Commentary

by

R O B E R T   G O R D I S

REVISED AND AUGMENTED EDITION.

KTAV PUBLISHING HOUSE, INC
NEW YORK

Library of Congress Cataloging in Publication Data

Gordis, Robert, 1908-
  The Song of songs and Lamentations.

  A revision, with new material, of the author's The
Song of songs (1954) and of A commentary on the text
of Lamentations (1958).
  Includes bibliographies.
  1. Bible. O.T. Song of Solomon—Commentaries. 2.
Bible. O.T. Lamentations—Commentaries. I. Bible. O.T.
Song of Solomon. English. Gordis. 1974. II. Bible. O.T.
Lamentations. English. Gordis. 1974. III. Title.
BS1485.3.G64   223'.9'066   74-4194
ISBN 0-87068-256-3

MANUFACTURED IN THE UNITED STATES OF AMERICA

TABLE OF CONTENTS
The Song of Songs

Lamentations

THE SONG OF SONGS

FOREWORD

Books have their own peculiar destinies, a Latin proverb informs us. Every student of human nature knows how wide are the fluctuations in fashion and interest affecting men's attitudes toward works of literature, art, and music.

In this regard, the *Song of Songs* is a shining exception. For over twenty centuries it has retained its appeal to men's hearts. To be sure, the book has been variously interpreted during its long career. Earlier ages, perhaps more devout than our own, read the *Song of Songs* as an allegory and saw in it an expression of the ideal relationship of love subsisting between God and man. However, as the full scope and character of Biblical literature became evident, this traditional view, in spite of its inherent charm and religious significance, became less and less popular. Only a few scholars have retained this position today. They have sought to save the theory by maintaining that the Scriptures are to be interpreted on several levels simultaneously, so that both the literal and the allegorical interpretation of the *Song of Songs* are to be regarded as valid.

By and large, the allegorical theory has been abandoned today. Within the last few decades, however, the allegorical view favored by tradition has been revived, though in a special, highly untraditional form. Some modern scholars have sought to interpret the *Song* as the ritual of a pagan fertility-cult. That this effort cannot be pronounced a success is, I believe, demonstrated in this study.

Today it is generally recognized that the book is to be understood literally, its theme being human love, a view which was, indeed, adumbrated in ancient times. Yet even now there is no unanimity with regard to the meaning and character of the book. Some scholars treat the book as a drama, with either two or three characters. This theory is still frequently encountered in popular treatments of the *Song,* but it, too, I believe, cannot sustain critical examination.

As the results of archaeological and literary research continue to mount, it becomes increasingly clear that the *Song* cannot be understood in isolation, however splendid and exalted. The life and faith of ancient Israel are, on the one hand, part of the culture-pattern of the ancient Near East and, on the other, markedly distinct from it. Unless both elements of this ambivalent yet perfectly natural relationship are fully taken into account, we obtain a distorted picture of reality. Only when the Bible is set within the larger framework of the Fertile Crescent can we gain an adequate appreciation both of its place in the world from which it emerged and of its unique character. For the Bible is both the record of God's revelation to man and of man's aspiration toward the Divine.

When the *Song of Songs* is studied without preconceived notions, it emerges as a superb lyrical anthology, containing songs of love and nature, of courtship and marriage, all of which revel in the physical aspects of love and reveal its spiritual character. The two Greek terms, *eros,* "carnal love," and *agape, "caritas,* spiritual love," reflect a dichotomy that has entered into classical Christian theology. The classical Hebrew outlook, on the contrary, finds it entirely proper to apply the same root, *'ahabah,* to all aspects of love. The ideal relationship of man to God, "You shall love the Lord your God" (Deut. 6:5), the love of one's fellow man, "You shall love your neighbor as yourself" (Lev. 19:18), "You shall love him (the stranger) as yourself" (Lev. 19:34), and the love of man and woman. "How fair and how pleasant you are, O love, with its delights!" (Song of Songs 7:7)—all are expressed in the Bible by the same Hebrew word.

This healthy-minded attitude toward life and love undoubtedly played an important role, even if subconsciously, in the acceptance of the *Song of Songs* into the canon of Scripture. For, as is demonstrated in the body of this book, the Rabbis were well aware of the literal interpretation of the book as dealing with human love.

Other factors contributed to the same result. References to Solomon in the text, which led to the assumption that he was the author of the book, undoubtedly played an important part. Yet there were many Jewish writings attributed to Biblical worthies of greater piety than Solomon, including at least one deeply religious book ascribed to the king himself, *The Wisdom of Solomon,* that were never accepted into the Hebrew canon and remained in the Apocrypha. The allegorical interpretation of the *Song* is unquestionably another central element in the process of its canonization. Yet it is by no means clear which is cause and which is effect—whether the acceptance of the book into the corpus of Scripture led to the allegorizing of its contents, or whether the allegorical interpretation made possible its admission into the canon. Conceivably both processes went on simultaneously. That the Rabbis rejected the literal view and canonized the book was undoubtedly due, in no small measure, to its innate charm and appeal.

Nor was this all. On the profoundest level, Rabbinic Judaism saw in love, the most intimate of human relationships, not merely a legitimate activity, but a Divine imperative, the fulfillment of the will of God. Thus it was possible for a rabbinic student, who was found hiding in his master's bedchamber and observing his teacher's intimate behavior, to declare, "This, too, is Torah, and I wish to learn" (B. Berakhot 62a).

The acceptance of the *Song of Songs* as sacred is entirely in consonance with the basic Hebrew conception of the organic unity of the human person. The Bible and the Talmud regarded body and soul, flesh and spirit, not as antagonistic elements, but as complementing and fulfilling each other.

John MacMurray has written that "the Hebrew form of thought rebels against the very idea of a distinction between the secular and the religious aspects of life." This acute observation does not go far enough. Classical Hebrew thought in its greatest creative eras, embodied basically in the Bible and the Talmud, did not rebel against the dichotomy; it never recognized its existence.

Even in the Middle Ages, when asceticism gained ground in the Western World, the classical Jewish attitude did not completely disappear. Whether or not the medieval work *Iggeret Hakodeš* is authentically that of the great legist, commentator, and mystic, Moses Nahmanides (1194-1270), it expresses this viewpoint with clarity and vigor: "We who are the descendants of those who received the sacred Torah believe that God, blessed be He, created everything as His wisdom dictated, and He created nothing containing obscenity or ugliness *(genai o kiyyur)*. For if we were to say that intercourse *(ha-hibbur)* is obscene, it would follow that the sexual organs are obscene. . . . And how could God, blessed be He, create something containing a blemish or obscenity, or a defect? For we would then find that His deeds are not perfect, though Moses, the greatest of the prophets, proclaims and says, 'The Rock, whose work is perfect' (Deuteronomy 32:4). However, the fact is, as it is said, that 'God is pure-eyed, so that He sees no evil' (Habakkuk 1:13). Before Him there is neither degradation nor obscenity; He created man and woman, fashioning all their organs and setting them in their proper function. with nothing obscene in them." (Hayyim Dov Chavel, *Kitbhei Rabbenu Moshe ben Nahman,* Jerusalem, 5724 = 1964, II, p. 323; translation mine). For all the vast differences in the idiom employed, the Jewish sages would have understood John Donne's words, "Love's mysteries in souls do grow, but yet the body is his book."

A careful study of the *Song of Songs,* its vocabulary, its syntax, its prosody, the geographical locales mentioned in the text, and its handful of national references, makes it clear that it is an anthology emanating from at least five centuries' of Hebrew history, from the days of Solomon to the Persian period. The *Song* thus constitutes a parallel, though of considerably smaller compass, to the *Book of Psalms,* which is a florilegium of man's yearning and love for God. If the two basic imperatives of religion are the love of God and the love of man, the *Song of Songs,* no less than the *Book of Psalms,* deserves its place in Scripture.

A word on the scope of the present work on the *Song of Songs* is in order. The Introduction traces the history of the interpretation of the *Song* and presents the conclusions as to the nature and content of the book which have commended themselves to me on the basis of long study. The technical question of date is difficult to establish in a lyrical work, but fortunately is not basic to its appreciation. On the other hand, it is essential to determine the extent and meaning of each component song in the collection, besides indicating the significance of the work as a whole. For the *Song* is an integral element in the world-view of ancient Israel, to which modern men are justly turning in increasing measure. All these aspects are treated briefly in the Introduction. A fresh Translation of the Hebrew text with a prefatory comment on each song then follows, which, it is hoped, will make the book both intelligible and attractive to the general, non-technical reader. This version is followed by the philological and textual Commentary, which sets forth the grounds for the various positions adopted in the Translation.

From this summary, the reader may recognize that the present study follows the general pattern of the author's previous works, on Ecclesiastes *(Koheleth—The Man and His World,* New York, 1951, 1955, 1968) and on Job *(The Book of God and Man—A Study of Job,* Chicago, 1965, 1966, and *The Book of Job—A Commentary and Translation* (now in process of publication).

While not attempting to exhaust the exegetical literature, I have tried to set forth alternative views which possess merit or interest, particularly on difficult passages. For each student can scarcely hope to do more than make a slight advance in the interpretation of a Biblical book— but this is reward enough. To disregard the work of others is not only morally indefensible; it is a grave disservice to the cause of truth.

At the farthest possible remove from the *Song of Songs* is another gem in the Biblical diadem, the *Book of Lamentations.* The dominant mood of the *Song of Songs* is joy—its sorrows are those of love yearning for fulfillment. It gives matchless expression to the love-experience of individual men and women; the national note is all but absent, and group concerns are totally lacking.

On the other hand, the *Book of Lamentations,* as its name indicates, is a collection of elegies composed after the capture of Jerusalem at the hands of the Babylonians in 587 B. C. E. It laments the burning of the Temple and the cessation of the priestly cult, the exile of the king and the silencing of prophecy, the devastation of the land and the hopelessness of the future—all of which are accepted as God's punishment upon a sinful people. The poignant cries of misery are punctuated by flashes of indignation at the rejoicing of Israel's foes and by passionate pleas for Divine favor and national restoration.

Of the five elegies, only one, chapter 3, which may well be called "The Job Lament," agonizes over the suffering of the individual. Yet here, too, the theme is closely interwoven with the tragedy of the nation as a whole, through the fundamental Biblical concept of "fluid personality," which is discussed in the special Introduction to chapter 3.

Thus these two small books, the *Song of Songs* and *Lamentations,* one expressing the happiness of the individual, the other the suffering of the nation, span the entire gamut of human emotion, from the heights of joy to the depths of grief. Both books, called *Megillot,* "Scrolls," in the Jewish tradition, are read publicly in the synagogue, the *Song of Songs* on the feast of Passover, and the *Book of Lamentations* on the Fast of Tisha B'ab. By the variety of their contents and the beauty of their form, both books exemplify the incredible richness of the Bible which has made it the Book of Books.

The elegies that have entered the *Book of Lamentations* were composed twenty-five hundred years ago. This Foreword is being written on the twenty-fifth anniversary of the founding of the State of Israel. There is a causal and not merely a coincidental relation between these two events. For twenty-five centuries these laments have been intoned by an exiled and wandering people, who thus kept alive the memory of Jerusalem, the love of the Holy Land, and an unshakable faith that the Guardian of Israel would yet bring about the restoration of His people to its homeland. The sorrows so poignantly expressed in the *Book of Lamentations* were the seedbed from which sprang the miracle of national restoration in our time, *'athalta digeulta,* "the beginning of redemption." May the day not be far distant when the prayer of the poet will come to fruition in all its fullness, both for Israel and for all humanity, "Turn us to Yourself, O Lord, and we will return; renew our days as of old."

It remains to point out that this study of *Lamentations* follows essentially the same pattern as the *Song of Songs*. It consists of an introduction, a new translation, and a philological and exegetical commentary. Unlike the *Song of Songs*, the Book *of Lamentations* has been relatively neglected by modern scholarship. It is hoped that the appended Bibliography will prove helpful to readers and students.

A note should be added on the rather complex history of both parts of the present volume. In the case of the *Song of Songs*, the introduction, the translation, and the commentary originally appeared in the *Mordecai M. Kaplan Jubilee Volumes*, edited by Moshe Davis (New York, 1953). Because of the widespread interest in the subject, it was republished in 1954 as Volume XX of *Tests and Studies of the Jewish Theological Seminary*, on the faculty of which I have been serving since 1937. This independent volume, which appeared in 1954 and subsequently in 1961, was amplified by a bibliography. As a result of additional research, the present edition contains new material in the commentary and a supplementary bibliography, as well as by some significant changes in the Translation, the result of new insights.

The Commentary on *Lamentations* originally appeared in two installments, the first in the *Seventy-Fifth Anniversary Volume of the Jewish Quarterly Review* (Philadelphia, 1967, Vol. 57, pp. 267-86), and the second in the July, 1967, issue (Volume 58, pp. 14-33). It then appeared in separate form under the title *A Commentary on the Text of Lamentations* (New York, 1968). Originally it contained only a brief introduction followed by philological and textual notes. For this edition a new translation with introductory comments, was prepared, incorporating the insights and conclusions that have been achieved as a result of fresh research.

Poetry is, by its very nature, not translatable. However, Biblical verse is based primarily upon two principles: the parallelism of stichs or cola, and meter-patterns based upon stressed words or thought-units. Biblical poetry, therefore, lends itself to translation to a greater degree than classical or traditional Western verse, both of which operate with syllable meter, though in different forms. I have sought in the English version of *Lamentations* to capture as much as possible of the haunting cadences of the Hebrew. Though many nuances are inevitably lost, I venture to hope that some of the poignancy and power of the original has carried over into the Translation.

Not only is the Translation completely new, but the Commentary has been substantially expanded. This extensive new material has been integrated into the original text. The publisher has made every effort to harmonize the appearance of the printing of the new and the old. However, the reader may be able to notice differences in the physical form between the two "strata" of the work.

The research and writing entailed in the preparation of this volume would not have been possible without a period of freedom from academic duties. I am deeply grateful to the Trustees of the John Simon Guggenheim Memorial Foundation, who granted me a Fellowship during the year 1973 and thus made it possible for me to concentrate on creative, scholarly activity. This book is one of the products of this period.

Once again, my devoted friend, Dr. Abraham I. Shinedling, out of his boundless friendship, has placed his extraordinary gifts of wide learning and exemplary accuracy at my disposal. He has read the manuscript, corrected the page proofs, and contributed greatly to the quality of the present work as a whole.

In the original edition of the *Song of Songs*, the Foreword concluded with a tribute to my beloved wife, Fannie, on the twenty-fifth anniversary of our marriage. Two decades later, I can only repeat what was set down there. Our forty-five years of married life have brought us the conviction that the *Song of Songs* is a testament of truth as well as a hymn to joy. As we look toward our golden jubilee, the verse in the *Song of Songs* becomes a prayer in our hearts: "Golden beads shall we make Thee, with studs of silver." But our lives are in His hands, and we are content.

Robert Gordis

Yom Ha'atzma'ut, 5733
May 7, 1973
New York, N.Y.

INTRODUCTION

I. A Unique Book

"The entire universe is not as worthy as the day on which the Song of Songs was given to Israel, for all the Writings are holy, but the Song of Songs are the Holy of Holies."[1] In these passionate words, Rabbi Akiba was upholding the right of the Song of Songs to a place in the Scriptures. The warmth of his defense testifies to the vigor of the challenge to which it was subjected, probably stronger than in the case of Esther, Koheleth and Job.[2]

The Song of Songs is unique among the books of the Bible in spirit, content and form. It is the only book in the canon lacking a religious or national theme, the Divine name occurring only once and then only as an epithet (8:6). To be sure, Esther also makes no direct mention of God, but its national emphasis is unmistakable. Even that is lacking in the Song of Songs. The reason for the doubts as to its canonicity is not hard to discover. Fragments of secular poetry are imbedded in the Bible,[3] but this is the only complete work which is entirely secular, indeed, sensuous, in character.

As in the case of Koheleth,[4] more than one factor helped to win admission for this little book into the canon of Scripture. While the charm and beauty of its contents played their part, if only on the subconscious level, there were two basic factors operating consciously. First was the occurrence of Solomon's name in the text,[5] which led to the attribution of the whole book to him, as witness the title: "The Song of Songs, which is Solomon's" (1:1). The several references to "the king"[6] were, naturally enough, identified with Solomon as well. Second was the allegorical interpretation of the book, according to which the love of God and Israel is described under the guise of

---

[1] For the entire passage in M. Yad. 3:5, see note 38 below.

[2] On the canonicity of these contested Biblical books, see F. Buhl, *Canon and Text of the O. T.* (Edinburgh, 1892), pp. 3–32; H. E. Ryle, *Canon of the O. T.* (2nd ed., London, 1909); as well as the suggestive treatments of Max L. Margolis, *The Hebrew Scriptures in the Making* (Philadelphia, 1922), pp. 83–96, and S. Zeitlin, "An Historical Study of the Canonization of Hebrew Scriptures," in *Proceedings of the American Academy for Jewish Research*, vol. III (1932), pp. 121–58. See also R. H. Pfeiffer, *Introduction to the O. T.* (New York, 1941), pp. 50–70.

[3] See below, sec. VI.

[4] See R. Gordis, *Koheleth — The Man And His World* (New York, 1951), chap. IV (later referred to as *KMW*).

[5] In 1:1, 5; 3:7, 9, 11; 8:11–12.

[6] In 1:4, 12; 7:6.

1

a lover and his beloved.⁷ This seemed reasonable since wise King Solomon would surely occupy himself only with recondite, spiritual concerns. Hence the Solomonic authorship of the book undoubtedly strengthened, if it did not create, the allegorical interpretation of the Song. This interpretation found Biblical warrant in the frequent use by the Prophets of the metaphor of marital love to describe the proper relationship of Israel to its God.⁸ This combination of factors overcame all doubts about the sacred character of the Song of Songs, and its canonicity was reaffirmed at the Council of Jamnia in 90 C. E., never to be seriously challenged again.⁹

II. THE ALLEGORICAL INTERPRETATION

The allegorical view of the Song of Songs to which we owe its inclusion in the canon and therefore its preservation was already well established in the first century C. E. The Apocryphal book *IV Esdras* uses the figures of "lily," "dove," and "bride" to refer to Israel (5:24, 26; 7:26). While the comparison to a bride might conceivably be based on other Biblical passages, like Jer. 2:2; Isa. 62:5, the references to "lily" and "dove" point unmistakably to our book. The only passage in the *Septuagint* which may point to a mystical interpretation is the rendering of *mērōsh 'amānāh* in 4:8 as "from the beginning of faith," but this is far from certain, since *'amānāh* has the meaning "faith" in Neh. 10:1. The Mishnah cites the description of Solomon's wedding in 3:11 and refers it to the giving of the Torah and the building of the Temple.¹⁰ The same view underlies the Targum on the book, and the Midrash *Shir Hashirim Rabbah*, as well as many talmudic interpretations of various verses in the book.

Medieval Jewish commentators like Saadia and Rashi accepted

---

⁷ After the preliminary draft of this study was completed, Professor H. H. Rowley sent me his new book, *The Servant of the Lord and other Essays on the O. T.* (London, 1952). It contains a characteristically thorough yet engrossing study of "The Interpretation of the Song of Songs" (pp. 189–234), incorporating two earlier papers of the author in *JThS*, vol. 38 (1937), pp. 337 ff., and *JRAS* (1938), pp. 251 ff., and supplemented with valuable references to recent literature, from which I have profited greatly. On p. 232, note 3, he cites the older surveys of the history of the interpretation of the *Song*, from C. D. Ginsburg and Salfeld to Vaccari and Kuhl, to which he acknowledges his own indebtedness.

⁸ Cf. Hos., chaps. 1–2; Jer. 2:2; 3:1–3; Isa. 50:1 f.; 54:5; 62:4 f.; Ezek., chaps. 16, 23; II Esdras 9:38; 10:25 ff.

⁹ In Christian circles, Theodore of Mopsuestia, who opposed its place in the canon, was excommunicated as a heretic.

¹⁰ Cf. M. Ta'an. 4:8.

its assumptions unhesitatingly. It is possible that the unconventional Abraham Ibn Ezra may be expressing his secret doubts on the subject by the method he employs in his commentary, which he divides into three parts, the first giving the meaning of the words, the second the literal meaning of the passage, and the third the allegorical interpretation.[11] Commentators differed as to details, but the general approach was clear. The book narrates, in symbolic fashion, the relationship of God and Israel from the days of the Patriarchs and the Exodus, extols the steadfast love and protection that God has given His beloved, and describes the fluctuations of loyalty and defection which have marked Israel's attitude toward its divine Lover.

When the Christian Church accepted the Hebrew Scriptures as its Old Testament, it was easy to transfer the parable from the old Israel to the New Israel, though there were variations of attitude. The first known allegorical treatment was that of Hippolytus of Rome, written early in the third century. He precedes Origen, Jerome, and Athanasius, who referred the book to Christ and the Church, while Ambrosius and Cornelius a Lapide identified the Shulammite with the Virgin Mary. Other figurative theories also were not lacking. Some of the older commentators, like Origen and Gregory of Nyassa, saw in it an allegory of the mystical union of the believing soul with God, a particularly congenial view, since mysticism has often expressed itself in strongly erotic terms.[12] Luther saw in it an allegory of Christ and the Soul.

The allegorical theory has been generally abandoned by modern scholars in its traditional guise. Yet a few contemporary Roman Catholic scholars[13] and some Orthodox Jewish writers[14] still interpret the book as an allegory of Israel's history.

---

[11] To be sure, in dealing with a similar procedure by Origen in his *Commentary on the Song*, Rowley (*op. cit.*, p. 200) denies that it implies any adherence to a literal meaning of the text. But what may be true of the 3rd century Church Father is not necessarily true of the medieval Jewish commentator, who frequently felt compelled to disguise his adherence to heterodox views, and even to polemize against ideas that he found attractive.

[12] Cf., for example, R. A. Nicholson, *The Mystics of Islam* (London, 1914); G. Scholem, *Major Trends in Jewish Mysticism* (New York, 1946).

[13] Cf. P. Joüon, *Le Cantique des Cantiques* (1909); A. Robert, "Le genre littéraire du Cantique des Cantiques," in *Revue Biblique*, vol. 52 (1943–44), pp. 192 ff.; E. Tobac, "Une page de l'histoire de l'exégèse," in *Revue d'histoire ecclésiastique*, vol. 21, part 1, 1925, pp. 510 ff., reprinted in *Les cinq livres de Salomon* (1926); G. Ricciotti, *Il Cantico dei cantici* (1928).

[14] Cf. J. Carlebach, "Das Hohelied," in *Jeschurun*, vol. 10 (1923), pp. 97 ff., especially pp. 196 ff.; R. Breuer, *Das Lied der Lieder* (1923).

Other forms of the allegorical theory have not been lacking. Isaac Abrabanel and his son Leo Hebraeus, basing themselves on the fact that Wisdom is described in *Hokmah* literature as a beautiful woman, who is contrasted with the "Woman of Folly" in Proverbs,[15] interpreted the beloved in the Song as a typological symbol of Wisdom, a view suggested in modern times by Godek and Kuhn. However, the details in the Song of Songs are both too concrete and too numerous to support this or any other allegorical view, which has accordingly found few adherents.

III. The Cult Theory

The most modern form of the allegorical theory regards our book as the translation of a pagan litany. In 1914, O. Neuschatz de Jassy suggested that it is a version of an Egyptian Osiris ritual, while Wittekindt proposed the view that it is a liturgy of the Ishtar cult.[16] The theory was most vigorously propagated by T. J. Meek,[17] who, in 1922, published the theory that the Song is a liturgy of the Adonis-Tammuz cult, the rites of which were undoubtedly practised in Palestine and were denounced by the prophets.[18]

The influence of Mowinckel and others[19] has popularized the view that the poetry of the Old Testament is in large measure cult-material, most of which was taken over from Canaanite religion.[20] Once the

---

[15] Cf. Prov. 8:1 ff.; 9:1 ff., 22 ff.; B. S. 14:23; 15:2; Wisdom of Solomon 8:2 ff., and see *per contra* Prov. 9:13 ff.

[16] Cf. Neuschatz de Jassy, *Le Cantique des Cantiques et le mythe d'Osiris-Hetep* (1914); Th. J. Meek (see the following note for references); W. Wittekindt, *Das Hohe-Lied und seine Beziehung zum Istarkult* (Hanover, 1925); L. Waterman, in *JBL*, vol. 45 (1936), pp. 171–87; Graham and May, *Culture and Conscience* (1936), pp. 22 f. The same theory underlies the excellent commentary of M. Haller, *Die fünf Megillot* (Tuebingen, 1940).

[17] Cf. his papers, "Canticles and the Tammuz Cult," in *AJSL*, vol. 39 (1922–23), pp. 1 ff.; "The Song of Songs and the Fertility Cult," in W. H. Schoff ed., *The Song of Songs, a Symposium* (Philadelphia, 1924), pp. 48 ff.; "Babylonian Parallels for the Song of Songs," in *JBL*, vol. 43 (1924), pp. 245 ff. In private correspondence he later informed Professor Rowley that he had modified his views, without indicating in what direction. Cf. Rowley, *op. cit.*, p. 213, note 5.

[18] Cf. Isa. 17:10 f.; Ezek. 8:14; Zech. 12:11. On the other hand, it is doubtful whether Jer. 22:18 refers to the ritual, and Isa. 5:1–7 surely is not connected with it.

[19] S. Mowinckel, *Psalmenstudien*, vol. 2 (1922), pp. 19 ff.; Hempel, *Die althebraeische Literatur und ihr hellenistisch-juedisches Nachleben* (Wildpark-Potsdam, 1930–34), pp. 24 ff.; O. Eissfeldt, *Einleitung in das A. T.*, pp. 94 ff.; E. H. Leslie, *The Psalms*, pp. 55–62.

[20] Cf. L. Kohler, *Theologie des A. T.* (Tuebingen, 1936), pp. 169, 182;

theory was set in motion, not merely the Psalms, but also the books of Hosea,[21] Joel,[22] Nahum,[23] Habakkuk[24] and Ruth,[25] have been interpreted, in whole or in part, as liturgies of the fertility-cult, and the end of the process is not yet in sight. Thus Haller declares that the Song of Songs was originally a cult-hymn for the spring festival of Ḥag Hamazzot, which the Canaanites observed with a litany glorifying Astarte as "the beloved" and Baal as Dod "the lover." The Song, we are assured, is part of the widespread Near Eastern ritual of the dying and reviving god.[26] Deuteronomic theologians are then assumed to have profanized the orginally sacred text, so that today it appears as a collection of erotic lyrics of a secular character. The impact of recent archaeological discoveries, particularly of Ugaritic literature, have given this view a new vogue.

Nevertheless, the cult-theory of the book can not be sustained, we believe, when subjected to analysis.[27] It begins with a hypothetical approach to the Hebrew Bible which is highly dubious. That the Old Testament contains only *Kultdichtung* is a modern version of the attitude which regards the Bible exclusively from the theological standpoint, instead of recognizing it, in A. B. Ehrlich's succinct phrase, as the Hebrews' "national literature upon a religious foundation."[28] Undoubtedly the religious consciousness permeated all aspects of the national life in ancient Israel, but the existence of secular motifs can not be ignored, particularly in the area of Wisdom, to which the art of the Song belonged, and with which it was identified.

There are other telling objections to the view that the Song of Songs is a liturgy of the dying and reviving god. That the Ḥag Hamazzot was such a festival in Israel is a gratuitous assumption, with

G. Hoelscher, *Geschichte der israelitischen und juedischen Religion* (Giessen, 1922), pp. 62 ff.

[21] Cf. H. C. May, "The Fertility Cult in Hosea," in *AJSL*, vol. 48 (1930), pp. 73 ff.

[22] Cf. I. Engnell, in *Svenske Biblikst Uppslagsverk*, vol. 1 (1948), col. 1075 f.

[23] Cf. P. Humbert, in *ZATW*, NF, vol. 3 (1926), pp. 266–80; *idem*, in *RHPR*, vol. 12 (1932), pp. 1 ff.

[24] Cf. E. Balla, in *Religion in Geschichte und Gegenwart*, 2nd ed., vol. 2 (1928), col. 1556 f.; E. Sellin, *Einleitung in das A. T.* (7th ed., 1935), p. 119.

[25] Cf. W. E. Staples, in *AJSL*, vol. 53 (1936), pp. 145 ff.

[26] The difficult וְדִגְלֹח in 6:4, 10, he regards as a textual error for *Nergal*. On this passage, see *Commentary ad loc.*

[27] Cf. the trenchant criticism of N. Schmidt, "Is Canticles an Adonis Liturgy?", in *JAOS*, vol. 46 (1926), pp. 154–64; and H. H. Rowley, in *JRAS* (1938), pp. 251–76, now amplified in his *The Servant of the Lord*, pp. 219–32.

[28] Cf. his *Kommentar zu Psalmen* (Berlin, 1905), p. V.

no evidence in Biblical or in post-Biblical sources. The proponents of the theory are driven to adduce as proof the synagogue practice of reading the Song of Songs during Passover. The oldest reference to the custom, however, is in the post-Talmudic tractate *Sopherim*, which probably emanates from the sixth century C. E.,[29] at least a millennium after the composition of the book. Its liturgical use at Passover can be explained without recourse to far-fetched theories. It is eminently appropriate to the festival, both in its literal sense and in the allegorical interpretation which has been official for centuries. Its glorification of spring (cf. 2:11 ff.; 7:11 ff.) was congenial to the "festival of Abib" and the Midrash refers many passages in the text to the Exodus, with its moving spirits, Moses and Aaron. Efforts have indeed been made to find vestiges of the Ishtar-cult in the text, but none of them are at all convincing.[30] The Song of Songs makes no references to

[29] Cf. Sopherim 14:16 (ed. Higger, p. 270), which apparently refers to its reading on the *last* two days of the festival, as observed in the Diaspora: בשיר השירים קורין :אותו בשני לילי ימים טובים של גליות האחרונים חציו בלילה אחד וחציו בלילה שני. On the date of the tractate, see Higger, *op. cit.*, Introduction. The reason is indicated in *Maḥzor Vitry*, p. 304: ולכן אנו אומרים בפסח על שם ששיר השירים מדבר מגאולת מצרים שנא׳ לסוסתי ברכבי פרעה וכל העניין מדבר מארבע גליות למבין: The medieval *piyyuṭim* which have entered the Passover liturgy are largely based on the *Song of Songs*, as in the cycle of hymns which begin with ברח דודי (Cant. 8:14).

[30] It has been argued that *zāmīr* in 2:12 must mean a "ritual song" (cf. Meek, in Schoff, *op. cit.*, pp. 49 f.). Actually, the root *zāmar* means "sing, make music," generally used in the Bible of ritual song, to be sure, but only because of the Bible's preoccupation with religious themes. The noun is used in a secular sense in Isa. 25:5, זְמִיר עָרִיצִים, "the tyrants' song of triumph"; note the parallelism. See also Isa. 24:16; Job 35:10. It is noteworthy that the Talmud interprets Ps. 119:54, זְמִרוֹת הָיוּ־לִי חֻקֶּיךָ, in a specifically secular sense and criticizes David for treating God's laws as mere song: מפני מה נענש דוד בעוזא מפני שקרא לספר תורה זמרות היו לי חקיך, "Why was David punished in the incident of Uzzah (II Sam., chap. 6)? Because he called the scroll of the Law mere 'songs' " (B. Sotah 35a; Yalkut Shimeoni, Psalm 119, sec. 480d). Actually, זָמַר is cognate to the noun זָמִיר (cf. קֶדֶם, קָדִים; זֶרֶם, זָרִים, Jer. 18:14, on which see Gordis, in *JThS*, vol. 41, 1940, pp. 37 ff.). The root is used to refer to a secular song *in direct connection with our book*; cf. Tos. Sanh. 12:10: רבי עקיבא אומר המנענע קולו בשיר השירים בבית המשתאות ועושה אותו כמין זמר אין לו חלק לעולם הבא, "He who gives his voice a flourish in reading the Song of Songs in the banquet-halls and makes it a *secular song* has no share in the world to come."

The 10th century agricultural calendar of Gezer lists ירחו זמר, "two months of vine-pruning." The Vav is best taken as a dual, status construct (so I. G. Février, in *Semitica*, vol. 1, 1948, pp. 33 ff.; W. F. Albright, in J. E. Pritchard, *Ancient Near Eastern Texts*, Princeton, 1950, p. 320a), rather than simply as the old nominative ending (so D. Diringer, *Le iscrizioni anticho-ebraiche Palestinesi*, 1934, p. 5; Th. C. Vriezen-J. H. Hospers, *Palestine Inscriptions*, Leyden, 1951, pp. 12 f.). However, *yrhw zmr* comes after ירחו קץ and therefore, as Dalman (*PEFQS*, 1909, p. 119) points out, "it cannot be the first pruning which comes in March, but the second,

this spring festival or any other, or, for that matter, to any ritual observance.

Proponents of the theory are in diametrical disagreement on a fundamental issue, whether the alleged pagan ritual in the Song has remained in its original and unmodified form[31] or whether it has been drastically reworked as part of the JHVH cult.[32] If the former is the case, it is an insuperable difficulty that the entire book makes no references to dying[33] nor to weeping for the dead god[34] nor to the decay of

in June or July." Rowley (p. 229 f.) follows him in interpreting *Song* 2:12 as a reference to this second pruning. But this is very unlikely, since, according to the poem, the winter and the rain are just over and the first bloom is taking place. For this, June-July is too late. So, too, the parallelism with "the voice of the turtle-dove" strengthens the view that *zāmīr* refers to "singing." Accordingly, there is no basis for interpreting it either as a ritual song or as meaning "pruning," which is against the parallelism and the context (against Ehrlich).

Another *locus classicus* of the cult-theory has been מַה־דּוֹדֵךְ מִדּוֹד (5:9), which is rendered, "Who but Dod is thy beloved?" (Meek, in Schoff, *op. cit.*, p. 55; Witte-kindt, *op. cit.*, p. 82). Meek argues that *mah* means "who" in Babylonian, or that it is a textual error for מִי. But even this assumed correction does not suffice to yield the required sense, which would have been expressed by some such phrase as מִי דוֹדֵךְ כִּי־אָם דּוֹד; cf. Isa. 42:19, מִי עִוֵּר כִּי אִם־עַבְדִּי, "Who is blind but My servant?" Actually, there is no real evidence for Dod as a divine name used in Israel. Conversely, Meek's objection to the usual interpretation is not valid. He argues that the rendering "What is thy beloved more than another beloved?" requires the addition of "other." I do not know of an exact analogy in Hebrew for the construction, on either view, but supplying "other" is justified. Cf. Gen. 3:1: וְהַנָּחָשׁ הָיָה עָרוּם מִכֹּל חַיַּת הַשָּׂדֶה, "The serpent was wiser than all *other* beasts of the field"; cf. *ibid.* 3:14; 37:3; Deut. 7:7; 33:24, בָּרוּךְ מִבָּנִים אָשֵׁר, "Blessed above all *other* sons is Asher"; Judg. 5:24; Ps. 45:3. The usual rendering, literally, "What is thy beloved above (the class of) lover," is therefore eminently satisfactory.

The difficult כַּנִּדְגָּלוֹת (6:4, 10) is emended to כְּנֵרְגַל, "like Nergal," the Babylonian god of the underworld, who was the partner of Ninurta, the summer sun, and "whose powerful gaze is contrasted with the milder light of the dawn and the moon (Haller)." Even if this attractive suggestion be adopted, it offers no real support to the cult-theory. Ritual texts and mythological allusions may employ the same figures, but they are worlds apart in their outlook, as Homer and Milton, or Vergil and Dante, abundantly attest. Biblical writers use Leviathan, Tehom, Mot, Reseph, and other elements of pagan religion, but for them, unlike the Babylonian and Ugaritic epics, these are mythological references, not religious verities. This is particularly true with regard to astronomical phenomena. Cf. the Babylonian names of the months in the Hebrew calendar, which include the god Tammuz himself, or the modern names of the planets, the days of the week and the months. Actually, there are some important objections to the emendation. For these and for an alternative interpretation, see the Commentary *ad loc.*

[31] So de Jassy, *op. cit.*, p. 90.
[32] So Meek, in *Song of Songs — a Symposium*, p. 53.
[33] "Death" and "Sheol" are mentioned in 8:6 purely as similes.
[34] As, e. g., in Ezek. 8:14 ff., where it is clearly condemned as a foreign rite.

nature. If the latter alternative is true, there is the additional problem of a JHVH liturgy in which the Divine name is absent, either explicitly or as an allusion.

It is human love, not that of a god, which is glorified in the Song, and that with a wealth of detail, which rules out an allegorical interpretation. The entire book deals with concrete situations, whether of love's repining, or its satisfaction, of lovers' flirtations, estrangement and reunion. Moreover, the frequent references to specific localities in the topography of Palestine effectively rule out the likelihood that this material could have been used for liturgical purposes. For the essence of a liturgy is that it is typological, being concerned with a generalized and recurrent pattern of activity.[35]

One is, of course, at liberty to assume that our book represents a secular reworking of a no longer extant litany of an assumed Israelite cult which has left no record of its existence behind it. Such a complex of unsubstantiated hypotheses recalls the argument that the ancient Hebrews must have known of wireless telegraphy, because archaeologists in Palestine have found no wires in their excavations.

Neither the older nor the more recent allegorical interpretations of the Song of Songs are convincing explanations of the original character of the book. In favor of the traditional Jewish and Christian allegories is the fact that they have their own independent charm, which the cult-theory does not possess.

It may even be granted, as Rowley well says, that "we, for our profit, may rightly find in the images of the Song, as in all experience, analogies of things spiritual," but that "does not mean that it was written for this purpose and that the author had any such idea in mind."[36] The key to the book must be sought in a literal interpretation of the text, as the surest basis for true understanding and lasting appreciation of its greatness.

IV. THE LITERAL INTERPRETATION

While the allegorical view of the Song of Songs early became official, it is noteworthy that the Rabbis were well aware that in many circles it was being interpreted literally. That the allegorical view had difficulty in winning universal acceptance is clear from the warmth

---

[35] This consideration disproves the hypothesis that Psalm 2 is part of a liturgy of enthronement. The historical background is clearly that of a revolt of subordinate rulers, much too specific a situation for a recurrent litany of royal enthronement.

[36] *Op. cit.*, p. 201.

of the statement in the Tosefta:[37] "He who trills his voice in the chanting of Song of Songs and treats it as a secular song, has no share in the world to come."

Obviously, too, the literal view of the book lay at the basis of the doubts expressed in the Mishnah as to its canonicity:[38] "The Song of Songs and Koheleth defile the hands (i. e. are canonical). Rabbi Judah says, The Song of Songs defiles the hands, but Koheleth is in dispute. Rabbi Jose says, Koheleth does not defile the hands and the Song of Songs is in dispute. . . . Rabbi Simeon ben Azzai said, I have a tradition from the seventy-two elders on the day that Rabbi Eleazar ben Azariah was appointed president of the Academy that both the Song of Songs and Koheleth defile the hands. Said Rabbi Akiba, Heaven forfend! No one in Israel ever disputed that the Song of Songs defiles the hands. For all the world is not as worthy as the day on which the Song of Songs was given to Israel, for all the writings are holy, but the Song of Songs is the Holy of Holies. If they differed at all, it was only about Koheleth. Rabbi Johanan ben Joshua, the brother-in-law of Rabbi Akiba, said, Both the division of opinion and the final decision accorded with the statement of Ben Azzai, i. e. they differed on both books and finally decided that both were canonical."

Nevertheless, the literal view, which was rejected on the conscious level, won a measure of unconscious acceptance even in Rabbinic circles. That the book deals with human love is implied in the well-known statement: "Solomon wrote three books, Proverbs, Koheleth, and the Song of Songs. Which did he write first? . . . Rabbi Hiyya the Great said, He wrote Proverbs first, then the Song of Songs, and then Koheleth. . . . Rabbi Jonathan said, The Song of Songs he wrote first; then came Proverbs, and then Koheleth. Rabbi Jonathan proved it from normal human behavior. When a man is young, he sings songs. When he becomes an adult, he utters practical proverbs. When he becomes old, he voices the vanity of things."[39]

---

[37] Cf. Tos. Sanh. 12:10. The text is quoted in note 30 above.

[38] Cf. Mishnah 'Eduy. 5:3; Tos. Yad. 2:14. In M. Yad. 3:5, the final decision in its favor is registered: שיר השירים וקהלת מטמאין את הידים ר' יהודה אומר שיר השירים מטמא את הידים וקהלת מחלוקת ר' יוסי אומר קהלת אינו מטמא את הידים ושיר השירים מחלוקת ר' שמעון אומר קהלת מקולי בית שמאי ומחומרי בית הלל אמר ר' שמעון בן עזאי מקובל אני מפי שבעים ושנים זקנים ביום שהושיבו את ר' אלעזר בן עזריה בישיבה ששיר השירים וקהלת מטמאין את הידים אמר רבי עקיבא חס ושלום לא נחלק אדם מישראל על שיר השירים שלא תטמא את הידים שאין כל' העולם כולו כדאי כיום שניתן בו שיר השירים לישראל שכל הכתובים קודש ושיר השירים קודש קדשים ואם נחלקו לא נחלקו אלא על קהלת אמר ר' יוחנן בן יהושע בן חמיו של ר' עקיבא כדברי בן עזאי כך נחלקו וכך נגמרו:

[39] Midrash Shir Hashirim Rabba 1:1, sec. 10. רבי יונתן אומר שיר השירים כתב תחילה

In the Christian Church, too, the literal view was known and fought. The position of the fourth-century Theodore of Mopsuestia was declared a heresy by the Second Council of Constantinople in 353. His objections to the book were repeated, in 1544, by Chateillon, who wanted it expunged from the canon as immoral. It is character-istic of the broader conception of canonicity in Judaism that no such demand for its elimination was made, even by the anonymous French Jewish commentator of the twelfth century or by a few other medieval Jewish writers who regarded it as a song written by Solomon for his favorite wife.[40] In the sixteenth and seventeenth centuries various scholars suggested that the book was a collection of eclogues, and analogies with the Idylls of Theocritus were frequently invoked. It was Herder who, in 1778, explained it as a collection of songs extolling the joys of human love. This view, however, receded in popularity for over a century thereafter.

V. The Dramatic Theory

In the eighteenth century, years before Herder, several scholars, like Wachtel (1722) and Jacobi (1771), espoused the view that the book is a drama. This view is perhaps foreshadowed by two Greek manuscripts of the fourth and fifth centuries C. E., which actually supply speakers for the various verses of the book. It is the dramatic theory which was the first to win wide acceptance among modern scholars and readers in two variant forms. According to the first, adopted by Delitzsch, there are two main characters, King Solomon and a rustic Shulammite maiden, and the book consists substantially of expressions of love by the two principal characters. According to the other view, first propounded by J. S. Jacobi and elaborated by Ewald, there are three characters, a beautiful maiden, her shepherd lover, and King Solomon, who on a visit to the countryside discovers her and becomes enamored of her beauty. The luxuries of the royal court and the blandishments of the king are powerless to shake her love. At length the young rustic lovers are reunited, and the play ends with a song on the lips of the maiden and her shepherd lover.[41]

ואחר כך משלי ואח״כ קהלת ומייתי ליה ר' יונתן מדרך ארץ כשאדם נער אומר דברי שיר הגדיל אומר
דברי משלות הזקין אומר דברי הבלים:

[40] Cf. Rowley, p. 206, n. 4.

[41] The division of the book according to both views is conveniently set forth by S. R. Driver, *Introduction to the Literature of the O. T.* (New York, 1906), 12th ed., pp. 437–43.

It is obvious that the second view has a dramatic tension lacking in the first, and it has been increasingly espoused by those who favor the dramatic theory.[42]

Nonetheless, the theory suffers from several grave drawbacks which must be clarified, since this view is still taken for granted in most popular treatments of the book:

1. That speakers must be supplied for the various lines would be natural and constitutes no difficulty. The crux lies in the fact that *the entire plot must be read into the book and the natural intent of the words be ignored again and again.* One or two instances must suffice. Thus Driver, following Ewald, attributes the opening section, 1:2–7, to the maiden in these words:

> "Scene I. (The Shulammite and Ladies of the Court.) — The Shulammite, longing for the caresses of her absent shepherd-lover, complains that she is detained in the royal palace against her will, and inquires eagerly where he may be found."

Now none of this reconstruction is in the actual text. The opening verses 2–4 make no reference to the lover as being absent. Moreover, the complaint in verse 7, which is addressed directly to him, is not that she is detained against her will by the king, but that she can not find him among his fellow-shepherds. Finally, this interpretation does not do justice to the text of verses 5 and 6. The proud words of these verses, in which the maiden praises her own beauty and explains her dark hue, are hardly the words appropriate to one who wants to flee the court and the king's advances, in order to be reunited with her shepherd lover.

The remainder of chapter 1 is assigned to Scene II as follows:

> Solomon (9–11) seeks to win the Shulammite's love. The Shulammite (12, aside) parries the king's compliments with reminiscences of her absent lover.— Solomon (15) — The Shulammite (v. 16, aside) takes no notice of the king's remark in v. 15 and applies the figures suggested by it to her shepherd-lover.

Now verses 9–11 might *conceivably* be Solomon's words as he seeks to win her love, but there the plausibility of the reconstruction ends. Verse 12, "while the king sat at his table (or couch), my spikenard

---

[42] Thus only the older commentators, Hengsterberg, Keil, and Kingsbury, favor the first. The second is accepted by Driver (*op. cit.*). The catena of commentators who share this view is given in R. H. Pfeiffer, *Introduction to the O. T.* (New York, 1941), p. 715.

sent forth its fragrance" (JV), can not naturally mean (*pace* Driver) that "while the king *was away from me*, at table with his guests, my love (for another) was active" (italics Driver's). Nor is there anything to suggest that vv. 13–14 *parry* any of the king's compliments or that she has more than one lover in mind at all. Finally, assigning v. 15 to the king and v. 16 to the maiden, who is *referring to her absent lover*, means to divide what is obviously a single literary unit, both in form and in content. The love-dialogue is clear:

"Thou art fair, my beloved, thou art fair, thine eyes are doves."
"Thou art comely, my lover, and sweet, and our couch is fragrant."

There are many other instances where the exigencies of the dramatic theory artificially divide obvious literary units. Thus 2:2 is assigned to Solomon, while 2:3 is again attributed to the maiden as an *aside*.

2. Incidents which in a drama should have been acted out are narrated, as in 2:8; 5:1, 4. This is perfectly comprehensible in a lyric, but not in a play.

3. The climax of the plot is assumed to be 8:11 ff. Here the young lovers spurn the luxury of Solomon's court in favor of the delights of love, contrasting the high financial returns of Solomon's vineyard with the "vineyard" of the beloved's person and charm. But precisely here the dramatic form is totally lacking. Solomon is not addressed at all, which is what one should have expected in a dramatic confrontation of king and commoner as they contend for the maiden's hand. Instead, it is clear from the narrative phrase, "Solomon had a vineyard at Baal-Hamon," that Solomon is *not* present, and the adjuration in v. 12 is therefore rhetorical and not actual.

4. The distribution of the name "Solomon" in the book is worthy of note. Aside from the superscription (1:1), the name occurs six times more — in 1:5, where it is used generically,[43] and in two other sections, i. e. in chapter 3 (vv. 7, 9, 11) and in chapter 8 (vv. 11, 12), and *nowhere else*. The full significance of this fact will be discussed below. Suffice it to note that if Solomon were a principal protagonist of the drama, we should expect a more consistent use of his name

---

[43] יְרִיעוֹת שְׁלֹמֹה means "Solomonic curtains," being parallel to "Arab tents," like our phrases "Louis Quatorze furniture," "Queen Anne fashions," and the like. On the meaning and poetic structure, see the Commentary *ad loc.*, and see Gordis, "Al Mibneh Hashirah Haivrit Haqedummah," in *Sefer Hashanah Liyhudei Amerikah* (New York, 1944), pp. 151 ff.

throughout the book than the existing. pattern. As for the noun "king," *hammelek*, which might conceivably be an epithet for Solomon in the drama, it is also very rare in the book, occurring in only three additional passages (1:4, 12; 7:6) besides its use together with "Solomon" in two cases (3:9, 11).

5. That the book is a drama presupposes that it is a literary unit. This is, however, ruled out categorically by linguistic considerations. The noun *pardēs* (4:13) is of Persian origin, and the passage in which it occurs can not, therefore, be older than the Persian period (6th century B. C. E.). On the other hand, in 6:4 the lover compares his beloved to Tirzah and Jerusalem. The parallelism makes it clear that the poet must be referring to Tirzah, the old capital of the Northern Kingdom of Israel, which was replaced with Samaria by Omri in the first half of the ninth century B. C. E.[44] A lover does not usually praise his beloved by comparing her to a city ruined centuries earlier! Hence this passage can not be later than the ninth century B. C. E.[45] It is obvious that if at least one passage in a book can not be earlier than the sixth century, and another can not be later than the ninth, the work is manifestly not a literary unit, and the dramatic theory is conclusively ruled out.

VI. Song as a Branch of Wisdom

In the Hebrew Bible, the Song of Songs finds its place in the third section, the Hagiographa, in proximity to Psalms and Lamentations on the one hand, and to Proverbs and Job on the other. This third section is not a heterogeneous collection but, on the contrary, possesses an underlying unity, being the repository of *Hokmah* or Wisdom. Wisdom was much more than a branch of literature. It included all the technical arts and practical skills of civilization. The architect and the craftsman, the weaver and the goldsmith, the sailor and the magician, the skillful general and the wise administrator of the state, are all described as *hakāmīm*, "wise."[46] In Rabbinic Hebrew the epithet *hakāmāh* is applied also to the midwife.[47]

---

[44] Cf. I Kings 16:23 f. Oesterley-Robinson, *History of Israel* (Oxford, 1932), p. 463, dates the accession of Omri to the throne as 886 B. C. E. W. F. Albright, in L. Finkelstein, ed., *The Jews* (New York, 1949), p. 33, places it as circa 876 B. C. E.

[45] The grounds for maintaining that there is even older material in the book, going back to the 10th century B. C. E., will be presented below.

[46] Cf. Gen. 41:8; Ex. 28:3; 35:25, 31; 36:1; Isa. 10:13; 29:14; 44:25; Jer. 9:16; 10:9; 49:7; Ezek. 27:8; Ps. 107:27.

[47] Cf. M. Shab. 18:3; M. R. H. 2:5; B. 'Er. 45a.

While all these phases of *Hokmah* disappeared with the destruction of the material substratum of ancient Hebrew life, it was these practical and technical aspects of *Hokmah* that were primary, and its more theoretical meaning to designate metaphysical and ethical truths embodied in literature is a later development. This semantic process from the concrete to the abstract, which is universal in language, is validated also for the Greek *sophia*, which is strikingly parallel in its significance.[48] The basic meaning of the Greek word is "cleverness and skill in handicraft and art," then "skill in matters of common life, sound judgment, practical and political wisdom," and ultimately, "learning, wisdom and philosophy."[49] The adjective *sophos* bears the same meanings, being used of sculptors and even of hedgers and ditchers, but "mostly of poets and musicians."[50] The noun *sophistes*, "master of a craft or art," is used in the extant literature of a diviner, a cook, a statesman, and again of poets and musicians. From Plato's time onward, it is common in the meaning of a professional teacher of the arts.[51]

The Hellenic culture-area serves as a valuable parallel, shedding light not only on the origin and scope of ancient "Wisdom," but also on the development and function of the teachers and protagonists of the discipline, but that is not our concern here.[52]

One of the most frequent uses of the term *Hokmah* refers it to the arts of poetry and song, both vocal and instrumental, for the composition and the rendering of songs, which were often done by the same individual, required a high order of skill. Thus the women skilled in lamentation at funerals are called *hakāmōth* by Jeremiah (9:16).

[48] Cf. Gordis, *KMW*, pp. 18 ff., 30 ff., for a full discussion of the parallels between Greek *sophia* and Hebrew *Hokmah*.

[49] In its first meaning, *sophia* is applied to Hephaestus, the god of fire and the arts, to Athena, to Daedalus, the craftsman and artist, and to the Telchines, a primitive tribe who are represented under three aspects: 1) as cultivators of the soil and ministers of the gods; 2) as sorcerers and envious demons, who had the power to bring on hail, rain, and snow, and to destroy animals and plants; and 3) as artists working in brass and iron. (Gen. 4:20–22 offers a suggestive parallel.) *Sophia* is used of such crafts as carpentry, driving a chariot, medicine and surgery. It is used preeminently of singing, music and poetry (*Homeric Hymn to Mercury*, lines 483, 511; Pindar, *Odes*, 1, 187; Xenophon, *Anabasis*, 1, 2, 8). On the usage of all three terms here discussed, cf. Liddell-Scott, *Greek Lexicon*, s. v.

[50] Pindar, *Odes*, 1, 15; Euripides, *Iphigenia in Tauris*, 12:38; Plato, *Laws*, 696c. See Liddell-Scott, *op. cit.*, s. v.

[51] Pindar, 1, 5, 36; Aeschylus, *Fragmenta*, 320; cf. Liddell-Scott, *op. cit.*, s. v.

[52] For a characterization of Wisdom, see Gordis, "The Social Background of Wisdom Literature," in *HUCA*, vol. 18 (1944); *KMW*, pp. 16–38.

The relationship between Wisdom and Song was so close that the terms were used interchangeably. Thus in I Kings 5:10–12 we read: "And Solomon's wisdom excelled the wisdom of all the children of the east, and all the wisdom of Egypt. For he was wiser than all men: than Ethan the Ezrahite, and Heman, and Calcol, and Darda, the sons of Mahol; and his fame was in all the nations round about. And he spoke three thousand proverbs; and his songs were a thousand and five."[53] Ethan and Heman, who are here described as "wise,"[54] are the eponymous heads of the musical guilds in the Temple in Jerusalem. Note, too, that the same Biblical passage attributes both "proverbs" and "songs" to Solomon.

The songs of the prophet Balaam are called *māshāl* (literally, "parable, proverb"), perhaps because the poems are replete with comparisons (Num. 23:7, 18; 24:3, 15, 20, 21, 23). But essentially the term is a synonym for "song." Thus the unknown poets, whose military epic is cited in the fragment in Num. 21:27–30, are called *mōshelīm* (literally, "makers of *mashal*"). The term *hīdāh*, "riddle, mysterious saying," together with *māshāl*, is applied to the song played on the *kinnōr*, "the lyre" (Ps. 49:5; 78:2). The recently discovered evidence from Ugaritic sources corroborates the Biblical tradition, previously dismissed as anachronistic, which declares that these guilds of singers are very ancient. In fact, they probably go back to the Canaanite period.[55]

Now Wisdom literature as a whole began on a secular note and only gradually took on a religious coloration. This is clear from the chronology of the best attested branch of Oriental Wisdom, that of Egypt, where religious motifs are late in appearing. Similarly in Israel, as Pfeiffer correctly says, "We know positively that the secular school (of Wisdom) flourished before the pious."[56] The oldest popular Hebrew proverbs and the Wisdom fragments imbedded in the Historical books are all secular in character.[56a]

A similar development may be postulated for that branch of Wisdom called *shir*, which includes both poetry and music. The Song certainly played an important role in religious ritual, at sacrifices processions and festivals, but it was not limited to these areas. Actu-

---

[53] Or, "five thousand," with the Septuagint.

[54] Cf. I Kings 5:10–12 with I Chron. 15:19 and the superscriptions of Psalms 88 and 89, and see Gordis, *KMW*, p. 17.

[55] So W. F. Albright, in an unpublished paper, "The Canaanite Origin of Israelite Musical Guilds."

[56] Cf. Pfeiffer, *op. cit.*, p. 650.

[56a] Cf. I Sam. 10:12; 24:14; II Sam. 14:14; I Kings 20:11; II Kings 14:9; Jer. 23:28; 31:29; Ezek. 16:44; 18:2.

ally, it was coextensive with life itself, dealing with all the normal secular concerns of life, such as combat and victory,[57] the opening of a well, vintage and harvest,[58] feasting and carousing,[59] the glory of nature and the tragedy of death.[60]

Undoubtedly the poems of national significance, like those of war and victory, were given a religious character, as in the "Song of the Sea" (Ex. 15) or the "Song of Deborah" (Judg. 5), since the historical experience of Israel was conceived as reflecting the will of God. But it is noteworthy that many of the briefer snatches of song which are preserved in prose narratives and are explicitly quoted from older collections, like the *Book of the Wars of the Lord* (Num. 21:14) and the *Book of Jashar* (probably the "Book of Heroes," Josh. 10:13; II Sam. 1:18; I Kings 8:53 in the Greek), are purely secular in content. The Song, like Wisdom, as a whole, later developed a religious stamp, but it remained an acquired characteristic.

For self-evident reasons, the secular note would be more likely to be preserved in the area of love and courtship, which has inspired more poetry and music than any other field of human interest. Into this area, where the sensual and the physical play so important a part, the traditional religious coloration would have the greatest difficulty in penetrating. The existence of secular love-songs in ancient Egyptian and Akkadian literature,[61] as well as among contemporary Arab peasants and city dwellers,[62] strengthens this contention, besides offering many a key to the understanding of the Biblical song.[63]

VII. THE SONG OF SONGS AS A COLLECTION

If the Song of Songs be approached without any preconceptions, it reveals itself as a collection of lyrics. This view of the book was taken by a Middle High German version of the 15th century, which

---

[57] Cf. Gen. 4:23; Judg. 15:16; I Sam. 18:7.

[58] Cf. Num. 21:17 ff.; Isa. 16:10; 22:13; 27:2.

[59] Cf. Amos 6:5; Isa. 5:12; Job 21:12; Ps. 69:13.

[60] II Sam. 1:19 ff.; 3:33; cf. Amos 5:16; Jer. 9:16 (מקוננות, חכמות, יודעי נהי).

[61] Cf. A. Erman, *Literature of the Ancient Egyptians*, tr. by Blackman (London, 1927); J. B. Pritchard, *Ancient Near-Eastern Texts Relating to the O. T.* (Princeton, 1950).

[62] For a collection of these songs, containing text, translation, and notes, see the extremely valuable study of St. H. Stephan, *Modern Palestinian Parallels to the Song of Songs* (Jerusalem, 1926).

[63] Cf. Gordis, *KMW*, pp. 16 ff., and note R. H. Pfeiffer's judicious statement on the subject (*Introduction*, p. 712): "There must have existed in Palestine during the last centuries of our era a considerable amount of erotic poetry of which our book alone survives by accident."

divided it into 54 songs. A long catena of modern scholars have adopted the same position, though naturally differing on the division of the book.[64]

A great step forward in the interpretation of the Song was taken in 1893, when J. G. Wetzstein, Prussian consul in Damascus, called attention to the nuptial customs of the Syrian peasants, who have the couple sit on a "throne" during the wedding-meal as "king" and "queen," while the guests sing songs of praise (wasf), glorifying the bride and groom. In some cases, the bride also executes a "sword dance" during the festivities. The affinities with several passages in the Song are obvious, and many scholars were accordingly led to interpret the entire collection as emanating from such wedding celebrations.[65]

That the praise of the bride on her wedding day was a regular feature of Jewish weddings in Second Temple days, and that these songs of praise were a technical art and therefore part of Hokmah, is clear from an ancient Talmudic tradition. It reads as follows: "How is one to dance before (i. e. praise) the bride? The Shammaites declare: 'By praising her for the qualities she actually possesses.' The Hillelites say: 'By saying of every one, O bride, beautiful and gracious.' "[66] The same function continued to be performed by the badḥān or humorous rhymster at East-European weddings until our day.

On the other hand, it is clear that some of the lyrics in the Song of Songs are not connected with wedding ceremonies or with married love at all.[67] The only justifiable conclusion is that the Song of Songs,

---

[64] Jastrow and Budde each finds 23 songs, though they differ on the subdivisions. Haller finds 26, Bettan 18. We divide the book into 28 songs, several of which are fragmentary and some of which may be doublets. Popular songs frequently circulate in many versions.

[65] So Wetzstein, Budde, Stade, Cornill, Kautzsch, Jastrow, Cassuto, Goodspeed, and others. Cf. Pfeiffer, op. cit., p. 716.

[66] B. Ket. 16b: כיצד מרקדין לפני הכלה בית שמאי אומרים כלה כמות שהיא בית הלל אומרים כלה נאה וחסודה.

[67] At the same time, Gebhardt's objection to the view in toto is much too extreme. The doubts which have been raised by H. Granquist as to the existence of such a custom as a "king's week" among the Arabs of Palestine overlook the clear-cut references in Jewish practice to שבעת ימי המשתה, "the seven days of feasting" following the wedding, which are observed to the present day with a repetition of the Seven Nuptial Blessings first recited at the marriage. Moreover, Rothstein's objection that the bride is never called "queen" in the Song loses part of its force when it is recalled that while Rabbinic literature cites and elaborates on the proverb חתן דומה למלך, "The bridegroom may be compared to a king" (Pirke de Rabbi Eliezer, chap. 16), there is no corresponding phrase about the bride. However, the Sabbath is described

like the Psalter, is an anthology, running a wide gamut of its emotions. It contains songs of love's yearning and its consummation, of coquetry and passion, of separation and union, of courtship and marriage.

The division of the songs will depend upon the changes in theme, viewpoint, background or form. These criteria will not always be sufficiently exact to command universal assent. Much will be dependent upon the literary taste and insight, as well as upon the knowledge, of the interpreter. But this is simply a restatement of the truth that exegesis is essentially an art, which rests upon a foundation of scientific knowledge.

VIII. Solomon in the Song of Songs

If the Song of Songs is an anthology of love poems, how are the seven instances of Solomon's name in the text to be explained? For on this view he is neither the author of the book, as the traditional view claims, nor its hero, as is maintained by the dramatic theory.

Several of these instances are easy to explain. In the opening verse of the book (1:1), we have a later superscription by an editor who had already accepted the theory of Solomon's authorship.[68] In three other passages, the use of the name is authentic. These are in 1:5 ("Solomonic hangings"), where it is a descriptive term like our "Louis XIV furniture," and in 8:11 and 12, where Solomon is used to typify a possessor of great wealth, as the ancients used "Croesus" or as moderns might use the name of a multi-millionaire like Vanderbilt or Rockefeller.

The other three examples of Solomon's name, it is generally suggested, are glosses which were induced by these authentic occurrences of the name in the text, and were reinforced by the tradition of Solomon as the "great lover" (I Kings 11:1 ff.). It would therefore be natural to believe that he was also intended by the word *melekh*, "king," in the Song, though the word actually referred to the bridegroom. Hence "Solomon" was added as a gloss in three more verses (3:7, 9 and 11).

For all its apparent plausibility, however, this approach is not adequate. Not only do we find "Solomon" used without the word "king" in 3:7, but the word "king" occurs several times in the book without the gloss "Solomon" (1:4, 12; 7:6). The clue to the solution

as both "queen" and "bride" in Talmudic and post-Talmudic sources; cf. Shab. 119a and Solomon Alkabetz' famous hymn *Lechah Dodi*.

[68] Hence the use of the relative *še*, instead of *'asher*, and the high valuation on the book expressed in the title. See the Commentary *ad loc.*

lies in the observation that the only three passages in the book in which Solomon is apparently unauthentic (3:7, 9, 11) *all occur in the same poem.*

This poem (3:6–11) is generally regarded as a rustic wedding song. But if it is scrutinized carefully, a variety of problems arise:

The poem contains many descriptive traits which, literally viewed, can not apply to a simple peasant wedding. The pillars of smoke (v. 6) and the sixty heroes trained in war (v. 7) are often dismissed as poetic hyperbole. However, v. 10, "he made its pillars of silver, the top thereof of gold, its seat of purple, its inside being inlaid with ivory,"[69] is much too explicit to be merely the product of a poet's heightened imagination. A country lover might describe the open fields as his fresh couch, the cedars as the walls of his home and the sycamores as his rafters (1:16 f.), but the circumstantial description of a luxurious palanquin, far beyond the reach of a rustic couple, would be a mockery rather than a tribute of praise to the lovers.

Another difficulty is the explicit national note to be found only here. Not only do we have a reference to "the daughters of Jerusalem" (3:10), which is familiar from other passages in the Song (2:7; 3:5; 5:8, 16; 8:4), but "the daughters of Zion" (3:11) are mentioned in this poem, and nowhere else. Most important of all, while the Palestinian locale pervades the entire book, the only national reference, that to "Israel," occurs in 3:7.

Moreover, the occurrence of Solomon's name in these verses is not easily solved by deletion. In 3:7, "king" does not occur and "Solomon" can not be removed without leaving a lacuna. Hence the entire stich must be dropped. In v. 11 the deletion of "Solomon" irreparably destroys the rhythm of the verse.[70] Even in v. 9, the excision of the name is not required on rhythmic grounds.[71]

---

[69] Reading הַבְּנִים with Graetz and most moderns, or הַבְּים with Tur-Sinai; cf. I Kings 10:22; Amos 6:4. See the Commentary.

[70] The meter of the verse is 2:2:2 ‖ 3:3:3:. *B'yōm hᵃthunāthō* receives three beats, both because of its length and the exigencies of the meter. On this procedure, as well as on the technique of longer stichs at the end of a poem, cf. the study by Gordis cited in note 43 above, pp. 136–59, especially pp. 140 f., 145 f.

[71] The *kinah* rhythm is not limited to the 3:2 pattern, its basic trait being a longer stich followed by a shorter. Scholars have been led astray here by the conjunctive accents linking *hammelekh šelōmōh*, when actually the words belong to separate stichs, with a 4:3 meter for the verse, which is in climactic or complementary parallelism. Similarly, in Num. 23:7 the words *bālāq melekh mō'ābh*, though linked by conjunctive accents, belong to separate stichs. For a full discussion of the meter of the verse, cf. Gordis, "A Wedding Song for Solomon," in *JBL*, vol. 63 (1944), especially pp. 266 ff.

These difficulties, cumulatively viewed, all point to the conclusion that we have here no song for a rustic wedding but, quite the contrary, an epithalamium for a wedding of great luxury, one possessing even national significance. In fact, all the details cited are easily explained by one assumption — *that we have here a song composed on the occasion of one of Solomon's marriages to a foreign princess*, probably an Egyptian.[72]

Such a poem has survived in Psalm 45, in which an Israelite king is marrying a Phoenician princess.[73] Obviously, songs were composed for and sung at different stages of the wedding ceremony. Psalm 45 is addressed to the king (vv. 3–10) and to his new queen (vv. 11–14), perhaps after the marriage rites had been concluded. Our song, on the contrary, is a chorus of welcome addressed to the bride as her procession approaches from across the wilderness which separates Palestine on the east and on the southwest from its neighbors.

All the details of the poem are explained naturally on this simple premise. The princess travels with a large retinue, which encamps at night and sends up pillars of smoke (v. 6). Her palanquin was sent to her by Solomon and is escorted by the royal bodyguard, sixty of the heroes of Israel (v. 7; cf. II Sam. 23:8 ff.; I Kings 1:10). The litter is made of the finest cedarwood of Lebanon, one of the by-products of his commercial relations with Phoenicia. Its decorations of silver, gold, purple and ivory (v. 10) are in keeping with Solomon's penchant for luxury, and may well have been prepared by the noble ladies of Jerusalem (v. 11).

All the references to Solomon in the book, aside from the title, are thus authentic, including the three references in this song, which dates from Solomon's reign. The presence of this poem, in the collection, would serve as the nucleus for the tradition attributing the entire book to Solomon.

In connection with this early date for the song, two linguistic problems must be considered. Graetz derived the word *'apiriōn*, "litter, couch" (3:9), from the Greek *phoreion*, which would imply a

---

[72] On Solomon's foreign marriages in general, cf. I Kings 11:1 ff.; on his marriage to the Egyptian princess, cf. I Kings 3:1.

[73] The dating of Psalm 45 has been the subject of wide difference of opinion. While it has been referred to Solomon (Kirkpatrick), to Jehu (Briggs, ICC), to Ahab and Jezebel (Hitzig, Buttenwieser), or to Jehoram and Athaliah (Delitzsch), Pfeiffer's judgment that the king's name can not now be determined is the soundest view. Evidently, such compositions must have been common, though only one has survived in the Psalter. The preservation of another example in the *Song of Songs* is perfectly natural, in fact even more appropriate.

period considerably after Solomon's day. However, this etymology is far from certain. On independent grounds, many scholars prefer other derivations, the most plausible being from the Sanskrit *paryanka*, "sedan, palanquin."[74] That Solomon had regular commercial relations with India is being increasingly recognized, as scholars re-evaluate the Biblical evidence in the light of new extra-Biblical data.[75] Ac-

[74] So Robertson-Smith in Yule, *Glossary of Anglo-Indian Words*, p. 502; Brown-Driver-Briggs, *Lexicon*, s. v. Tur-Sinai (in his paper, p. 4, n. 1) adduces an Akkadian parallel *ap (p)aru*, meaning "hut of reeds" and also "head covering." Erbt and Wittekindt read *'appidyōn*, from Babylonian *'aphad* = "come as messenger." Zapletal reads *appadan*, Babylonian "tent," which occurs in Dan. 11:45. Tur-Sinai makes a new suggestion in *Halashon Vehasepher* (Jerusalem, 1951), p. 389, where he argues that a litter is too small an object and suggests that the word is actually a scribal combination of אף, "also," and an unknown word רין.

[75] The technical term "ship of Tarshish," which the book of Kings applies both to Solomon's vessel that sailed with Hiram's navy and brought back "gold, silver, ivory, apes and peacocks" (I Kings 10:22) and to the ships of Jehoshaphat which sailed from the southern port of Ezion-geber (I Kings 22:49), has been regarded as a generic term for a large vessel, no matter what its destination, like our English "Indiaman." Thus it could be used of vessels going eastward to Arabia, Africa, or even India. This, in spite of the fact that the place-name "Tarshish" has been generally equated with some port west of Palestine, such as Carthage (LXX on Ezek. 27:12), the Roman province of Africa (Targum on I Kings 22:49; Jer. 10:9), Tarsus in Cilicia (Josephus, *Antiquities*, 1, vi, 9), Etruscan Italy (Cheyne), Tharsis on the Black Sea (Desnoyers), Tharros in Sardinia (Covey-Crump), or, as is most generally accepted, Tartessos in Spain (first proposed by Eusebius and revived by Bochart; cf. W. Max Müller, *Dictionary of the Bible*, vol. 4, pp. 683 f.; Galling, *Biblisches Reallexikon*, pp. 510 f.).

On the other hand, it seems clear that the book of Chronicles thought of Tarshish as lying to the east of Palestine, since it uses the phrase "ships going to Tarshish" in its account of these same nautical enterprises of Solomon and Jehoshaphat (II Chron. 9:21; 20:36). This was long dismissed as another example of the unreliability of the Chronicler. Recent scholarship has, however, gone far in rehabilitating his credibility (cf., for example, Von Rad, *Die Geschichtsbildung der Chronistischen Werke*, Stuttgart, 1930; Martin Noth, *Ueberlieferungsgeschichtliche Studien*, Halle, 1943; W. F. Albright, *From the Stone Age to Christianity*, Baltimore, 1940, p. 268). It is, therefore, not impossible that the Chronicler's view of Tarshish is another example where his value was unduly discounted in the past. Thus Bochart's old attempt to validate the Chronicler's references by assuming that there were two localities referred to as "Tarshish," one in the Western Mediterranean, the other in the Indian Ocean, was dismissed summarily by scholars (cf. W. Max Müller, *Dictionary of the Bible*, vol. 4, p. 684n). On the other hand, J. Hornell recently contended vigorously that Tarshish refers to "a great mart on the west coast of India," from which gold, spices, pearls, and other gems were shipped westward (cf. his paper, "Naval Activity in the Days of Solomon and Rameses III," in *Antiquity*, vol. 21, p. 72). This view is favorably considered by Salo W. Baron (*A Social and Religious History of the Jews*, 2nd ed., New York, 1952, vol. 1, p. 321, n. 3.).

Whatever the identification of Tarshish, the Oriental provenance of *'apiriōn*,

cording to our sources (I Kings 10:22), Solomon's imports from the East included ivory, apes (*qōph*) and peacocks (*tūkī*). As the derivation of these words indicates (Sanskrit, *kapi*; Malabar, *toqai, toqhai*), India was the point of origin of these luxuries. In addition, Solomon's ships might well have imported the palanquin, or at least the materials from which it was constructed, from India, together with its native name.

The syntactic construction in 3:7 (*miṭṭāthō šelliš⁼lōmō*), which would seem to reflect Aramaic influence,[76] does not represent an insuperable objection to a Solomonic dating for the poem as a whole. Popular songs often tend to be supplemented and modified with time, so that a late phrase may enter an early poem, and inconsistencies result. The composite character of folk-poetry must always be kept in mind. Thus, in a modern Palestinian love-lyric, the girl Fulla is addressed as Jewish, Mohammedan and Christian, all in the course of the eleven stanzas of the song.[77] While she is called Serena, a popular name of Spanish-Jewish actresses (stanza 4), she is described as making her ablutions before prayers, a Mohammedan practice (stanza 6), while the marriage ceremony is described by a specifically Christian term (stanza 9).

Moreover, the evidence is constantly growing that an "Aramaic" usage is not necessarily late in Hebrew. Not only in Northern Israel, but even in the south, the close linguistic affinities of the two languages[78] were strengthened by continuous relations between Israel

rather than the proposed Greek etymology for the word, becomes increasingly more plausible.

[76] Cf. Dan. 3:26; 4:23, and such frequent Mishnaic locutions as רבונו של עולם.

[77] Cf. Stephan, *op. cit.*, pp. 35 f.

[78] That this affinity involved not only the vocabulary, but also the phonetic and morphologic structure of Hebrew, was conclusively demonstrated by Max L. Margolis. Cf. E. A. Speiser in *Max L. Margolis, Scholar and Teacher*, edited by R. Gordis (Philadelphia, 1952), pp. 31–34.

On the various categories of "Aramaisms," see *KMW*, pp. 59, 362 f. Cf. also Driver's judgment (*op. cit.*, p. 440) that "*še* and many words common in Aramaic are part of the northern dialect." They represent part of the North-West-Semitic vocabulary, common to both Aramaic and Hebrew, except that some words became common in the former and were used only sporadically in the latter. To this category of a common *Wortschatz*, we may assign, in addition to the relative (cf. Judg. 5:7; 6:17; 7:12; 8:26; II Kings 6:11), בְּרוֹת (1:17, instead of בְּרוֹשׁ; cf. סַבְלָת for שִׁבֹּלֶת in Judg. 12:6) and שַׁלָּמָה (1:7), a Hebraized form of the Aramaic דְּלְמָא.

Many others have classical Hebrew parallels: לכי (2:13 Kethib, cf. II Kings 4:2 Kethib); נטר (1:6; cf. Lev. 19:18; Amos 1:11, reading וַיִּטֹּר for וַיִּטְרֹף; Jer. 3:5, 12, etc.); קפץ, "leap" (2:8; cf. קפץ, "close, clench," Deut. 15:7; Isa. 52:15); הרהיב (6:5:

and Syria throughout the pre-Exilic period.[79] The usage may, accordingly, be older than can at present be documented in our extant sources.[80]

Moreover, related instances of pronominal anticipation occur in Biblical Hebrew and Phoenician.[81] Hence we are not forced to delete the entire clause from the poem, or even to assume that it was introduced later.[82]

Whatever approach be adopted on this detail, the unique features of this poem mark it as a royal wedding-song going back to Solomon's reign. It is at present the oldest datable unit in the book. By contributing to the growth of the tradition of Solomonic authorship, it helped to win inclusion for the entire Song of Songs in the canon of Scripture.

IX. Date of the Book

Being lyrical in character, with no historical allusions, most of the songs are undatable. There are, however, a few exceptions, which have already been noted. The song in which Tirzah, the early capital of North Israel, is referred to (6:4), must predate the year 876 B. C. E., when Omri made Samaria the capital of his kingdom, while the use of a Persian word like *pardēs* (4:13) can hardly antedate the 6th century. Yet even this latter inference must be qualified by the consideration already adduced above, that folk songs often undergo many

cf. Isa. 3:5; *Rahab* the mythological monster mentioned in Isa. 30:7; Job 9:13, etc.); Lamed accusative (2:15; 8:13; cf. Lev. 19:18, 34; II Sam. 3:30).

Authentic Aramaic borrowings seem to be חרכים (2:9); כתל (2:9); סתו (2:11); סמדר (2:13, 15; 7:13); פג (2:13); סנט (5:3); סנסנים (7:9); and סוגה (7:3), though new texts may change the picture. See note 80.

[79] Cf. A. T. Olmstead, *A History of Palestine and Syria* (New York, 1931).

[80] Thus the word 'aŝiāḥ occurs only in the Hebrew of Ben Sira (50:3) with no Biblical parallel, but it is found in the Mesha Inscription (Line 9) as 'aŝūaḥ. The late Biblical and Mishnaic word *nekhasim* occurs once, in Josh. 22:8. The root *kibbel*, occurring only in Job 2:10 and Esth. 9:27, and generally regarded as a late Aramaism, was recently found by Albright in the Tell-el Amarna Letters (*BASOR*, 89, Feb., 1943, pp. 29 ff.). On the conjunction ŝe, once regarded as a "late Aramaism," see note 78.

[81] In Biblical Hebrew, pronominal anticipation occurs a) with a verbal suffix (Ex. 2:6; 35:5; Jer. 9:14; Ecc. 2:21); b) with a nominal suffix, which resembles our usage more closely (Ezek. 10:3; Prov. 13:4; Job 29:3; Ezra 3:12; possibly also Num. 23:18; 24:3, 5) and c) after the preposition Lamedh (Ezra 9:1). That the usage is early in origin is attested by its occurrence in Phoenician in the Karatepe Inscription of Azitawadd (9th or 8th century B. C. E.); cf. Text C, I, lines 17–18, לשבתנם דדנים lit. "for the dwelling of them, of the Danunians"; III, line 4, לחתי בעל כרנתריש lit. "for the giving of him, of Baal Kalendris (?)". Cf. C. H. Gordon in *JNES*, vol. 8, 1949, pp. 113 f.; N. H. Tur-Sinai in *Leshonenu*, vol. 17, no. 4, p. 9.

[82] So Jastrow, H. L. Ginsberg (orally, to the writer), Haller.

changes with time, so that later words and expressions may well be
inserted into such older material. The grounds for attributing one
song (3:6–11) to the period of Solomon have already been set forth.
Thus the datable material in the' Song spans five centuries. The
period begins with Solomon's accession to the throne (c. 960 B. C. E.),
includes the early days of the Northern Kingdom (c. 920–876), and
reaches down to the Persian era (6th–5th century).

The variations in language, which point to a considerable difference in the dates of the different songs, are only one factor, though
decisive, in making it impossible to agree with Rowley, who has "the
impression of a single hand" in the Song with "a corresponding unity
of theme and style."[83] So, too, the varying geographical locales, from
the Lebanon mountains in the north to the Dead Sea region in the
south, from Transjordan to the central valleys, plainly point to a
different provenance for the various songs. The change from rustic
simplicity in some lyrics to the sophistication of the city in others
points in the same direction.

It is most probable that the other songs in the book fall within
the same four centuries as the datable units, with the bulk of the
material being pre-Exilic rather than post-Exilic. The freshness of
the poetry, the naturalness of the references to the Palestinian land-
scape, and the unabashed attitude toward love all seem to point to
the period before the Babylonian Exile. No national disaster has
yet cast its shadow over the temper of the people, and there is no echo
as yet of the deepening of the religious consciousness which followed
the Restoration under Cyrus and the reforms of Ezra and Nehemiah.
That most of the place-names are northern and eastern also points
to the pre-Exilic era, in fact to the period preceding the destruction
of the Northern Kingdom in 722 B. C. E., since the Jewish settlements
were restricted largely to Judah in the south during the Persian and
pre-Maccabean period. The book was redacted in the Persian period,
the heyday of Wisdom literature, not later than the fifth century.

X. HEBREW ELEMENTS IN THE SONG OF SONGS

Love lyrics are, as we have seen, difficult to date because their
basic emotion knows no limit of time. Since the sentiment is not
limited in space, love songs are not specifically national. In this
respect, the Song of Songs shares the qualities of Wisdom literature
as a whole, which is the most secular and least particularist element
of Hebrew literature.

[83] *Op. cit.*, pp. 212 f.

Nonetheless, some specific *national* coloring is to be found in the book. The reference to "the heroes of Israel" (3:7) is needed in this epithalamium of a foreign princess to indicate the nationality of her bodyguard. The "tower of David" upon which the shields of the heroes are hung (4:4) testifies to the widespread living character of the tradition of David's band of heroes, which is now embodied in the lists in II Sam. 23:8 ff.

The only other national notes are *geographical*, the cities, hills, and valleys of the country. Principally, the book reflects the background of Northern Israel. It is the northern mountain range which appears in Hermon and Senir (modern Jebel esh-Sheikh) as well as in Lebanon (now Jebel Libnan) and 'Amana (the modern Jebel Zebedâni).[84] The central territory of Northern Israel appears in Shunem,[85] in Carmel and Sharon, as well as in Tirzah, if its location is to be sought at Tel-el-Fâr'ah. Transjordan appears in Ḥeshbon (modern Hesban), in the south, in the districts of Gilead, and possibly in Bashan to the north.[86] On the other hand, the territory of Judah is sparsely represented. Aside from the references to the daughters of Zion (3:11) and of Jerusalem (3:5; 5:8), only En-gedi on the Dead Sea is mentioned (1:14).

The preponderantly northern coloring of the book, as already noted, is significant in strengthening the view that the songs are predominantly pre-Exilic. The northern provenance of the songs also explains the Aramaisms in the book, which reflect the close proximity of the pre-Exilic Kingdom of Israel to Syria. Foreign products and articles bear foreign names, whether Sanskrit or Persian.[87]

Attention to the geographical locale is sometimes helpful in delineating the literary unit. The passage 1:9–17 is often regarded by commentators as one song.[88] However, the references to Pharaoh's horses and chariots (v. 9), which were most likely to be seen in Southern Palestine, and the mention of the vineyards of En-gedi on

---

[84] On the modern identification of these sites, see Wright-Filson, *Historical Atlas to the Bible* (Philadelphia, 1945), pp. 107 ff. While Deut. 3:9 informs us that Senir was the Amorite equivalent for Hermon, the Song (4:8) treats them either as distinct mountain peaks or as a wider designation for the Anti-Lebanon range.

[85] The equivalence of "Shulammite" with "Shunemite," long maintained, is attested by *Sulem*, the modern Arabic name of *Shunem*. On other recent theories, see the Commentary *ad loc.*

[86] If כְּמִגְדַּל הַשֵּׁן in 7:5 is to be read as הַבָּשָׁן, in view of the other geographical similes in the *waṣf*.

[87] Thus פַּרְדֵּס (4:13) is not a garden, but a park. Of the spices mentioned, קִנָּמוֹן, אֲהָלוֹת and כֹּפֶר are probably Indian, like אַרְגָּמָן and אַפִּרְיוֹן. אֵגוֹז may be Persian. See the Lexicons of Brown-Driver-Briggs and Baumgarten-Kohler, *s. v.*

[88] So e. g., Jastrow, Haller. Pfeiffer (*op. cit.*, p. 710) regards vv. 12–17 as a unit.

the western shore of the Dead Sea (v. 14), point to Judah in the south. On the other hand, the reference to the lovers' meeting in the forest, their "house walled with cedars" (v. 17), must necessarily reflect a North Israelite locale, since cedars never grew in southern Palestine.[89] So, too, the Aramaized form *berōthīm*, "sycamores," for the more common Hebrew *berōšīm* (v. 17), points to the Northern Kingdom, which was more exposed to Aramaic influence. It is therefore clear that the passage consists of two independent songs (1:9–14 and vv. 15–17).

When this is recognized, other divergences which tended to be overlooked or misunderstood receive a natural and unforced explanation. The first song speaks of the beloved as luxuriously decked out in jewels (vv. 9–11), and the lover is called "king" (v. 12) and is therefore the bridegroom. He is probably speaking during the festivities of the bridal week and hence uses the plural (*na'aseh*, v. 11) in the presence of his friends. Hence, too, the frank reference to sexual intimacy (vv. 12–13). The second song, on the other hand, reflects the simplicity of an outdoor tryst of lovers (note *dōd*, v. 16), not of the bride and groom, hence the delicate reticence regarding their relationship.

Religious motifs are even rarer in the book than specific national references. In the noun *šalhebhethyāh*, "flame of God" (8:6), the Divine name is used to express the superlative, and the word is equivalent in meaning to "a mighty flame." This usage has many analogies in Biblical Hebrew.[90]

We believe that Hebrew religious attitudes, hitherto unrecognized, lie at the base of a unique phenomenon in the book, the adjuration "by the gazelles and the hinds of the field" (2:7; 3:5), "not to disturb love until it be sated." That the gazelle and the hind were symbolic of love is, of course, clear from Biblical and post-Biblical Hebrew, where they were used as metaphors for a graceful and loving young woman.[91] Ebeling, in his study of Babylonian magic, calls attention to the Babylonian practice of tying a gazelle to the head of the bed and a ram at the foot as a magical rite to induce potency, with the formula, "like that ram may my husband love me."[92]

---

[89] Cf. *Enzyklopedia Miqrait* (Jerusalem, 1950), vol. 1, p. 554b.

[90] Cf. מַאְפֵּלְיָה, "deep gloom" (Jer. 2:31); מֶרְחַבְיָה, "great enlargement" (Ps. 118:5); גִּבּוֹר צַיִד לִפְנֵי ה', "an exceedingly mighty hunter" (Gen. 10:9); אַרְזֵי אֵל, "mighty cedars" (Ps. 80:11).

[91] Cf.l אַיֶּלֶת אֲהָבִים וְיַעֲלַת חֵן (Prov. 5:19). These and similar terms are frequent in the love poetry of Jehudah Halevi, Immanuel of Rome, and other medieval Hebrew poets.

[92] Cf. J. Ebeling, "Liebeszauber im alten Orient," in *Mittheilungen der altorientalischen Gesellschaft*, I (1905), pp. 27, 33.

This is, however, far removed from an oath "by the gazelle," particularly for the strongly monotheistic Hebrews. A closer parallel is afforded by the Greek custom, practiced by no less a figure than Socrates, of swearing by an animal, as e. g. "by the dog," "by the goose," or by any nearby plant or object, such as "by the caperberry," "by the almond" and "by the cabbage."[93] The Greek philosophers defended this usage by asserting that the Greeks never intended to swear by the animals as gods, but used the animals as substitutes for gods. This was no mere apologetics, but a reflection of the widespread fear of the consequence of an unfulfilled oath. Hence arose the desire for an "escape formula."

Another factor, however, often enters into the choice of a substitute, which has been overlooked — *a similarly sounding term, even if irrelevant or virtually meaningless, is often chosen.* Thus the Rabbinic vow-term *ḳorbān* would frequently be replaced by *ḳōnām*.[94] In contemporary colloquial English, this phenomenon can be clearly observed. "Gosh darn" does duty for "God damn," "Gee," for "Jesus," "Jiminy Crickets" for "Jesus Christ," "Holy Cow" for "Holy Christ," etc.[95] Older substitutions of the same kind that entered English literature are "zounds" for "By God's wounds," "Marry" meaning "indeed," for "By Mary," "Dear me," probably for "Dio Mio," "By Cripes" for "By Christ." The German replaces "Gott" by "Potz" in "*Potzwelt*," "*Potzwetter*" and "*Pottsblitz*." The Frenchman changes "Dieu" into *bleu* in "Corbleu," "Morbleu," "Sambleu," and avoids the name of God altogether by swearing by "nom de nom."

Of the common speech of the Hebrew populace, little, if any, has reached us, and so the only extant example of this phenomenon is to be found in our book.

The most solemn Hebrew adjuration would be *be'lōhei ṣebhā'ōth* or *beʿēl šaddai*, "by the Lord of Hosts" or "by the Almighty."[96] The

---

[93] Cf. the discussion in S. Lieberman, *Greek in Jewish Palestine* (New York, 1942), pp. 125–27, who cites some of the abundant material assembled in P. Meinhardt, *De forma et usu iuramentorum*, pp. 77 ff., and Hirzel, *Der Eid*, p. 96, note 2.

[94] Cf. Lieberman, *op. cit.*, p. 129, note 106.

[95] Cf. Burgess Johnson, *The Lost Art of Profanity* (New York, 1948); esp. pp. 26, 101, 116, 117. I am indebted to Professor Mario A. Pei for this reference. I was unable to consult *A Dictionary of Profanity and Its Substitutions* by M. R. Walter, on deposit in manuscript form in the Princeton University Library, to which Johnson refers.

[96] The most popular oaths naturally invoked the God of Israel: a) 'חי ה, "As JHVH liveth" (I Sam. 14:39, 45; 19:6, and often; I Kings 1:29; 2:24, and often; Jer. 4:2; 5:2, and often; Ruth 3:13); (אלהים) נשבע בה' (Josh. 2:12; 9:19; I Kings 1:17; 2:8, etc.). b) חי האלהים (II Sam. 2:27); נשבע באלהים (Gen. 21:23). c) (rarely)

deepseated reluctance to use the Divine name, which finds expression in the Third Commandment (Ex. 20:7), became increasingly felt with time. This tendency is mirrored in such Biblical books as Esther and Ecclesiastes, as well as in the editing of Psalms, and finds varied expression in Rabbinic literature.[96a] The desire to avoid mentioning God's name would be particularly strongly felt in connection with an oath concerned with the physical aspects of love. Hence, the lover replaces such customary oaths as *bē'lohei ṣ̌ebhā'ōth* or *bᵉ'ēl šaddai* by a similarly sounding phrase *biṣᵉbhā'ōth 'ō bᵉ'ayᵉlōth hassādeh*, "by the gazelles or the hinds of the field," choosing animals, which symbolize love, for the substitutions. It is likely that the Septuagint retained some recognition of the oath by rendering the unique Hebrew phrase "in (or, by) the powers and the forces of the field."[97] The Midrash also recognized the irregular character of the oath in the Song and identified "the gazelles and the hinds" with "the hosts of heaven and earth."[98] Here, as elsewhere, the homily rests upon a fine perception of the essential meaning of the text.

חי אל (Job 27:2). d) חי ה' אלהיך (I Kings 17:12; 18:10); נשבע לה' (Zeph. 1:5; Ps. 132:2).

Additional solemnity undoubtedly attached to oaths with more elaborate formulas as a) חי ה' אלהי ישראל (I Sam. 25:34; I Kings 17:11); b) חי ה' צבאות, "As JHVH, Lord of Hosts, liveth" (I Kings 18:15; II Kings 3:14); ונשבעות לה' צבאות (Isa. 19:18). A possible double oath occurs in only one poetic passage: חי ה' וברוך צורי, "God liveth and my Rock is blessed" (II Sam. 22:47 = Ps. 18:47). So also the oath בְּחֵי הָעוֹלָם, "By Him who liveth eternally" (Dan. 12:7).

To avoid mentioning JHVH, oaths by His name became common: בשם ה' (Isa. 48:1); בשמו (Deut. 6:13; Jer. 12:16); בשמי הגדול (Jer. 44:26); בשמי (Jer. 12:16).

Joint oaths invoking God and a human being also occur: a) חי ה' וחי נפשך, "As God lives and as does your soul" (I Sam. 20:3; 25:26; II Kings 2:2; 4:30); b) חי ה', וחי אדני המלך, "As God lives and as does my lord, the king" (II Sam. 15:21).

The Lord Himself swears by His own being: a) חי אני, "As I live" (Num. 14:21; Jer. 22:24; Ezek. 5:11; 14:16, and often; Zeph. 2:9). b) חי אנכי (Deut. 32:40); בי, "By Myself" (Gen. 22:16; Isa. 45:23; Jer. 22:5; 49:13). c) בקדשו, "By His holiness" (Amos 4:2); בקדשי, "By My holiness" (Ps. 89:36). d) בנפשו, "By His essence, literally, soul" (Jer. 51:14; Amos 6:8). e) בימינו, "By His right hand" (Isa. 62:8). f) בגאון יעקב, "By the glory of Jacob," an epithet for God (Amos 8:7).

[96a] Cf. now the illuminating study by S. S. Cohon, "The Name of God, a Study in Rabbinic Theology," in *HUCA*, vol. 23, 1950–51, Part I, pp. 579–604.

[97] Reading ἐν ταῖς δυνάμεσι καὶ ἐν ταῖς ἰσχύσεσι τοῦ ἀγροῦ. Cf. Siegfried *ad loc.*

[98] Cf. Midrash Shir Hashirim Rab. 2:7: במה השביען ר' אליעזר אומר השביען בשמים ובארץ. בצבאות בצבא של מעלה ובצבא של מטה. "By what did he (*sic*) adjure them? R. Eliezer says, 'He adjured them by heaven and earth. *Biṣᵉbhā'ōth* means by the host (*Ṣᵉbā'*) above and by the host below.'"

In this reticence with regard to the use of the Divine name, particularly in the context of sensual love, as well as in its pervasive delicacy of expression, which will be discussed below, the Song reveals itself as authentically within the Jewish tradition.

At times, the differences between the Hebrew poet and his Oriental confrères prove highly revealing of the Hebrew *ethos*. Moreover, what the Song does not say is often as significant for its Israelite outlook as any overt Hebrew element.

Thus, hunting was a favorite sport in Egypt and Mesopotamia, as literary sources and archaeological discoveries abundantly indicate.[99] In a love-song emanating from "the Golden Age" of Egyptian lyric poetry in the 18th dynasty,[100] the maiden expresses the yearning for her lover:

> "How good it would be,
> If thou wert with me
> When I set the trap."

She is referring to a small trap set for bird-catching. It is noteworthy that in all the references to nature in the Song, hunting is not mentioned. Nimrod and Esau were hunters, but the taking of animal life for sport was not popular in ancient Israel,[101] an attitude crystallized further in Rabbinic Judaism.[102]

Even more characteristic of the Hebrew spirit is the absence of the personification of nature in the Song. In the Egyptian poem "The Tree in the Garden" the poet goes on to say, "The tree speaketh."[103] For the Hebrew poet, nature serves as the glorious background for human love, but never as more, exactly as nature is the manifestation of the creative power of God for the Psalmist and for Job.[104]

The age-old relationship of wine, women, and song finds its reflection, of course, in the Song, for wine-drinking was widespread in Israel. Nonetheless, references in our book to the first member of

---

[99] Cf. K. Galling, *Biblisches Reallexikon* (Tuebingen, 1937), pp. 286 ff.

[100] Cf. J. A. Wilson, in Pritchard, *op. cit.*, p. 468a.

[101] Cf. W. H. Bennett, in Hastings, *Dictionary of the Bible*, vol. 2, pp. 437 f.; K. Galling, *Biblisches Reallexikon* (Tuebingen, 1937), pp. 286 ff. On the other hand, killing animals in self-defense was naturally practised (cf., for example, Judg. 14:6; I Sam. 17:34 ff.), and some game animals were used for food (Deut. 12:15, 22; I Kings 5:3).

[102] The Jewish laws of *shehitah*, which prescribed slaughter with a knife, effectively ruled out the use of birds or animals killed in the hunt.

[103] Cf. Erman, *op. cit.*, p. 249.

[104] Cf., *inter alia*. Psalms 19 and 105; Job, chaps. 38–41.

the triad are very few.[105] Nothing is to be found resembling these
lines of an Egyptian love song:[106]

> "Her lover sitteth at her right hand,
> The feast is disordered with drunkenness."

The absence of this theme in the Song may, of course, be the
result of the choice of poems in the collection. It is at least equally
likely that it reflects a negative attitude toward drunkenness, which
became traditional in Judaism.

Another common aspect of love-poetry, virtually missing here, is
the motif of faithlessness and jealousy.[107] On the other hand, the
Egyptian maiden complains:[108]

> "What meaneth it that thou wrongest another heart and me?"

To be sure, coquetry and the maiden's resistance to the lover's advances occur as themes,[109] but no "love triangle" is to be met with
in our book. This absence, however, must be accidental, or the result
of the editor's choice — the human emotion involved is ubiquitous
and must have existed in ancient Israel.

XI. EXTRA-HEBREW PARALLELS TO THE BOOK

The universality of love as an emotion and an experience, which is
responsible for the absence of any considerable degree of specific
Hebrew coloration in the book, should make us wary about postulating
direct borrowings from other peoples in these songs. Mere resemblances of theme are not sufficient. What is methodologically required
is a special sequence of theme or some other unusual feature, not
explicable in terms of Hebrew background. A few centuries later, the
Palestinian city of Gedera was the home of the gifted Greek poets
Meleager and Philodemus the Epicurean, who flourished in the 1st
century B. C. E. It is a purely gratuitous assumption that the lyric

---

[105] Note that in 1:4 and 7:10, wine is used merely as a comparison, while in
1:6 and 8:12, the vineyard is a symbol for love. The difficult closing phrase of 5:1
is the only direct reference to heavy drinking in the Song (šikhᵉrū, literally "become
drunk"). See the Commentary on this passage.

[106] Erman, op. cit., p. 251.

[107] The noun kin'āh in 8:6, as the parallelism indicates, means "passion." The
possibility of other lovers is raised in 1:7. See the Commentary ad loc.

[108] Erman, op. cit., p. 248.

[109] As e. g. 2:14; 4:12 ff.; 5:2 ff.; 8:8 ff.

gift was limited to the Greek inhabitants of the country and that the Hebrews were congenitally incapable of love-poetry.

With the all but universal rejection of a Greek date for the book today, scholars have turned instead to the Egyptian culture-milieu in seeking evidence of borrowing in the Song of Songs. Thus, it has been argued that the use of *'āḥōth*, "sister," for "beloved" is an Egyptian usage. Being unhebraic, the word was glossed by *kallāh*, "bride," everywhere except in the last passage (4:9, 10, 12; 5:1, 2).[110] Actually, the assumption of glossing is not supported by the meter. Of the five passages where the term occurs, it is not accompanied by *kallāh* in one (5:2), and it can not be a gloss in two others (4:9, 12), because its deletion would destroy the rhythm of the text.[111] In the other two passages (4:10; 5:1), metric considerations can not be invoked at all, since either the retention or the deletion of *'āḥōth* would produce an acceptable rhythmic pattern.[112]

The entire assumption that the usage is unhebraic, however, is unjustified. The Hebrew nouns *rē'a* and *ra'yāh* (*r'ʿūth*), which are common in the meanings "friend" and "neighbor," also signify "beloved."[113] Similarly, the synonyms *'āḥ* and *'āḥōth*, "brother, sister," develop the parallel meanings of "friend, neighbor" and "beloved."[114] *Aḥōth* therefore means "beloved" in the Song, when the lover, in an outburst of emotion, heaps up terms of endearment, coupling "sister"

---

[110] Cf. Pfeiffer, *op. cit.*, p. 711. As a matter of fact, *'āḥōth* occurs in the meaning of "beloved" with no gloss, in another song, 8:8. See Commentary *ad loc.*

[111] The MT in 4:9 has a 3:3:3 meter. The deletion of כַּלָּה would create 2:3:3, a rare, if not impossible, pattern, since as a rule closing stichs are longer than the opening ones only at the end of a literary unit, for the purpose of creating a strong close. See the following note for an example, and cf. the study cited in note 43, p. 146. In 4:12, the rhythm is 2:2:2:2, which would also be destroyed by deleting כַּלָּה, to create a 3:4 meter.

[112] In 4:10, the MT is 4:3:3, a common form of the *kīnāh* rhythm. With the deletion it would be the frequent 3:3:3 meter. In 5:1, the MT exhibits the 4:3:3:3 pattern; with the deletion of *aḥōtî*, it would be 3:3:3:3. The closing stich, אִכְלוּ רֵעִים שְׁתוּ וְשִׁכְרוּ דוֹדִים, which is widely regarded as out of place, is in 2:3 rhythm, normal at the close of a poem. See note above on the metric principle involved, and see the Commentary *ad loc.*

[113] On רַע as "friend," cf., *inter alia*, Gen. 38:12; as "fellow, neighbor," cf. Ex. 2:13; Lev. 19:18; as "lover," cf. Jer. 3:1. On רַעְיָה (רֵעוּת) as "friend," cf. Judg. 11:37 *Kethib*; as "fellow, neighbor," cf. Ex. 11:2; Jer. 9:19; Esth. 1:19; as "beloved," cf. Song 1:9, 15; 2:2, 10, 13; 4:1, 7; 5:2; 6:4.

[114] On אָח as "friend," cf. II Sam. 1:26; I Kings 9:13; as "fellow, neighbor," cf. Lev. 19:17. On אָחוֹת as "fellow, neighbor," cf. Ex. 26:3, 5, 6, 17; Ezek. 1:9, 23; 3:13.

either with "bride" or with "friend."[115] So too, the Hebrew and
Arabic word for "daughter," *bat*, *bint*, means "girl" and is not restricted
to the specific family relationship.[116]

Nor is there any objective ground for assuming that the feeling
for nature was an exclusively Egyptian trait. The God speeches in
Job manifest a loving insight into nature unparalleled elsewhere,
and the prophets and psalmists disclose a love and observation
of the external world which needed no foreign influence or literary
borrowing.[117]

Of direct borrowings in the authentic sense, there is no evidence.
Nonetheless, since love is the same anywhere, the reactions and
forms of expression of love-lyrics everywhere will resemble each
other. Accordingly, Oriental love poetry, ancient and modern, often
sheds light upon the background of the Hebrew poem. Because of
the close relationship of love to magic and religion[118] which modern
psychology and anthropology have revealed, ancient incantation
texts also add considerably to our understanding of the Song.[119]

Tur-Sinai[120] has called attention to the background underlying 8:9:

> If she be a wall,
> We will build upon her a turret of silver;
> And if she be a door,
> We will enclose her with boards of cedar.

[115] On the equivalence of אָח and רֵעַ, cf. Ps. 35:14, כְּרֵעַ כְּאָח־לִי הִתְהַלָּכְתִּי; Job
30:29, אָח הָיִיתִי לְתַנִּים וְרֵעַ לִבְנוֹת יַעֲנָה.

[116] Tur-Sinai calls attention to this fact, *op. cit.*, p. 367. This usage is not restricted to Biblical Hebrew (Gen. 30:13; Isa. 32:9; Prov. 31:29), but is common in
modern Israeli Hebrew as well.

[117] Cf., on the appreciation of beauty in the Bible, the eloquent presentation of
S. Goldman, *The Book of Books*, vol. 1 (New York, 1948).

[118] Cf., *inter alia*, J. G. Frazer, *The Golden Bough* (New York, 1922); A. E.
Crawley, *The Mystic Rose* (New York, 1927); B. Z. Goldberg, *The Sacred Fire*
(New York, 1930).

[119] Cf. J. Ebeling, "Liebeszauber im alten Orient," in *Mittheilungen der alt-
orientalischen Gesellschaft*, vol. 1 (1925); *idem*, "Aus dem Tagewerk eines assyrischen
Zauberpriesters," in *MAOG*, vol. 5 (1931). It is the merit of N. H. Tur-Sinai, in
his paper "Shir Hashirim," now reprinted in his *Halashon Vehasepher*, vol. II
(Jerusalem, 5711), pp. 351–88, to have utilized this material for the interpretation
of our book with great brilliance. At times, however, his deductions, like his basic
view of the *Song* as part of a gigantic prose-poetic history of Israel (cf. p. 388), do
not carry conviction.

[120] *Op. cit.*, p. 367. We are, however, unable to accept his interpretation (p. 368)
that *šeyᵉdubbar bāh* (8:8) means "when incantations are pronounced upon her."

Charms warding off all types of perils were couched in this form.
Thus, for example, the Assyrian charm against a crying baby was as
follows:

> It it is a dog, let them cut off morsels for him!
> If it is a bird, let them throw clods of earth upon him!
> If it is a naughty human child, let them adjure him with
>   the oath of Anu and Antu!

Even more apposite, because it demonstrates that *ḥomah*, "wall,"
and *deleth*, "door," "bar," in 8:9 are synonymous and not antithetic,
is the following charm against an enemy:[121]

> If he is a door, I will open thy mouth,
> If he is a bar, I will open thy tongue.[122]

Obviously there is no incantation implied any longer in the Song,
but the formula has survived as a love motif.

While several *waṣfs* in praise of the beloved occur in the book,
only one waṣf praising the lover is to be met with (5:10–16). In part
the description is highly extravagant and goes beyond the limits of
metaphor. Thus, for example, 5:11, 14, 15:

> "His head is fine gold . . . .
> His hands are rods of gold, set with topaz . . . .
> His thighs are pillars of marble
> Set upon sockets of gold . . . .

Perhaps these phrases are more than mere poetic hyperbole. This
is suggested by a Babylonian adjuration for the recovery of a sick
person from illness:[123]

> Like lapis lazuli I want to cleanse his body,
> Like marble his features should shine,
> Like pure silver, like red gold,
> I want to make clean what is dull.

The Biblical *waṣf* may therefore be extolling the health and potency
of the lover.

A long-standing difficulty in the Song is presented by 5:1. The
first four stichs of the verse speak of the lover enjoying the myrrh,

---

[121]Ebeling, "Aus dem Tagewerk," p. 19.

[122] Ebeling's rendering "seine Zunge" is a *lapsus calami*. The Akkadian is
lisânaka.

[123] *Ibid.*, p. 37.

honey, wine and milk that symbolize the delights of love. The fifth
stich of the verse is couched in the plural:

'ikhᵉlū rēʿīm šᵉthū vᵉšikhᵉrū dōdīm

"Eat, friends, drink abundantly, O loved ones." It is, of course, in-
conceivable that either the love-struck youth or the maiden would
invite others to enjoy the same pleasures as the loved one, and the stich
has therefore been emended either to the masculine singular[124] or to
the feminine,[125] either procedure requiring no less than five changes.
Some have regarded the stich as a misplaced fragment of an independent song.[126] A solution to the problem through an illuminating
parallel is offered by an Arab song, widely known all over Palestine
and Syria, which would indicate that the poet may address the individual lover in the plural, as well as in the singular:

> Examine me,
>   O physician,
> As to what I suffered
>   On behalf of the beloved one.
>
> By God, O Lord!
>   This is a wondrous thing;
> Yet my heart melted
>   For the beloved ones.[127]

The Hebrew text of 5:1 is therefore in order and the stich is in place.

---

[124] Ehrlich reads: .אֱכֹל רַעִי שְׁתֵה וּשְׁכַר דּוֹדִי
[125] Haller reads: .אִכְלִי רַעְיָתִי שְׁתִי וְשִׁכְרִי דוֹדִים
[126] So Budde, who deletes the stich entirely, also Jastrow.
[127] Cf. Stephan, *op. cit.*, p. 80. The text reads as follows:

> *Ykšif ʿalayya*
> *Ya tabīb*
> *ʾAla-lli atāni*
> *Min il-ḥabīb*
> *Wàllah ya râbb*
> *ha-l-àmru ʿajīb*
> *Wàna ʾalbi dâb*
> *ʾAla l-aḥbâb.*

Stephan (note 3) suggests that the plural *aḥ-bâb* is used for the sake of the rhyme
(with *dâb*). That is hardly a compelling reason, since the singular *ḥabīb* would be
an excellent rhyme for *ʿajīb*, and the second and fourth lines of the stanza would be
in rhyme, exactly as in the preceding stanza, *ḥabīb* rhymes with *tabīb*.

XII. MOTIFS AND PATTERNS IN THE COLLECTION

Because of the degree of subjective judgment which must enter
into the delimitation of the songs, unanimity is not to be expected.
Our own study of the book indicates that it contains twenty-eight
songs and fragments, which fall into several patterns, though they
often overlap. To mark each basic theme, we have added descriptive
titles:

A. SONGS OF YEARNING

The Call to Love (1:2–4)
The Rustic Maiden (1:5–6)
Tell Me Where My Love (1:7–8)
Love's Proud Proclamation (2:4–7)
Would Thou Wert My Brother (8:1–4)
Let Me Hear Thy Voice (8:13–14)[128]

B. SONGS OF FULFILLMENT

Love's Barriers — a Duet (4:12 to 5:1)
How Delightful Is Love (7:7–10)
The Beloved's Promise (7:11–14)[129]
Love Under the Apple-Tree — a Duet (8:5)
Surrender (2:16–17)

C. SONGS IN PRAISE OF THE BELOVED

Bedecked in Charm — a Duet (1:9–14)
My Beloved Is Perfect (4:1–7)
Love's Enchantment (4:9–11)
The Power of Beauty (6:4–7)
The One and Only (6:8–9)

---

[128] V. 14 is best taken as a quotation of the words which the lover wishes to hear
(הַשְׁמִיעִנִי: בְּרַח דּוֹדִי), an invitation to enjoy the delights of love (so Haller; slightly
differently Bettan).

[129] The entire passage 7:7–10 and 11–14 may constitute a single song in duet
form, the first portion being spoken by the lover, the second by his beloved. However, there is no direct plea to the beloved in 7–10, which is essentially a poem of
praise, and vv. 11–14 do not constitute a direct answer. We therefore prefer to
regard these passages as two independent poems.

D. DUETS OF MUTUAL PRAISE

Our Walls Are Cedars (1:15–17)
Who Is Like My Love (2:1–3)
The Lover's Welcome (2:14–15)

E. LOVE IN THE WORLD OF NATURE

The Time of Singing Is Come (2:8–13)
Call From the Mountains (4:8)
Love's Dawning (6:10–12)[130]

F. DREAM SONGS

The Dream of the Lost Lover (3:1–5)
Love's Trial and Triumph (5:2 to 6:3); see below.

G. THE GREATNESS OF LOVE

The Seal of Love (8:6–7)
The Finest Vineyard (8:11–12)

H. SONGS OF COURTSHIP AND MARRIAGE

A Wedding Song for Solomon (3:6–11)
The Maiden's Dance (7:1–6)[131]
The Ramparts of Love (8:8–10)

I. LOVE'S SORROWS AND JOYS

Love's Trial and Triumph (5:2 to 6:3)

This, the most elaborate and perhaps the most beautiful song in the collection, is a blending of several patterns: (a) the *dream motif* (5:2), which incorporates the themes of coquetry (5:3) and longing (5:4 ff.); (b) the *waṣf* in praise of the lover (5:10 ff.); and (c) praise of the delights of love (6:2 f.).

---

[130] It is possible that these verses may be independent fragments. V. 12 is completely untranslatable in its present form. See the Commentary for some of the emendations proposed.

[131] That this is a dance is clear from the fact that the description of the bride begins with her feet. That the occasion is a wedding is highly probable, both from the frank description of her physical charms, by far the most outspoken in the book, and from the reference to the "king," i. e. the bridegroom, in v. 6.

In several instances, the units seem very short and we have merely fragments,[132] perhaps only titles of songs, which are no longer extant in their full form. On the other hand, it must always be remembered that in these charming lyrics we lack the music to which they were invariably sung. The number of words and lines required for a song would therefore generally be fewer than in the case of poetry designed to be read. One has only to compare the few words in the popular Israeli song or traditional Hasidic melody with the longer texts of modern poetry in Hebrew or any other language to see the difference. The longest lyric in the book (5:2 to 6:3), which consists of eighteen verses, is, as has been noted, a highly complex blending of several literary motifs.

In a collection such as this, it is to be expected that phrases and verses will reappear more than once.[133] Glosses are, of course, not to be ruled out *a priori*, but deciding which words are secondary is a particularly precarious undertaking in a collection of popular folk-songs, where additions are natural.[134] Thus the two dream-songs (3:1–5 and 5:2 ff.) repeat the theme of the city watchmen, but the second passage introduces a variation, which is in thorough keeping with the more elaborate development of the song as a whole.

XIII. SYMBOLISM AND ESTHETICS IN THE SONG

It is of the essence of poetry that it employ *symbolism* to express nuances beyond the power of exact definition. This is particularly true of love poetry, where the reticences imposed by social convention add both urgency and piquancy to the use of symbols. Hence the beloved will be compared to a flower (2:1 f.), and the lover to a tree (2:3). The delights of love will be described as fruit (2:3), wine (1:4;

---

[132] Cf., for example, 8:5 or 8:13 f. Albright has made the suggestion that Psalm 68 may contain the titles of a collection instead of being the text of a single poem.

[133] Such are the three adjurations of the daughters of Jerusalem (2:7; 3:5; 8:4), the first two of which include the reference to the hinds and the gazelles of the field. So, too, the same text is repeated in 2:5 and 8:3; the phrase seems less relevant in the second passage. The two dream songs (3:1–5 and 5:2 ff.) repeat the theme of the city watchmen (3:3; 5:7) with a variation in the latter.

[134] Cf. Pfeiffer, *op. cit.*, p. 710, for a list of alleged glosses. Some are essential to the text and need only to be interpreted correctly (as e. g. 5:6). Most rest upon considerations of meter which of themselves do not suffice to justify excisions in the text. Not only is there great uncertainty concerning all theories of Biblical meter proposed (cf. W. H. Cobb, *A Criticism of Systems of Hebrew Meter*, Oxford, 1905), but our lack of the accompanying music makes it impossible to tell what words were repeated or lengthened in the chanting of the songs.

5:1), or perfume (5:1), as milk and honey (5:1), as a garden (4:12; 5:1; 6:2), or a vineyard (8:12). The maiden's resistance to the lover's advances will lead to the metaphor of a sealed fountain (4:12) or a high wall (8:9),[135] and the beloved "enemy" will be attacked with the power of charms (8:8 ff.). The invitation to the lover will be couched in the form of a call to enjoy the vineyard (2:15), the fountain (4:15), or the garden (4:16), while the confession that love's demands have been met will be expressed by the figure of a vineyard unguarded (1:6) or of a gazelle upon the mountains of spices (2:17; 8:14).

Symbolism is much more profound than allegory. In allegory, the imaginary figures that are chosen as equivalents for the real characters and objects involved have no independent reality of their own. The language of symbolism, on the other hand, is superior to literal speech as well, because its elements possess both existential reality and a representational character. When, for example, the maiden, in 2:4 f., announces that she is faint with love and asks to be sustained with raisins and apples, she is calling for concrete food, to be sure, but *at the same time*, by her choice of fruits that are symbolic of love, she is indicating that only the satisfaction of her desires will bring her healing. To cite another instance, when the beloved speaks of awakening her lover who is asleep under the apple-tree (8:5), the tree is real enough, but, at the same time, it symbolizes her wish to rouse the dormant desire of her lover. When the girl declares, "I am a wall and my breasts are towers" (8:10), the simile is especially apt, because it expresses both her inaccessibility to the many suitors who are besieging her, and her maturity and readiness for love when her true lover appears.

Nor is the potency of symbolism exhausted by this trait alone. It is characteristic of the delicacy of the songs that the woman in each case expresses her desire for love by indirection. While a blunt avowal would repel by its crassness, the use of symbolism, which conceals as it reveals, heightens by its subtlety the charm of the sentiments expressed. Psycho-analytic theory has offered a highly plausible explanation for this powerful appeal of symbolism to the human spirit. According to psycho-analysis, the "unconscious" persistently seeks some avenue of expression which will elude the "censor" who stands guard over the conscious mind. Symbolism performs this liberating function for the unconscious admirably, because, in its very nature,

---

[135] Thus, in Palestinian Arabic, a girl deprived of her virginity is described as *maftûḥa* (see Stephan, p. 16). Cf. also the Talmudic phrase פתח פתוח מצאתי (Ket. 9b) as a charge of unchastity.

it expresses far more than it says; its nuances are at least as significant as its explications. Its overt meaning has nothing in it to arouse the vigilance of the censor, and meanwhile its deeper content is able to cross the threshold of consciousness.

Modern psychological research has also shed considerable light on the intimate relationship between love and pain. This connection is expressed in the great "Dream-Song" (5:2 to 6:3). When the love-sick maiden wanders through the city, in search of her lover, the watchmen beat her (5:7).

Stephan cites an old *ḥaddâwiyye* from Jaffa, which affords a striking parallel:[136]

> "The quarrel rose between me and him:
> They dragged me to the *sarai*;
> They beat me a thousand strokes;
> They beat me on my ankles."

An Egyptian love song of the New Kingdom[137] expresses the same theme of the lover's devotion in the face of physical attack:

> "I will not let go of thy love
> Even if I am beaten,
> As far as the land of Palestine with *shebet* and clubs
> And on to the land of Ethiopia with palm-ribs
> As far as the hills with sticks
> And unto the fields with cudgels."

The variations in date and geographical provenance do not exhaust the variety to be found within this small book. The songs reflect the simplicity of rustic scenes, the sophistication of the great city, the poverty of the shepherd's hut, and the luxury of the royal palace. Hence it is possible for one scholar to find in the book "the simplest kind of ballads scarcely touched by the polishing efforts of the self-conscious poet,"[138] while another declares that the Song is to be classed "as belles-lettres rather than as folk-songs," and finds them "only less artificial than the idylls of Theocritus."[139] Actually, the book contains both the simple and unrestrained outpourings of un-tutored love and the elaborated literary expressions of the same basic impulse.

[136] *Op. cit.*, p. 18.
[137] Cf. A. Erman, *op. cit.*, p. 241.
[138] Cf. Jastrow, *op. cit.*, p. 13.
[139] Cf. Pfeiffer, *op. cit.*, p. 711.

Frequently the point is made that the boldness of expression in the book with regard to sexual intimacy and bodily description is not in keeping with modern taste. It is true that the description of the maiden's charms in 7:3 is more explicit and franker than has been customary in Occidental poetry, but this passage is unique in the Song. Elsewhere, the description of physical beauty is frank without crassness. To evaluate it fairly, the Song should be judged against its Oriental background. Actually, its delicacy is at least as striking as its lack of inhibitions. The symbolism used in describing the manifestations of love throughout the book adds piquancy without offending. It should also be noted that some of the most outspoken passages are to be found in songs relating to married love.[140] Yet even here we have none of the crassly physical references to be found in the Akkadian love-charms,[141] in Sumerian love-poems,[142] or in contemporary Arabic love-songs.[143]

Esthetic standards are notoriously prone to change. In describing the beauty of a woman today, we would not think of her as resembling a city or a mare (1:9), yet we do compare a city to a woman,[144] and we refer to a beautiful horse by the feminine pronoun. A horse was, of course, not a beast of burden, but the cherished comrade of kings and nobles.[144a] Sociological and economic factors undoubtedly influence tastes in feminine pulchritude. The ancients liked their women large, as the Venus de Milo demonstrates and as is clear from the Song, even after allowance is made for poetic hyperbole (see 4:4; 7:5). Undoubtedly this taste for an ample woman reflected the emphasis upon child-bearing as woman's chief task. On the other hand, the modern preference for thin, "stream-lined" figures testifies to the present position of women as associates, and even as competitors,

---

[140] Thus 1:12, 13 and 7:3 f. both occur in poems where the lover is "king," i. e. the bridegroom (1:12; 7:6).

[141] Cf. Ebeling, "Liebeszauber," *passim.* See especially the direct references to the *membra* (pp. 11, 33) and to sexual congress (pp. 21, 43).

[142] See the Sumerian "Love Song to a King" (S. N. Kramer, in Pritchard, *op. cit.*, p. 496).

[143] Cf. Stephan, *op. cit.*, pp. 21, 39, for examples of such crudity in modern Arabic poetry.

[144] A striking instance where a city is compared to love occurs in Egyptian poetry:

"I will go to Memphis and say, 'Give me my sister tonight,
Memphis is a dish of love-apples, set before the Fair of Face.' "

(The last epithet is a name of Ptah, god of Memphis). Cf. Erman, *op. cit.*, p. 245.

[144a] See the description of the horse in Job 39:19 ff. and Horace, *Odes*, III, 2.

with men in all fields of activity in a society of small families, where child-bearing plays a considerably less important role. Yet in this area the French proverb has particular cogency: "Plus ça change, plus c'est la même chose." The love of a man for a maid is a perennially fresh theme in literature, because it is a constant of human nature.

XIV. Some Stylistic Traits in the Song

Our understanding of the Song of Songs is helped considerably when certain characteristics of style are kept in mind. One of these is the *use of quotations*, without any external formula or phrase to indicate that the words are being quoted. Elsewhere we have shown how widespread this usage is in Biblical, Rabbinical and Oriental literature generally.[145] Several passages in the Song are best explained as instances of this use of quotations.

In 1:7–8, Tur Sinai[146] plausibly explains v. 8 as the words of the shepherds who want to draw her affections away from her lover:

> Tell me, O thou whom I love,
> Where dost thou feed and rest thy flock at noon?
> Why should I be a wanderer
> Among the flocks of thy friends,
> *Who would mock me and say, if I asked about thee:*
> "If thou dost not know, O fairest among women,
> Go forth in the tracks of the flocks
> And feed thy kids near the shepherds' tents."

The closing verses of the Song, 8:13 f., are explained by Haller as containing the words that the lover wishes to hear from his beloved:

> O thou who sittest in the garden
> With friends listening,
> Let me hear thy voice
> *Saying to me,*
> "Hasten, my beloved, and be as a gazelle,
> Or as a young hart
> Upon the mountains of spices."

In 1:4, the third stich, "We will rejoice and be merry with thee," may well be the quotation of the words of the bridegroom to his

---

[145] Cf. "Quotations As a Literary Usage in Biblical and Oriental Literature," in *HUCA*, vol. 22 (1949); see also *KMW*, pp. 95 ff.

[146] *Op. cit.*, pp. 365 f.

beloved, who responds in the following stichs, "We shall inhale thy love more than wine."

This use of quotations without a *verbum dicendi* is illustrated in a popular modern Palestinian Arab song, current in several versions:[147]

> "If you should visit me one night, O perfection of my
> happiness,
> I would rejoice and mortify the envious (saying:),
> "My friend regales me."

The use of similes and metaphors in the Song also requires a word of explanation. When the poet uses a figure of speech, he often continues to elaborate upon it for its own sake, without reference to the subject for the sake of which it was invoked. The figure, so to speak, develops its own momentum and has its own independent existence. Thus, in 4:2,

> "Thy teeth are like a flock ready for shearing
> Who have come up from washing,"

the second stich describes the sheep, without being related back to the teeth. Similarly, in 4:4,

> "Like the tower of David is thy neck,
> Built as a landmark,"

the second stich likewise refers not to the neck, but to the tower of David.

The difficulties and obscurities of the Song are due, in large measure, to the fact that it is an expression of a segment of Israelite life, which is largely unknown to us otherwise. Reference has already been made to variations in esthetic standards. These factors should caution us against facile emendations and transpositions in the text. Only in a small number of passages does emendation of the Masoretic text seem justified on the basis of our present state of knowledge.[148]

---

[147] Stephan, *op. cit.*, p. 60:

> *lô zurtani fard lêle yâ kamâl sa'di*
> *afraḥ v'akîd il-'azul: — "ḥubbi mhannîni."*

[148] The following changes from the Masoretic text underlie our version:
1:2 For יַשְׁקֵנִי read יְשַׁקְּנִי
3:6 For כְּתִימְרוֹת read בְּתִימְרוֹת (doubtful)
4:15 For גַּנִּים read גַּנִּי
5:13 For מִגְדְּלוֹת read מְגַדְּלוֹת
    For עֲרוּגַת read עֲרוּגוֹת
6:12 For שָׂמַתְנִי מַרְכְּבוֹת read שָׁם תְּנִי מֹרֶךְ בַּת
7:14 For דּוֹדִי read דּוֹדַי
8:2 For תְּלַמְּדֵנִי read וְאֶל חֶדֶר הוֹרָתִי (see the Commentary)

XV. The Song of Songs in Holy Writ

Undoubtedly, the allegorical interpretation of the Song of Songs, aided by the ascription of the book to King Solomon who is mentioned in the text, led to its inclusion in the Biblical canon. That Pharisaic Judaism admitted the book into the canon because it was "an ancient book, a religious book, and one that had always been religious"[149] as part of a pagan fertility cult, is unlikely to the point of impossibility. Had there been any recollection of such a use of the material, those who objected to the canonicity of the book would not have hesitated to mention it, and its chances for inclusion would have been nil.

The view against which Rabbinic Judaism levelled its strictures and which led to lengthy discussions as to its canonicity was the widely held literal interpretation, with which the Rabbis were very familiar, as has been noted. That all objections were overridden and the Song admitted into the canon indicates that on the subconscious level, at least, another factor operated, as was the case with Ecclesiastes:[150] a genuine affection for the book. It was this attitude which refused to permit its exclusion from Scripture, an act that would have spelled its ultimate destruction. As Jastrow well says: "It entered the canon not by vote, but because of its inevitable human appeal. Love is sacred even in passionate manifestations, when not perverted by a sophisticated self-analysis."[151]

The physical basis of love is extolled in the Song without shame or pruriency. Yet it serves as the foundation for the spiritual relationship, which is adumbrated in many an incidental phrase and reaches its climax in the great paean to love[152] in 8:7:

> Many waters can not quench love,
> Neither can the floods drown it.
> If a man would give all the substance of his house for love,
> He would be laughed to scorn.

[149] Cf. Meek, in Schoff, *op. cit.*, pp. 52 f.

[150] Cf. Gordis, *KMW*, pp. 121 f.

[151] *Op. cit.*, p. 16.

[152] Tur-Sinai, *op. cit.*, pp. 383 f., refers the "love" which is the subject in 8:7 not to the relationship of a maiden and her lover, but to the effort of an interloper to steal the affections of a married woman from her husband. The passage is interpreted to mean that it is impossible to make monetary restitution for this heinous sin. This is highly ingenious, but we find it unconvincing. There is a clear-cut reference to the wronged husband in Prov. 6:27 ff., which Tur-Sinai adduces as a parallel, but it is entirely lacking here.

It is in this sense that the modern reader, who is not likely to read it as an allegory, will echo Akiba's passionate description of the book as "the Holy of Holies," for it is, in Herder's words, "holy as a song of pure natural love, the holiness of human life."

Over and beyond its eternal youthfulness and inherent charm, the Song of Songs, precisely because it is within the canon of Scripture, serves to broaden the horizons of religion. It gives expression, in poetic and hence in deathless terms, to the authentic world-view of Judaism, which denies any dichotomy between body and soul, between matter and spirit, because it recognizes them both as the twin aspects of the great and unending miracle called life.

THE SONG OF SONGS, WHICH IS SOLOMON'S

I

THE CALL TO LOVE

In passionate accents, the beloved voices her desire for the presence of her bridegroom, who is here called "king," in accordance with a common West-Semitic and Jewish usage.

This song emanates not from the countryside, but from the city. Hence the background of many-chambered houses, the abundance of wine and oil and the presence of many maidens (1:2–4).

> Let me drink of the kisses of his mouth,
> For thy love is better than wine!
> Thine oils are a delight to inhale,
> Thy presence — as oil wafted about,
> Therefore do the maidens love thee.
>
> Draw me after thee, let us hasten —
> The king has brought me to his chambers,
> Saying, "We will rejoice and be merry with thee!"
> We shall inhale thy love rather than wine!
> As fine wine do they love thee.

II

THE RUSTIC MAIDEN

A country girl addresses the sophisticated women of the capital with a mixture of naivete and coquetry, of modesty and pride. Her skin, unlike that of the well-kept women of the capital, is dark. She has been exposed to the sun's rays, because she has been compelled to guard the vineyards of her brothers, who were angry with her. Their displeasure stemmed from the fact that she had left her own "vineyard" unguarded, being too prodigal with her favors (1:5–6).

Swarthy am I, but comely, O daughters of Jerusalem,
Swarthy as Kedar's tents,
Comely as Solomonic hangings.
Do not look askance upon me, for being swarthy,
For the sun has tanned me;
My brothers were incensed against me,
They set me a keeper over the vineyards;
But my own vineyard I did not keep.

III

TELL ME WHERE MY LOVE

*The maiden pleads with her lover, to tell her where he is
guarding his flocks. She gives him a gentle warning that if
she must seek him herself, his fellow-shepherds are likely to
make overtures for her affection* (1:7–8).

Tell me, O thou whom I love,
Where dost thou pasture thy sheep,
Where dost thou let them lie at noon?
Why, indeed, should I be a wanderer
Among the flocks of thy comrades,
Who would say to me:
"If thou knowest not, fairest among women,
Follow the footprints of the sheep,
And pasture thy kids
Near the tents of the shepherds."

IV

BEDECKED IN CHARM

*In this duet, the locale of which is southern Palestine, the
"king" praises the beauty of his bride, bedecked in gold and
silver ornaments, and compares her to a steed in Pharaoh's
chariots. The comparison, somewhat strange to our habits of
thought, is characteristically Semitic. It should be recalled
that the horse was not a beast of burden in the Orient, but
the cherished companion of kings and nobles in war and the
chase. The bride responds by extolling the joys of love with her
"king" (1:9–14).*

THE BRIDEGROOM: To a steed in Pharaoh's chariots
Do I compare thee, my beloved.
Thy cheeks are beautiful with banglets,
Thy neck, with strings of jewels.
Golden beads shall we make thee
With studs of silver.

THE BRIDE: While the king was on his couch,
My nard gave forth its fragrance.
A bag of myrrh is my beloved,
Lying between my breasts.
A cluster of henna is my beloved to me
From the vineyards of En-gedi.

V

OUR WALLS ARE CEDARS

This simple lyric is of North-Israelite origin. The lovers make their tryst in the forest, with the cedars and cypresses as their home (1:15–17).

THE LOVER: Thou art fair, my beloved, thou art fair,
              Thine eyes are doves.

THE BELOVED: Thou art handsome, my beloved, yea sweet,
              And our couch is green.

BOTH: The beams of our house are cedars,
              And our rafters are cypresses.

VI

WHO IS LIKE MY LOVE

*In this brief duet, the maiden describes her charms in modest
terms, which the lover turns into a triumphant praise of her
beauty. She counters by extolling his handsome presence,
describing the joy she finds in his company (2:1–3).*

THE MAIDEN: I am but a rose in Sharon,
             A lily of the valleys.

THE YOUTH: As a lily among thorns,
             So is my beloved among the young women.

THE MAIDEN: As an apple-tree among the trees of the
                  wood,
             So is my love among the young men.
             Under its shadow I delight to sit,
             And its fruit is sweet to my taste.

VII

LOVE'S PROUD PROCLAMATION

The maiden proudly announces her love before all who are assembled in the tavern, and asks for refreshment, for she is faint through passion. She adjures the daughters of Jerusalem by a solemn oath to leave the lovers undisturbed, till their desire be spent (2:4–7).

He has brought me to the banquet-hall,
And his glance upon me was loving.
Strengthen me with dainties, sustain me with apples;
For I am love-sick.
His left hand is beneath my head,
While his right embraces me.
I adjure you, O daughters of Jerusalem,
By the gazelles and the hinds of the field,
That you disturb not, nor interrupt our love,
Until it be satiated.

VIII

THE TIME OF SINGING IS COME

This lyric is perhaps the most beautiful expression of love in the spring to be found in literature. It is worth noting that the point of origin is the city rather than the country. That nature discloses her charms primarily to the urban dweller rather than to the rustic has long been suspected. The appreciation of nature and the creation of nature-poetry are the products of urban culture, whether it be ancient Israel, the Hellenistic Age, the Silver Age of Roman literature, or the modern Romantic movement.

The city maiden, ensconced in her house, sees her lover coming to her and calling her to go out with him to the country-side, so that they may greet the spring in all its loveliness (2:8–13).

> Hark! my beloved! here he comes,
> Leaping over the mountains, skipping over the hills.
> My beloved is like a gazelle or a young hart;
> Behold, he stands behind our wall,
> Looking through the windows,
> Peering through the lattices.
> My beloved spoke, saying unto me:
> "Rise up, my love, my fair one, and come away.
> For lo, the winter is past,
> The rain is over and gone;
> The flowers have appeared on the earth;
> The time of singing is come,
> And the voice of the turtle-dove is heard in our land.
> The fig-tree puts forth her green fruits,
> And the vines in blossom give forth their fragrance.
> Arise, my love, my fair one, and come away."

IX

THE LOVER'S WELCOME

That a new song begins here seems clear. The beloved is here pictured as hiding among the cliffs, instead of being in her city home, and the lover calls upon her not to go out with him to the countryside, but to show herself to him. Her response is expressed cryptically. Little foxes have been devouring the vineyards already in bloom. Does she mean that young men have already found their way to her? (2:14–15).

THE LOVER: O my dove, in the clefts of the rock, in
                the shadow of the cliff,
              Let me see thy face, let me hear thy voice;
              For sweet is thy voice, and thy face is
                comely.

THE BELOVED: The foxes have seized us, the little foxes
                that spoil the vineyards;
              For our vineyard is in blossom.

X

SURRENDER

The maiden speaks of the love binding her and her lover, and invites him to taste the joys of love until dawn (2:16–17).

My beloved is mine, and I am his, who feeds among
    the lilies.
Until the day break, and the shadows flee,
Turn, my love, and be like a gazelle or a young hart
Upon the mountain of spices.

XI

THE DREAM OF THE LOST LOVER

The pathos of love's separation is movingly described in this song. Dreaming of her absent lover, the beloved wanders through the streets seeking him, until she finds him and holds him fast. She too, like the happy maiden in 2:7, adjures the daughters of Jerusalem not to disturb their love — but her reunion with her lover is only in a dream. The repetition of those passion-charged words highlights the pathos of the lovers' separation.

The sorrowful echo of an imaginary fulfillment recalls the scene in Christopher Marlowe's play, "Dr. Faustus," when the hero, in the last few hours before the Devil comes to claim his soul, repeats the words of Ovid, spoken by a lover in the midst of his revelry, "O lente, lente, currite noctis equi," "O slowly, slowly, run on, ye coursers of the night" (3:1-5).

On my couch at night I sought him whom I love,
Sought him, but found him not.
"I will rise now, and go about the city,
On the streets and highways,
I will seek him whom I love."
I sought him, but I found him not.
The watchmen making their rounds in the city found me.
"Have you seen him, whom I love?"
Scarcely had I passed them,
When I found him whom I love.
I held him, and would not let him go,
Until I had brought him into my mother's house,
Into the chamber of her that conceived me.
"I adjure you, O daughters of Jerusalem,
By the gazelles, and by the hinds of the field,
That you disturb not, nor interrupt our love,
Until it be satiated."

XII

A WEDDING SONG FOR SOLOMON

This song is the oldest datable unit in the collection. It was written to mark the ceremonies connected with King Solomon's marriage to a foreign princess, perhaps from Egypt, across the desert. Another example of a royal wedding hymn, not connected with Solomon, is to be found in Psalm 45. Here the arrival of the princess' elaborate entourage is described by the court poets (3:6–11).

Who is this coming from the wilderness,
Like thick clouds of smoke?
Perfumed with myrrh and frankincense,
With all powders of the merchant?
Behold, it is the litter of Solomon;
Sixty heroes round about it,
Of the heroes of Israel,
All skilled with the sword,
Expert in war.
Every man has his sword at his side
To ward off the terrors of the night.
A palanquin has the king made for himself,
Solomon, of Lebanon-wood.
He has made its pillars of silver,
Its inlay of gold,
Its seat of purple,
Its inner side lined with leather
By the daughters of Jerusalem
Go forth, O daughters of Zion,
And gaze upon king Solomon,
Arrayed in the crown with which his mother
    has crowned him
On his wedding-day,
On the day of his heart's gladness.

XIII

MY BELOVED IS PERFECT

A characteristic waṣf *in praise of the physical perfection of the beloved. Both the standard of feminine beauty that is extolled and the mode of expression that is employed are characteristic of the ancient Orient. See the Introduction for details* (4:1–7).

Thou art fair, my love, thou art fair!
Thine eyes are as doves behind thy veil,
Thy hair is as a flock of goats,
Streaming down from mount Gilead.
Thy teeth are like a flock ready for shearing,
Who have come from the washing,
All paired alike, and none missing among them.
Thy lips are like a scarlet thread
And thy mouth is comely;
Thy temples are like a slice of pomegranate,
Seen behind thy veil.
Thy neck is like the tower of David
Which is built as a landmark,
A thousand shields hanging upon it,
All the armour of the heroes.
Thy two breasts are like two fawns,
Twins of a gazelle,
Feeding among the lilies.
Until the day break
And the shadows flee,
I will get me to the mountain of myrrh,
And to the hill of frankincense.
Thou art all fair, my love;
And there is no blemish upon thee.

XIV

CALL FROM THE MOUNTAINS

From the Lebanon mountain range at the northern extremity of Israel comes the lover's call to his bride (4:8).

> With me from Lebanon, my bride,
> With me from Lebanon shalt thou come.
> Leap from the top of Amana,
> From the top of Senir and Hermon,
> From the dens of the lions,
> From the mountains of the leopards.

XV

LOVE'S ENCHANTMENT

*The charm of the beloved has quite ravished her lover, who
finds her presence more fragrant than wine and perfume, or
the strong, clean smell of Lebanon's cedars, and her kisses
sweeter than milk and honey. On the use of "sister" as a
term of endearment in this song and succeeding ones, see the
Introduction (4:9–11).*

Thou hast ravished my heart, my sister, my bride;
Thou hast ravished my heart with one of thine eyes,
With one bead of thy necklace.
How fair is thy love, my sister, my bride!
How much better thy love than wine!
And the smell of thine ointments than all perfumes!
Thy lips, O my bride, drop honey —
Honey and milk are under thy tongue;
And the smell of thy garments is like the smell
    of Lebanon.

XVI

LOVE'S BARRIERS

In this dialogue, the lover praises the delectable qualities of his beloved, but complains that he finds her a closed garden, a sealed fountain. She responds by declaring that, on the contrary, she is a free-flowing fountain, and implies that her lover has been backward. She therefore calls upon the winds to waft her fragrance to him, that he may come and enjoy the fruit of his garden. He accepts her invitation with alacrity, and finally announces the joy of love's consummation (4:12 to 5:1).

THE LOVER: A closed garden is my sister, my bride;
A closed spring, a fountain sealed.
Thy branches are a garden of
      pomegranates,
With precious fruits,
Henna with nard,
Spikenard and saffron, cassia and
      cinnamon,
With all trees of frankincense;
Myrrh and aloes, with all the chief spices.

THE BELOVED: The fountain in my garden is a well of
      living waters,
Flowing down from Lebanon.
Awake, O north wind;
And come, O south;
Blow upon my garden,
Let its spices flow out,
Let my lover come into his garden,
And eat its delightful fruits.

THE LOVER: I have come into my garden, my sister,
      my bride;
     I have gathered my myrrh with my spice;
     Eaten my honeycomb with my honey;
     Drunken my wine with my milk.

THE BELOVED: Eat, O my friend,
     Drink, yea, drink abundantly of love.

XVII

LOVE'S TRIAL AND TRIUMPH

*The longest and most elaborate song in the collection takes the
form of a dream-song. Within its framework, other patterns,
like the search for the absent lover and the* wasf *praising his
person, are skillfully interwoven.*

*The song reflects the sophistication and coquetry of the city
maiden, whose artifices fall away before the power of love. The
maiden is asleep, and in the dream she hears her lover knocking,
begging to be admitted. She playfully answers that she has
already retired for the night. Instead of continuing the badi-
nage, as she expected, he leaves her doorway. Yearning for
the sound of his voice, she runs out into the city streets, seeking
for him everywhere. The city watchmen, mistaking her for a
streetwalker, beat and wound her. She turns to the daughters
of Jerusalem — everything is possible in a dream — and begs
them to tell her lover that she is lovesick for him. How can
they distinguish her lover from all others? Triumphantly she
answers that he is unique for beauty, strength and charm. Im-
pressed with her description, the daughters of Jerusalem offer to
help find him. The maiden, however, feels that discretion is
much the better part, and that too much help from them may
be dangerous to her cause. She disclaims their assistance and
joyously announces that her lover has already found his way
to his garden. He is hers alone, and she is his (5:2 to 6:3).*

I was asleep, but my heart was awake.
Hark! my love is knocking:
"Open to me, my sister, my love, my dove, my
    perfect one,
For my head is filled with dew,
My locks, with the drops of the night."
"I have already put off my coat,
Why should I put it on again;

I have washed my feet,
Why should I soil them?"
My beloved withdrew his hand from the door's opening,
And my heart was stirred for him.
I rose to open to my beloved,
And my hands were dripping with myrrh,
My fingers, with flowing myrrh,
Upon the handles of the bar.
I opened to my beloved,
But my beloved was gone and away.
My soul longed for his word;
I sought him, but could not find him;
I called him, but he gave me no answer.
The watchmen going about the city found me,
They struck me, they wounded me,
The keepers of the walls stripped my mantle from me.
"I adjure you, O daughters of Jerusalem,
If ye find my beloved,
What shall you tell him?
That I am faint with love."
"What is thy lover more than any other,
O fairest among women?
What is thy lover more than any other,
That thou dost so adjure us?"
"My beloved is fair and ruddy,
Pre-eminent above ten thousand.
His head is the finest gold,
His locks are curled, black as a raven.
His eyes are like doves, beside the water-brooks,
Bathing in milk, sitting at a brimming pool.
His cheeks are as beds of spices,
Exuding perfumes,
His lips are as lilies,
That drop with flowing myrrh.
His arms are rods of gold
Set with beryl,

His body is a column of ivory,
Overlaid with sapphires.
His legs are pillars of marble,
Set upon sockets of fine gold,
His appearance is like Lebanon,
Lordly as the cedars.
His mouth is sweetness itself,
He is altogether a delight.
This is my beloved, and this is my friend,
O daughters of Jerusalem."
"Where is thy lover gone,
O fairest among women?
Where has thy lover turned,
That we may seek him with thee?"
"My beloved is gone down to his garden,
To the beds of spices,
To feed in the gardens,
And to gather lilies.
I am my lover's,
And my beloved is mine,
As he feeds among the lilies."

XVIII

THE POWER OF BEAUTY

This is a very old waṣf, *which can be dated during the first half-century of the Divided Kingdom (between 930 and 880 B. C. E.).   See the Introduction for details.   The lover praises his beloved's beauty, by comparing her to the two capitals of the country, Jerusalem in the south and Tirzah in the north. The repetition of several phrases that are familiar to us from earlier songs in the collection is natural in popular poetry* (6:4–7).

Thou art beautiful, O my love, as Tirzah,
Comely as Jerusalem,
Awe-inspiring as these great sights!
Turn thine eyes away from me,
For they have overcome me.
Thy hair is as a flock of goats,
Streaming down from Gilead.
Thy teeth are like a flock of ewes,
Who have come up from the washing;
All paired alike and none missing among them.
Thy temple is a slice of pomegranate
Seen behind thy veil.

XIX

THE ONE AND ONLY

The lover has heard of the resplendent ladies in the royal court, but for him there is only one, unique and perfect, the favorite even of her mother among all her children. No wonder all women unite in praising her (6:8–9).

There are threescore queens,
And fourscore concubines,
And maidens without number.
But my dove, my pure one, is one alone,
The only one for her mother,
The choice of her that bore her.
Maidens saw her, and called her happy,
Even queens and concubines, and they praised her.

XX

LOVE'S DAWNING

For the lover, the beauty of the maiden can only be compared to the hosts of heaven. Spring is here, and he resolves to go down to his garden, to see the fruit-trees in blossom. There his beloved will let him enjoy her fragrance.

The last verse is incomprehensible in the accepted text. For the emendation on which our rendering is based, see the Commentary (6:10–12).

Who is she gazing forth like the morning star,
Fair as the moon,
Bright as the sun,
Awe-inspiring like these great sights?
I have come into the garden of nuts,
To look at the tender shoots of the valley,
To see whether the vine has budded,
And the pomegranates are in flower.
I am beside myself with joy,
For there thou wilt give me thy myrrh,
O noble kinsman's daughter!

XXI

THE MAIDEN'S DANCE

*Among the Syrian peasants in our time, it is customary for
the bride to perform a sword-dance on her wedding day. Our
song has often been regarded as a Hebrew counterpart of this
Syrian practice. This may well be the case, since the "king,"
or bridegroom, is mentioned in the song, though there is no
reference to a sword in our text. What is certain is that the
maiden is dancing, revealing both her grace of movement and
her physical charms. She is referred to as the maid of Shulem,
after a town (Biblical Shunem, modern Arabic, Sulem) which
was famous for its beautiful women. This epithet "Shulammite" in Hebrew was mistaken for the proper name of a
rustic maiden with whom Solomon fell in love.*

*The song begins with the company's call to her to turn, so
that her comeliness may be observed. She modestly wonders
what they can see in her. They proceed, however, to describe
the beauty of her body in motion, from her dancing feet to the
crowning glory of her tresses (7:1–6).*

THE COMPANY: "Turn, turn, O maid of Shulem,
                        Turn, turn, so that we can see thee!"

THE MAIDEN: "What will you see in the maid of
                        Shulem?"

THE COMPANY: "Indeed, the counter-dance!
                        How beautiful are thy steps in sandals,
                        O nobleman's daughter!
                        The roundings of thy thighs are like
                                jewelled links,
                        The handiwork of a craftsman.
                        Thy navel is like a round goblet
                        In which the wine-mixture is not lacking.

Thy belly is like a heap of wheat,
Set about with lilies.
Thy two breasts are like two fawns,
Twins of a gazelle.
Thy neck is as a tower of ivory.
Thine eyes are pools in Heshbon,
At the gate of Bath-rabbim,
Thy nose is like the tower of Lebanon
Facing toward Damascus.
Thy head upon thee is like crimson,
And the hair of thy head like purple —
A king is held captive in its tresses!"

XXII

HOW DELIGHTFUL IS LOVE

In this rhapsody to love, the lover compares his chosen one to a slender and stately palm-tree and announces his intention of climbing up its branches and enjoying its delights (7:7–10).

The succeeding verses (7:11–14) may possibly constitute the beloved's reply. Since, however, our passage is not a plea directly addressed to the beloved, but rather a song of praise, and the next verses are not couched as a reply, it seems likelier that we have two independent songs here.

How fair and how pleasant art thou, love,
    with its delights!
Thy form is like a palm-tree,
Thy breasts, like clusters of grapes.
I said: "I will climb up into my palm-tree,
And take hold of its branches.
Let thy breasts be as clusters of the vine,
And the fragrance of thy face like apples,
For thy kiss is like the finest wine
That gives power to lovers,
And stirs the lips of the sleepers with desire."

XXIII

THE BELOVED'S PROMISE

*With a joyous affirmation of the love binding her and her
lover, the maiden calls upon him to come out into the fields
and vineyards, blooming in the glory of the spring. There,
she promises, she will give him her love (7:11–14).*

I am my beloved's,
And for me is his desire.
Come, my beloved, let us go forth into the field,
Let us lodge among the villages,
And rise early for the vineyards.
Let us see whether the vine has budded,
Whether the vine-blossom has opened,
And the pomegranates have flowered —
There will I give thee my love.
The mandrakes are giving forth their fragrance,
And at our door are all sweet fruits,
Both new and old —
There will I give thee my love,
Which I have laid up for thee.

XXIV

WOULD THOU WERT MY BROTHER

*The maiden has been exposed to the taunts of neighbors and
friends, when she has given public expression to her love. If
only her lover were her foster-brother, raised in the same home!
None could reproach her, then, if she were to kiss him in the
street, lead him to her mother's home and drink wine at his
side. In her reverie, she pictures the bliss in her lover's company, and calls upon the daughters of Jerusalem not to disturb
her imagined ecstasy (8:1–4).*

Would thou wert indeed my brother,
Who had suckled at my mother's breasts!
If I found thee outside, I could kiss thee;
Yet no one would despise me.
I would bring thee to my mother's house
Who had taught me,
I would give thee spiced wine to drink,
The juice of pomegranates.
His left hand would be beneath my head,
And his right hand would embrace me.
And I would exclaim,
"I adjure you, O daughters of Jerusalem:
Why should you disturb or interrupt our love
Until it be satiated?"

XXV

LOVE UNDER THE APPLE-TREE

This passage, which may be fragmentary, is not very clear, principally because of the symbolism employed. It seems to be a duet, where the company greets the advent of the maiden leaning on her lover. She, however, has no ear for their words, but addresses her lover. She reminds him that she woke him from his sleep under the apple-tree. It was at the self-same spot that he had come into the world, because of the love of his father and mother. The apple-tree, a familiar erotic symbol, is, as Jastrow notes, the sexual passion which passes from one generation to the next. The maiden is apparently calling him to respond to her love (8:5).

THE COMPANY: Who is this coming up from the wilderness,
Clinging to her beloved?

THE BELOVED: Under the apple-tree I woke thee,
There thy mother gave thee birth,
Yea, there she who bore thee brought
thee forth.

XXVI

THE SEAL OF LOVE

The maiden can not bear any separation from her lover. She therefore pleads to be as close to him as his seal. The ancients carried their seals either as a ring on the finger or as a necklace near the heart.

The frank and unabashed avowal of love throughout the book reaches its impressive climax here where it is described as a mighty force, the very flame of God. Thus the basic truth underlying the Song of Songs is emphasized, that natural love is holy (8:6–7).

Set me as a seal upon thy heart,
As a seal upon thine arm,
For love is strong as death,
Passion is unyielding as the grave.
Its flashes are flashes of fire,
A flame of God.
Many waters can not extinguish love,
Nor can the floods sweep it away.
If a man gave all the wealth of his house
In exchange for love,
He would be laughed to scorn.

XXVII

THE RAMPARTS OF LOVE

*The young maiden is surrounded by suitors who complain
that she is not ready for love and marriage. Their determination to break down her resistance they express by using the
formula of an oath (see the Introduction). If she remains
obdurate, like the wall of a city, they will lay siege to her. This
they plan to do in approved military fashion, by building
around her another temporary embankment, from which they
will launch the "attack." That their intentions are not hostile
is clear from the* materiel *of war that they intend to employ
in their campaign, silver and cedar-wood. These expensive
goods probably symbolize the gifts that they are showering
upon her.*

*She answers that she is indeed like a wall, impregnable to
their importunities, but not because she is too young for love.
On the contrary, she is ready for the great experience, but only
with him whom she loves and strives to please above all others*
(8:8–10).

THE SUITORS: We have a little sister,
But she has no breasts.
What shall we do with our sister,
On this day when she is being spoken for?
If she be a wall,
We will build a turret of silver against her;
If she be a gate,
We will besiege her with boards of cedar.

THE MAIDEN: I am a wall,
And my breasts are like towers,
Therefore am I in my lover's eyes
A true fountain of joy.

XXVIII

THE FINEST VINEYARD

The genuine joys of love are graphically contrasted with the illusory satisfactions of wealth. The lover recalls that King Solomon owned a large and fruitful vineyard containing a thousand vines. It was worked by tenant-farmers, who received one-fifth of the income for their labor. The lover may be poor in money, yet he is far richer than Solomon, for he possesses a priceless treasure, the vineyard of his beloved (8:11–12).

Solomon owned a vineyard at Baal Hamon
Which he gave over to tenants.
For its fruit one would give
A thousand pieces of silver.
But my vineyard, my very own, is before me.
You, Solomon, are welcome to your thousand,
And your vine-tenders to their two hundred!

XXIX

LET ME HEAR THY VOICE

The beloved, sitting in the garden, is surrounded by her companions. Her lover pleads with her to invite him to enjoy the delights of love. As he quotes the words that he wishes to hear her say, he employs the familiar figures of the young deer and the fragrant mountain to symbolize the lover and his beloved (8:13–14).

> Thou dwelling amid the gardens,
> While thy companions are listening,
> Let me hear thy voice, saying to me,
> "Make haste, my beloved,
> And be like a gazelle or a young hart
> Upon the mountains of spices."

COMMENTARY

1:1. The verse is the title of the book, added by the editor. Hence the use of the classical relative *'ašer* instead of *še* employed throughout the book (e. g. 1:6; 5:8; 6:5, etc.). The post-Exilic editor accepts the Solomonic theory of authorship, which made the acceptance of the book into the canon possible. Hence שיר השירים meant for him "the best of songs," and is a superlative like קדש הקדשים, "holy of holies," הבל הבלים, "vanity of vanities" (Eccl. 1:2), מלך המלכים, "king of kings," as it was for Rabbi Akiba, "For all the writings are holy, but the Song of Songs is the Holy of Holies" (M. Yad. 5:3).

1:2. Read, with many moderns, יַשְּׁקֵנִי. The change of person in the song is a characteristic of Biblical style; cf., *inter alia*, Micah 7:19. There is, therefore, no need to assume more than two characters in this song or to emend the vowels or suffixes in order to create a non-Biblical standard of consistency.

1:3. שֶׁמֶן תּוּרַק is best taken as "oil wafted about," literally "emptied, poured forth" (cf. LXX, V), though שֶׁמֶן is elsewhere masculine. Thus הָמוֹן, generally masculine, is feminine only in Job 31:34 and Eccl. 5:9 (reading תְּבוּאֵהוּ for תְּבוּאָה). See *KMW, ad loc.* תְהוֹם, generally feminine, is masculine in Ps. 42:8; 104:6 ("The deep — Thou hast covered it as with a garment") and in Job 28:14. Common in gender are מחנה, כיס, שמש, דרך, etc. There is, therefore, no need to read תָּמְרוּק (cf. Esth. 2:3, 9, 12) or מוּרָק (*BH*) or מוּּזָק, "purified" (Rothstein). שְׁמָךָ, "your name, being, presence." Cf. the figurative use of "the Name" for the presence or essence of God. On the assonance of *šem* and *šemen*, cf. Eccl. 7:1, and *KMW, ad loc.*

1:4. נַזְכִּירָה, not "we shall praise" but "we shall inhale"; on this meaning of the root, cf. Lev. 24:7; Isa. 66:3; Hos. 14:8; Ps. 20:4 (cf. I Sam. 26:19), as Ibn Janah recognized long ago. Hence there is no need to emend to נִשְׁכְּרָה, "we shall be drunk." אהבוך, 3rd person plural, is impersonal; cf. וגללו, Gen. 29:8; hence, "they love you, i. e. you are loved."

The traditional rendering for מישרים אהבוך, "rightly have they loved thee" (LXX, V, Rashi), is syntactically dubious and out of context. Deleting the phrase is a too easy solution; it destroys the rhythmic pattern which consists of 2 stichs (v. 2) followed by 3 (v. 3) and then of 3 stichs, followed by 2 (v. 4). What is required in the context is a reference to another element in the triad of wine, women and song. Accordingly, Ibn Ezra equates the word with "wine," in favor of which the parallelism may be adduced, as well as the occurrence of the word in connection with wine three times (here, in 7:10, and in Prov. 23:31). In the two other passages, the noun occurs with הלך: הלך לדודי למישרים and יתהלך במישרים; the noun, therefore, would seem to be the purpose or effect of the wine-drinking; see the Commentary on 7:10 for another suggestion. Here it may mean "strong wine" or refer to a special variety. Both because of the parallelism and the better syntax, it may be better to render the stich: "As fine wine do they love thee." On the other hand, Tur-Sinai (*op. cit.*, 369) interprets the word to mean "sexual potency," on the basis of Akkadian *mushartu*, which he interprets as "paramour," and *musharu*, "membrum virile." However, the etymology which he proposes is not borne out by the Akkadian (cf. M. Weir, *Lexicon of Accadian Prayers*, pp. 39, 221). Ben Jehudah also gives the word a sexual connotation, but his derivation is likewise doubtful (*Thesaurus*, VI, 2980 f.). Our word may, however, well mean "vigor, virility, strength," on the basis of indigenous Hebrew usage. Cf. the common Rabbinic phrase יְיָשֵׁר כֹּח, "May your strength be firm" (B. B. 14b), and the Biblical source *Sefer Hayašār*, probably "The Book of Heroes" (Josh. 10:13; II Sam. 1:18). The stich may therefore mean, "For thy manliness do they love thee."

1:5. The verse exhibits "alternate parallelism," a, b, a', b' (cf. Ex. 29:27; Deut. 22:25–27; Hos. 3:5; Ps. 33:20 f.; Ps. 113:5–6; Eccl. 5:17 ff., and cf. Gordis, "Al Mibneh Hashirah Haivrit Haqedumah," in *Sefer Hashanah Liyhude Amerika*, 1944, pp. 151 f., and *KMW*, p. 246). The opening stich does not mean "dunkel und doch hell" and is not a reference to the moon-goddess (against Hal., Wit.). Nor is the view that *šelōmōh* here refers to an Arab tribe *Shalmah* (e. g., T. H. Gaster, in *Commentary*, vol. 13, April, 1952, p. 322) acceptable. Not only does this hypothesis propose a strange meaning for a common Hebrew name, creating a *hapax legomenon*, but it destroys the alternate parallelism of the verse, "swarthy" being completed by "tents of Kedar," and "comely" by "Solomonic curtains." Since the first stich is antithetic and not synonymous, "swarthy but comely," the second must follow suit. Similarly, in Ps. 113:5–6, המגביהי לשבת המשפילי לראות בשמים ובארץ. The tents of the Bedouins, woven of goatskins, are dark-brown or black, and would be particularly familiar to the country-dwellers. "Solomon's curtains" is a generic term like זקן אהרן, Ps. 133:2, "an Aaronic beard;" cf. a "Van Dyke beard," "Louis Quatorze furniture," etc.

1:6. נְחָרוּ, from חרה, a variant vocalization for חָרוּ; cf. the reverse phonetic process in Judg. 5:28, אָחֲרוּ for אִחֲרוּ (against Hal.). For the vineyard as a symbol of the person of the beloved, cf. Isa. 5:1 f.;

Song 2:15; 8:12. The last-named passage, as here, employs "vineyard" in both the literal and the symbolic meanings.

1:7. שֶׁלָּמָה, literally, "for why?", a Hebrew equivalent for the
Aramaic דִּלְמָא, "lest," the use of še being principally, but not exclusively, North Israelite. Cf. אֲשֶׁר לָמָה (Dan. 1:10). כְּעֹטְיָה a) has been
rendered "wayward woman," from the verb עטה I, "cover, wrap"
(cf. I Sam. 28:14), hence "a robed woman, sign of a harlot" (cf. Gen.
38:14), and b) from עטה II, "delouse" (cf. Jer. 43:12 LXX; Von Gall,
ZATW, 24, p. 105). It is best taken as a metathesis or a scribal error
for טֹעִיָה (Sym., P, V, Tar.), "wandering one." The Kaph is asseverative, "Why indeed should I be a wanderer"; cf., for example, Num.
11:1, and see Gordis, in *JAOS*, vol. 63, 1943. The usage occurs again
in our book in 8:1 and probably in 7:1.

1:8. The verse is a quotation of the speech of the shepherd's
comrades used without a formula of citation, as Tur-Sinai recognizes,
p. 366. On the entire usage of quotations, cf. R. Gordis, in *HUCA*,
1949.

1:9. On the Judean origin of this song and on this type of simile,
see the Introduction. לְסֻסָתִי, "to a mare," ·with paragogic Yod;
cf. Lam. 1:1.,

1:12. עַד, "while, so long as"; cf., for example, Job 1:18. בִּמְסִבּוֹ,
not "table," but "couch"; cf. the Mishnaic use of הֵסַב, "to recline."

1:14. בְּכַרְמֵי, perhaps "from the vineyards," rather than "in the
vineyards"; cf. this meaning of Beth in Ugaritic. En-gedi, on the
western shore of the Dead Sea, was famous for its vineyards; cf.
Pliny, *Historia Naturalis*, XII, 14 and 24.

1:15. The deletion of עֵינַיִךְ יוֹנִים deprives the verse of its third stich.
Note the three stichs in the next verse.

1:16. עַרְשֵׂנוּ, generally rendered "couch," may possibly mean
"arbor." Cf. M. Kil. 6:1, עָרִיס. Deleting the third stich is unjustified.
See v. 15.

1:17. קֹרוֹת בָּתֵּינוּ is the plural of קוֹרַת בֵּיתֵנוּ, formed on the Mishnaic
model, where the plural of בֵּית כְּנֶסֶת is בָּתֵּי כְּנֵסִיּוֹת (Ehr.). Hence the MT
is to be rendered, not "the beams of our houses," but "the beams of
our house." בְּרוֹתִים, a dialectic pronunciation for the classical בְּרוֹשִׁים,
probably influenced by the Aramaic; cf. *sibōleth-šibbōleth*, Judg. 12:6,
and see the Introduction and note 78. It is the cypress (I. Low) or
the Phoenician juniper-tree (Koehler, *Lexicon*, s. v., according to
Pliny, XII, 78).

2:1. חֲבַצֶּלֶת has been identified with the narcissus (Dalman), the
colchicum autumnale, a flower of pale lilac-color (I. Löw), the saffron
(Jastrow), and the rose (Tar., Ibn Janah, Ibn Ezra). שׁוֹשַׁנָּה, generally

rendered "lily," is probably a red or dark purple flower; cf. 5:13. שָׁרוֹן, from יְשָׁרוֹן, "a valley, plain," was originally a common noun, and then was applied to the fertile central valley in Palestine, a process paralleled by *Carmel*; cf. the Commentary on 7:6.

2:2. בָּנוֹת = "girls"; cf. Prov. 31:29. On רַעְיָתִי, "beloved," see the Introduction, sec. XI.

2:3. חִמַּדְתִּי וְיָשַׁבְתִּי, "I delight to sit." Cf. Deut. 1:5; Hos. 5:11 for examples of this paratactic variant of the complementary infinitive.

2:4. וְדִגְלוֹ עָלַי אַהֲבָה, a difficult phrase which may perhaps contain a reference to a custom unfamiliar to us today. The traditional rendering, "His shield" (so Hal.) or, "his banner over me is love," is a bold and striking figure. The emendation וְדִגְלוּ, taken as an imperative plural verb, "serve me with love," on the basis of the Akkadian *dagâlu* (Del., Jastrow), does not commend itself, because we ˙expect a singular verb addressed to the lover and, in addition, the preposition is unhebraic.

Stich b, *vᵉdiglō ʿālay ʾahᵃbhāh,* is traditionally rendered, "his banner above me is love." Though highly resonant, the words are virtually meaningless. Some have sought to relate the phrase to a flag placed over taverns, like the signs with which we are familiar today. They render, "He has brought me to the banquet hall, and its banner above me is love." There is no evidence for any such practice. Haller renders, "His shield over me is love," but this is an *ad hoc* meaning for *diglō*. Some commentators have revocalized *hᵉbhîʾanī* and *vᵉdiglō* as imperatives, *hᵃbhîʾūnī* and *vᵉdiglū* respectively, and then rendered, "Bring me to the banquet hall and serve me with love."

Even after the two changes are introduced, several difficulties remain: (1) the meaning "serve" for *dāgal* is without parallel in Biblical Hebrew; (2) we should expect the preposition *lī,* not *ʿālay;* (3) the meaning of the clause "serve me with love" is unclear; (4) as indicated in the Comm., we would expect a singular verb addressed to the lover.

Actually, the solution lies in the primary meaning of the Akkadian root *dagâlu,* "look upon, gaze, behold," as in *du-gul-an-ni,* "look upon me" (W. von Soden, *Akkadisches Handwörterbuch,* vol. 1, p. 14b). I first called attention to this root in the interpretation of *nigdālōth* in 6:4 and 6:10 (see the Comm., pp. 90, 92), but it was not utilized for the elucidation of this passage. From this basic meaning "look upon, gaze," the Hebrew noun *degel* means (a) "an object looked upon, hence, banner," as in Nu. 1, 2, 10; and (b) "a look, glance," as in our passage, which is to be rendered, "His look upon me was in love, i.e., loving." The use of a

noun as an adverbial accusative or adjectivally is a well-known characteristic of Biblical Hebrew; cf. Ps. 120:7, *'aﾂī šālōm,* lit. "I am peace,
i.e., peaceful"; Hos. 14:5, *'ōhᵃbhēm nᵉdābhāh, lit.* "I shall love them as
a free gift, i.e. freely."

2:5. אֲשִׁישׁוֹת, "dainties," perhaps "raisin-cakes" (see Hos. 3:1).
רַפְּדוּנִי, not "spread out" (Job 17:13; 41:22), but "strengthen," on
the basis of the Arabic (Ibn Ezra, JPS). There is no need to change
the imperative verbs to the perfect singular, "he has strengthened me"
(against Hal.), since she is addressing the company in the banquet-
hall. Note the plural in v. 7. Raisin-cakes, which were used in fertility
rites (cf. Hos. 3:1), served, like the apple, as an erotic symbol on the
subconscious level, while on the conscious level they refer literally to
a source of physical refreshment. See the Introduction, sec. XIII.

2:7. On the oath and the symbolism employed, see the Introduction. תָּעִירוּ and תְּעוֹרְרוּ most naturally mean "arouse, stir up love"
(JPS), on the basis of which Bettan interprets the passage to mean
that the maiden opposes rousing love by artificial means in favor of
gentle, natural love. This is not likely. Not only is there no reference
to these artificial means in the text, but the context implies that she
is already experiencing passionate love in all its fullness. Hence the
verbs are best rendered "disturb, i. e. interfere with love" (so most
commentators). עַד שֶׁתֶּחְפָּץ, "until love wishes" (*scilicet* to be disturbed,
because it has been satisfied).

Another interpretation of the difficult closing phrase, *'ad ṣeteḥpāṣ,* may
be suggested: "that you disturb not nor interrupt love, while it is passionate." On *'ad,* "while," cf. Ex. 33:22; Jud. 3:26; Jonah 4:2; Job 7:19,
and see BDB, s.v. 2b (p. 724b). The verb *ḥāphēṣ* is used of desiring a
woman in Gen. 34:19; Deut. 21:14; Esther 2:14, 3:5, so that in our
context here it may mean "while love is desirous, i.e. active, passionate"
(my former student, Rabbi David Teitelbaum).

2:8. קוֹל = "hark." Cf. Gen. 4:10.
2:9. This verse is replete with Aramaisms and late Hebrew words.
For כֹּתָל, a *hapax legomenon* in the Bible, see the Targum to Lev. 1:15;
for חֲרַכִּים see the Targum on Prov. 7:6. מַשְׁגִּיחַ is also an Aramaism;
cf. Isa. 14:16; Ps. 33:14.
מֵצִיץ, in earlier Hebrew "sprout" (cf. Ps. 90:6) and "shine" (Ps.
132:18), here means "look, peep"; cf. the Mishnaic usage בן עזאי הציץ
ונפגע, "Ben Azzai looked in and was wounded" (M. Ḥag. 13:2). For
a parallel semantic development, cf. the German *glänzen,* English
glance.

2:10. The opening stich can not be deleted (against Hal.), as it leaves only one stich in the verse. Its presence militates strongly against the dramatic theory.

2:11. סְתָו, "winter," a *hapax legomenon*, is an Aramaism; cf. the Targum on Gen. 8:22, where it renders חֹרֶף. Some manuscripts and editions read סתו Kethib, סתיו Qere, an instance of the original function of the Kethib-Qere formula as a guide to the reader; see Gordis, *The Biblical Text in the Making* (Philadelphia, 1937).

2:12. On זָמִיר see the Introduction, note 30.

2:13. סְמָדַר, "in blossom," has Aramaic and Mandaic cognates, but no satisfactory etymology.

2:14. חַגְוֵי, singular חַגְוָ or חָגָה (cf. קָצֶה and קְצָוֵי), has the basic meaning "break, crack." It is used literally here, and figuratively in Isa. 19:17 in the meaning "destruction, calamity." מַדְרֵגוֹת, the terraces dug into the hillside for purposes of cultivation. Cf. Ezek. 38:20 for its use parallel to הָרִים.

2:15. The verse is patently symbolic. If the vineyard represents the maiden, the young foxes may be the young men who lay siege to her. אֶחֱזוּ is generally regarded as the imperative Qal, and the verse is then given two diametrically opposite interpretations: 1) "Catch the little foxes for us," a plea to save her chastity (so most commentators); and 2) "Take us, you little foxes," a plea for love (so Jast., Hal.). While the second view is far more appropriate to the theme, it is not satisfactory. In v. 14, the lover pleads to see his beloved; she is hardly likely to respond by calling upon many young men to take her. Even if verses 14 and 15 be treated as unrelated, the whole spirit of the *Song* militates against the idea of promiscuity in love, for everywhere the unique relationship of the pair involved is emphasized (cf. 6:9; 8:8 ff.; 8:11 ff.), while we do find complaints by the maiden of advances made by other youths, which she rejects (cf. 1:6 f.; 8:10). We prefer, therefore, to regard אֶחֱזוּ as a perfect and to render the entire clause as "Little foxes have seized us." Nor is it necessary to revocalize the verb as אָחֲזוּ, if it be recognized as a Piel, which occurs in Job 26:9, מְאַחֵז פְּנֵי כִסֵּה. On this form of the Piel perfect instead of the usual אִחֵזוּ, cf. Judg. 5:28, אֶחֱרוּ, the broader vocalization being due to the gutturals. לָנוּ is to be construed as the direct object; cf. Lev. 19:18; II Sam. 3:30. כְּרָמֵינוּ is a plene spelling for the singular: "our vineyard."

2:17. עַד שֶׁיָּפוּחַ הַיּוֹם, "until the day blows, i. e. in the morning"; note the parallelism, "and the shadows flee." On the night as the season for love, which really requires no Biblical references, cf. Prov. 7:18. It cannot mean "until evening," nor can the phrase "and the shadows flee" refer to nightfall, when the shadows lengthen and fade (against Bettan), since the context refers not to the lover's departure, but to his enjoyment of love. The gazelle and the hart are symbols of the lover. The precise meaning of הָרֵי בָתֶר is not clear. It has been 1) emended to הָרֵי בְשָׂמִים, "hills of spices" (cf. 8:14); 2) interpreted to *mean* "spices"; 3) emended to read הָרֵי הַמּוֹר, "hills of myrrh" (Jastrow); and 4) taken as a geographical reference to Bether (or Betar) in Judah (AV, RV), later the scene of Bar Kochba's heroic but fruitless Third War against Rome (132–35 C. E.). Hal. suggests that the place-name may have been derived from an aromatic plant, so that the phrase may virtually mean "spices" in our passage.

For the interpretation "until the day blow = until dawn," cf. the noun *nešeph*, "lit., the blowing time," which is used to refer both to the evening twilight (II Ki. 7:5, 7; Isa. 5:11; 59:10; Pr. 7:9; Job 24:15) and to the morning light, as in Ps. 119:147; Job 7:4, and cf. BDB, s.v. For the semantics of "blowing time = morning," cf. Shakespeare's *Antony and Cleopatra*, IV, 4, 11. 25-27:

> " 'Tis well-blown, lads,
> This morning . . .
> begins betimes."

3:1. While Jastrow deletes בְּקַשְׁתִּיו וְלֹא מְצָאתִיו, Hal. adds קְרָאתִיו וְלֹא עָנָנִי, following the LXX. Actually, the LXX's reading here is an example of "leveling," to bring our passage into agreement with 5:6. Neither change is necessary, the two dream-songs being similar but not identical examples of this genre. The MT is therefore to be preferred.

3:3. Reading מְצָאתִי for the opening word is unnecessary; in fact the MT is superior (against Ehr., Hal.).

3:5. This refrain is often deleted on the ground that it is appropriate to a genuine meeting of the lovers, but not to a dream. See the Introductory Comment on this song for the psychological appropriateness of the oath both here and in 8:4.

3:6. כְּתִימְרוֹת עָשָׁן, "like pillars of smoke," a reference to the dust of the procession traveling across the desert. In Joel 3:3, the phrase alludes to the pillar of cloud which accompanied the Israelites in the wilderness (Ex. 13:21 f.). Perhaps we should read בְּתִימְרוֹת, "with pillars of smoke," which would refer either to the smoke-wreaths of the campfire at night, or possibly to the smoke of incense burned in the bride's honor. רוֹכֵל, "merchant"; cf. קופת הרוכלים (B. Giṭ. 67a). The root is a metaplastic form for רגל, "go on foot"; hence both roots

develop the secondary connotation of "tale-bearing, slander"; cf.
Jer. 9:3; Ps. 15:3.

3:7. On the "Aramaic" form שֶׁלִשְׁלֹמֹה and on the usage of pronominal anticipation, see Intr., sec. VIII and n. 80. The first two
letters of שלשלמה may be a dittography.

3:8. אֲחֻזֵי חֶרֶב, the participle passive, is here used with middle
force; cf. חָגוּר in Judg. 18:11, and such Mishnaic forms as סבור, מדומה, סבור,
"thinking," etc. On the basis of the Akkadian, Perles interprets אחז as
"taught, skilled"; cf. the parallelism. The "terrors of the night" may
refer to evil spirits rampant particularly in those hours, or to desert
bandits, who might be tempted to attack the richly laden caravan
of a royal princess going to her wedding.

3:9. On the various foreign etymologies proposed for אַפִּרְיוֹן,
see the Introduction and note 74. It is probably Sanskrit in origin.
The Talmud uses the Biblical word occasionally (B. Sotah 49a), but
more often the Aramaic פּוּרְיָא. In spite of the accents, the caesura
belongs after הַמֶּלֶךְ; cf. Num. 23:7, where the pause comes after
בָּלָק, likewise against the accents. On the parallelism, see the
Introduction.

3:10. רְפִידָתוֹ, literally, "its bedding, inlay." מֶרְכָּבוֹ must be "the
seat" rather than the "body" (Jast.). תוֹכוֹ רָצוּף אַהֲבָה, generally rendered: "its parts are inlaid with love," is unsatisfactory (in spite of
such instances of the adverbial accusative as Hos. 14:5, אֹהֲבֵם נְדָבָה,
"I should love them freely"). The context requires a concrete substance, as the parallelism indicates, and most scholars accept Graetz's
emendation הָבְנִים, "ivory," for אַהֲבָה (cf. Ezek. 27:15). Tur-Sinai
proposes הַבִּים, from שֶׁנְהַבִּים (cf. I Kings 10:22). He bases his proposed
vocable on the Aramaic יב for the place-name "Elephantine." "The
daughters of Jerusalem" are the ladies of its court who prepared the
decorations of the palanquin.

The difficulties of stich d, tōkhō rāṣūph 'aʰbhāh, as well as the
better emendations that have been proposed for meeting them, are set
forth in the Comm. ad loc. It is pointed out there that the context requires
a concrete substance, a parallel to the other terms mentioned. The defini-
tive solution to this crux was presented by G. R. Driver (JBL, vol. 55,
1936, p. 111). He calls attention to an Arabic cognate 'hb, the root
of the nouns 'ihāʼb, "hide, raw skin," and 'ihaʼb, "soldier's equipment."
The noun in our passage therefore means "leather," and the stich receives
an excellent meaning, "Its innermost part being lined with leather." Our
translation has been revised accordingly.

3:11. Crowns were worn even by ordinary grooms and brides, until the defeats sustained in the War against Rome in 70, when they were abandoned as a sign of mourning (cf. B. Sotah 49a). Hence the Rabbinic proverb חתן דומה למלך (*Pirke deRabbi Eliezer*, chap. 16). The Vav of וּבְיוֹם need not be deleted (against Ehr.). On its use in parallel stichs with no sense of addition, cf. Zech. 9:9, עָנִי וְרֹכֵב עַל־חֲמוֹר וְעַל־עַיִר בֶּן־אֲתֹנוֹת. Here the failure to recognize the usage led to unusual consequences (cf. Matt. 21:2, 7). There is no need to transpose the order of the last four stichs (against Rothstein, Jast.).

4:1. There is no need to read עֵינַיִךְ כְּיוֹנִים (against Hal.). Much of the power of Biblical poetry derives from its directness, its preference for the metaphor over the simile, for the noun over the adjective.

נלשׁ, "trail down." The root is used in Rabbinic Hebrew of bubbling, boiling water (Pes. 37b) and of luxuriant tresses (Midrash Cant. Rab. 4:3).

4:2. The participle passive הַקְּצוּבוֹת has a gerundive force, "ready to be sheared," as Ehr. noted. Cf. Ps. 137:8, הַשְּׁדוּדָה, "destined to be despoiled." מַתְאִימוֹת, a Hiphil of condition, literally, "all in twins," a reference to the evenness of the two rows of teeth.

4:4. A large neck, like a prominent nose (cf. 7:5), was a mark of beauty to the ancients. Nonetheless, it is not the neck, but the tower of David, which is described as having room for a thousand shields. Shields were hung on towers for decoration and storing while not in active use; cf. Ezek. 27:11. On this use of similes in the *Song*, see the Introduction.

לְתַלְפִּיוֹת is an ancient crux, which the LXX did not understand and therefore transliterated (εἰς θαλπιώθ). The word has been rendered variously: 1) as "maneuvers," from the root אלף, "teach"; 2) as "landmark," from the same root (Ibn Janah); 3) as "armory" (AV, Jast.); 4) as "turrets," from תֵּל פִּיוֹת (?), "heap of points" (AV); 5) as "for looking afar off," from the Greek τηλωπος (Graetz). It is noteworthy, however, that the LXX did not recognize it as such, and the Tav generally reproduces the Greek Theta, not the Tau; 6) by metathesis and revocalization it is read לְתָלוֹת יְפִי, "to hang beautiful things upon" (Tur-Sinai, who compares Ezek. 27:11, שִׁלְטֵיהֶם תָּלוּ; 7) Read לַפְּתִילוֹת, which is taken to mean "built according to the (proper) lines," from פְּתִילָה, "thread" (Kuhn, Hal.). None of these views is strikingly persuasive.

4:5. שְׁנֵי is deleted by Jastrow, but this destroys the rhythm of the verse. The presence of the numeral emphasizes that both are alike.

4:6. There is no ground for eliminating this verse as a doublet of 2:17 (against Hal.). Refrains with variations are common in folk poetry. Nor need vv. 6 and 7 be reversed in order (against Rothstein, Jast.). The song ends with the theme with which it begins (v. 1), but with a slight variation in the refrain. This change in the refrain is a common characteristic of Biblical poetry; cf. Ps. 49:13, 21; Job 28:12, 20. The "mountain of myrrh" and the "hill of frankincense" are obvious symbols for the body of the beloved.

4:8. This verse may be a fragment of a song emanating from the mountain-ranges lying to the north of Israel. It is not necessary to emend the first אֲתִי to אֵתִי, "come" (against Hal.). The lover emphasizes "with me"; note the word-order. תָּשׁוּרִי is better derived not from שׁוּר, "look," but from the homonym "leap" (Aramaic שׁוור; Arabic سار). It occurs in Hos. 13:7. On the parallelism of "come" and "leap," cf. 2:8. It is, therefore, unnecessary to read תָּסוּרִי with Hal.

אֲמָנָה here refers to the mountain from which the rivers Amana and Parpar flow (II Kings 5:12). While Deut. 3:9 and 4:48 identify Hermon, Sirion, Senir, and Sion, I Chron. 5:23 apparently distinguishes between Senir, Hermon (and Baal Hermon), as does our passage. The names may refer to different peaks. Leopards are still to be found in the Lebanon range, but lions are now extinct.

4:9. לִבַּבְתִּנִי, a privative Piel: "thou hast stolen my heart away"; cf. דִּשֵּׁן, שָׁרַשׁ, עִקַּר. Ibn Janah interprets the verb as "pierced my heart," based on the Mishnaic עורות לבוביןּ, "pierced skins" ('Ab. Zarah 2:3). The Kethib באחד is a scribal error for בְּאַחַת, which is the reading (not the correction) of the Qere; cf. Gordis, *The Biblical Text in the Making — A Study of the Kethib-Qere* (Philadelphia, 1936). The error was induced by the following phrase. In בְּאַחַד עֲנָק the word-order is an Aramaism, which penetrated Hebrew to some degree. Cf. Neh. 4:11, בְּאַחַת יָדוֹ. עֲנָק has two meanings: 1) "neck" (cf. Aramaic ענקא), hence "with one turn of thy neck" (Jast.); 2) "jewel" (cf. Prov. 1:9), hence "with one jewel." The latter is preferable here. מִצַּוְּרֹנָיִךְ is a defective spelling for מִצַּוְּארֹנָיִךְ. The noun צַוְּרֹן is a derivative of צַוָּאר, "neck," with which the Versions and many commentators have confused it. It means not "neck," but "ornament for the neck, necklace." In modern Hebrew it is aptly used for "collar."

4:11. On the fragrance of the beloved's garments, cf. Ps. 45:9. The smell of Lebanon-wine is mentioned in Hos. 14:7; here the reference is to its cedars.

4:12. The two phrases גַּל נָעוּל and גַּן נָעוּל have often been regarded as identical. Thus the Versions read גַּן for the less familiar גַּל (LXX, P, V, also the Midrash). This is accepted by Kittel, *BH*, and by others

who overlook the process of "leveling" here at work. Conversely,
Hal. reads גַּל נָעוּל at the beginning of the verse and then deletes the
second phrase as a dittography. Actually, the MT is in perfect order.
The two figures of a sealed garden and a closed fountain are both
highly appropriate for expressing the idea that the lover is being
denied access to the delightful person of his beloved. Both themes
are taken up later in the maiden's response (vv. 15–16). Note, too,
that גַּל נָעוּל — a "sealed spring" (cf. Josh. 15:19; Judg. 1:15) — is an
ideal transition-word between גַּן, which precedes it and which it resembles in sound, and מַעְיָן, which follows it and which it resembles in
meaning. Moreover, the meter (2:2:2:2) effectively disposes of the
effort to delete any part of the verse (against Jast.).

4:13. שְׁלָחַיִךְ, apparently "branches"; cf. Isa. 16:8. Hal. plausibly
refers it to the arms or bosom. מֶגֶד, "blessing, sweetness"; cf. Deut.
33:13. The spices mentioned in these verses include several imports
from the East. See the Introduction and note 75.

4:15. The Masoretic reading מַעְיָן גַּנִּים makes this verse a continu-
ation of the lover's speech, but it then contradicts v. 12, for the
beloved is here described as "a well of *flowing* water," while above she
is called "a *sealed* fountain." It is therefore better to emend to מַעְיָן גַּנִּי,
"the fountain of my garden" (so Budde, Ehr., Hal., *BH*), so that v. 13
contains the lover's complaint, v. 15, her denial of his charge, and v. 16
her invitation to him to enjoy his garden's delights.

5:1. אָרִיתִי, "I gather"; cf. Ps. 80:13. יַעַר = "honey-comb." The
closing stich, אִכְלוּ רֵעִים שְׁתוּ וְשִׁכְרוּ דּוֹדִים, has occasioned much difficulty,
since the lover is not likely to invite his friends to enjoy the delights
of his beloved. Hence Ehr. emends it to the singular by five changes,
אֱכֹל רֵעִי שְׁתֵה וּשְׁכַר דּוֹדִי, "Eat, my friend, drink abundantly, my beloved,"
while Hal. changes the text even more drastically to the feminine
singular: אִכְלִי רַעְיָתִי שְׁתִי וְשִׁכְרִי דּוֹדִים, "Eat, my beloved, drink abundantly
of love." Others delete the stich entirely or regard it as a fragment of a
drinking song now out of place (Jast.). On the occasional use of the
plural for the singular in modern Palestinian love-poetry, see the
Introduction. If this usage occurs here, the stich represents the
closing response of the beloved, urging her lover to take his full measure
of joy.

Introductory Note — 5:2 to 6:3

On the structure of this long and elaborate song, see the Introduction and Introductory Comment. Scholars who separate the song

into three units, the dream-song (5:2–8), the *waṣf* (5:9–16), and the dialogue (6:1–3) (so Jastrow), or into two (5:2–7 and 5:8 to 6:3) (so Hal.), overlook the exquisite articulation of the three sections and deprive the song of much of its power. Actually, 5:8, addressed to "the daughters of Jerusalem," leads directly to their question in 5:9 and this in turn prepares for the maiden's response embodied in the *waṣf* in 5:1 ff. 6:1 then offers the natural reaction of "the daughters of Jerusalem" to the description of the lover's charms, and 6:2 her announcement that her lover has already found his way to her (so also Budde, Bettan).

The elaborateness of the contents is matched by the variety of meter. Efforts by scholars to force the entire poem into the Procrustean bed of the 3:2 *kinah* rhythm are untenable. That long poems in particular will have various meters was always clear from Biblical poetry and has been demonstrated anew by the Ugaritic epics. In our song, the *kinah* rhythm predominates, particularly in the *waṣf*, but is not the only meter employed. Its basic characteristic is that a long stich is succeeded by a shorter. Hence it may take the form of 3:2 (the most common) or a variation (3:2:2 or 4:3, or 3:3 ‖ 2:2). On the metric principles involved, see the paper cited in note 43 above.

The meter of the song is as follows:

5:2 — 4:3 ‖ 3:2 ‖ 3:3
5:3 — 4 ‖ 4 (or 2:2 ‖ 2:2)
5:4 — 4:3
5:5 — 4:3 ‖ 3:3
5.6 — 3:3 ‖ 3 ‖ 3:3 (The central stich, because of emotional
      impact, is an anacrusis, outside the
      meter.)
5:7 — 2:2:2 ‖ 3:3 (The close of the first section. Hence a
      longer closing distich. Accordingly, stich c,
      which consists of two long words, שֹׁמְרֵי הַחֹמוֹת,
      receives three beats.)
5:8 — 2:2 ‖ 2:2:2
5:9 — 3:2 ‖ 3:2 (The beginning of the *waṣf*.)
5:10 — 3:2 (To emphasize the description of the lover, the
     opening line has no parallel stich, adding to its
     force.)
5:11 — 3:2:2
5:12 — 2:2 ‖ 2:2

5:13 — 3:3 ‖ 3:3 (Stich b, מנדלות מרקחים, and stich c, שפתותיו
                    שושנים, each receives three beats, because of
                    the length of the words and the exigencies
                    of the meter.)
5:14 — 3:2 ‖ 3:2
5:15 — 3:3 ‖ 2:2
5:16 — 2:2 ‖ 2:2:2
6:1 — 3:2 ‖ 3:2
6:2 — 3:3 ‖ 2:2 (Stich b, לערוגת הבשם, probably receives three
                    beats because of its length; otherwise, the
                    meter is 3:2 ‖ 3:2.)
6:3 — 2:2:2

5:2. The call is hardly that of a husband, estranged from his
wife (against Bettan), but rather that of a lover seeking admission
to his sweetheart's home.

5:4. מן החור is extremely difficult. It is rendered by some "through
the door," but the context (besides the preposition מן) implies his
withdrawal, not his opening the door. There is no need to read שָׁלַף
(against Ehr., Jast.). "The hole" has been explained as a "lock"
(Haupt), "window" (Siegfried), "peering-hole" (Budde), or as an
obscene term for the vagina (Wittekindt, Hal.). The last view makes
nonsense of the preceding verses, which are a call by the lover to be
admitted to the house. The context requires an opening for the hand,
not a window or peering-hole. It probably refers to an aperture
through which the door can be opened from the outside. When the
lover hears her negative reply, he takes it at face-value, instead of
as coquetry. He therefore withdraws his hand, just as he was getting
ready to let himself in. On the bowels as the seat of strong emotions
in Biblical psychology, cf. Isa. 16:11; Jer. 31:19.

5:5. The myrrh dripping from her hands is taken by some to
refer to the perfume which her lover had left on the door-handle
(Jast., Hal.). It is better to think of her as having anointed herself
with perfume before retiring, because she had expected her lover, the
by-play in v. 3 being simply a flirtation (so also Ehr.). עבר, "dropping,
dripping."

5:6. חָמַק, a pluperfect, "had gone"; cf. Jer. 31:21. נפשי יצאה
בדברו is transposed by Hal. after 5a because the lover is obviously
not speaking here. The correct sense of this clause, which is crucial
for the understanding of the entire song, was proposed by Ehr.:
"My soul passed out with longing for his speaking," or (revocalizing

בְּדִבְרוֹ) "for his word," i. e., "I longed to hear his voice." On the Beth =
"for the sake of," cf. Exod. 10:12, נְטֵה יָדְךָ בְּאֶרֶץ, and the common
Beth pretii. Tur-Sinai's suggestion בְּדָבְרוֹ, "I went out to his pasturage"
(cf. Isa. 5:17; Micah 2:12), is not only prosaic, but is ruled out by the
pervasive city-background of the poem.

5:7. The city-watchmen, seeing her wandering about at night
and hearing her call for her lover, mistake her for a harlot, and beat
her. The cape was the outer garment, mentioned last in the "Cata-
logue of Finery" in Isaiah (3:23), where it may have had a more
specific meaning. Jast. deletes השמרים to get a 3:2 rhythm. Besides
being metrically unnecessary (see the Introductory Note), this
procedure creates an unclear sense, since we would have no subject
for the verbs.

5:8. מָה, literally, "what," rhetorically used, is equivalent to
"that" (Ehr., Jast.).

5:10. צַח, used of shining heat (Isa. 18:4), of a milk-white com-
plexion (Lam. 4:7), or of pure speech (Isa. 32:4), means "pure white,
fair." דָּגוּל, from Akkadian *dagâlu*, "see, look upon," whence דֶּגֶל,
"a flag, something visible." דָּגוּל means "outstanding, distinguished."
On כַּנִּדְגָּלוֹת (6:4, 10), which is to be taken similarly, see the Commentary
ad loc.

5:11. כֶּתֶם פָּז, rendered "fine gold," actually consists of two
synonyms used for greater effect; cf. the heaping up of epithets in
4:9–10; 5:2. The change to כֶּתֶר, "crown," is attractive, but not
necessary. קְוֻצּוֹתָיו, "locks." תַּלְתַּלִּים, "curled, heaped up," from תֵּל,
"heap." The Akkadian *taltallu* means "palm branches," a comparison
to be found also in Arabic love-poetry: the hair is here conceived of
as dark and wavy (Jast.).

5:12. The verse compares the dark pupil within the white iris
to doves bathing in milk or perched at a clear brook. The rendering
"fitly set" for יֹשְׁבוֹת עַל־מִלֵּאת (JPS) is inept. What is required is a noun
denoting a pool or watering-place (so Ehr., Jast., Hal.). Tur-Sinai
aptly cites Midrash Gen. Rab., section 95 (ms. Theodor), אזל למליתה,
"he went to the pool where the maidens draw up the water."

5:13. מִגְדְּלוֹת מֶרְקָחִים, "towers of spices, banks of spices" (Ibn
Ezra, JPS). It should be revocalized as מְגַדְּלוֹת, "raising, exuding
perfumes" (so LXX, V, Tar., and most moderns), as is clear from the
parallelism נֹטְפוֹת. כַּעֲרוּגַת should, accordingly, be revocalized as a
plural, כַּעֲרוּגוֹת (so some Mss.), so as to supply the proper subject for
the participle. Cf. 6:2 for the plural.

5:14. גָּלִיל, "rod, column." תַּרְשִׁישׁ has been identified with topaz, beryl (JPS), and rubies (Jast.). מֵעָיו, literally "reins," here represents the "skin" (Ibn Ezra, Hal.), or "the belly" (JPS). It probably refers to the entire central portion of the body. עֶשֶׁת (Akkadian *išitu*, "column"); cf. Ezek. 27:19. סַפִּירִים is not our sapphire, but lapis lazuli or azure, ultramarine blue in color.

6:2. It is not necessary to emend לָנוּ to לְנִי or to change בַּגַּנִּים to בַּגַּנִּפִים (*BH*, Hal.).

The imagery of a garden as the symbol of the delights of love, which the lover would rather not share with others, may be illustrated in a Viennese soldier's song:

> *"Was nutzet mir ein Rosengarten*
> *Wenn and're drin spazieren gehen?"*
>
> "What use to me a rose garden
> when others go walking in it?"
>
> (cited by Theodore Reik, *The Haunting Melody*, p. 83.)

6:4. The efforts made to identify תִּרְצָה with a famous beauty, now unknown (cf. Num. 27:1, where it occurs as a feminine proper name), and then to find another feminine name in כִּירוּשָׁלַם, such as יְרוּשָׁא (cf. II Kings 15:33), cannot be pronounced successful. The reference is to the ancient city of Tirzah captured by Joshua (Josh. 12:24), which served as the capital of the Northern Kingdom (I Kings 14:17; 16:8, 9, 15) until it was replaced by Omri (887–876 B. C. E.) with Samaria (II Kings 16:24). While it is mentioned (II Kings 15:14) as late as the reign of Menahem, the son of Gadi (745–736 B. C. E.), its juxtaposition with Jerusalem in our song suggests that it was still the capital. Hence this lyric emanates from the half-century between Jeroboam I (933 B. C. E.) and the reign of Omri. Curiously, both the LXX and Rashi render it "a beautiful structure."

אֲיֻמָּה כַּנִּדְגָּלוֹת is a famous crux. The traditional rendering, "terrible as an army with banners" (Ibn Ezra), is hardly satisfactory. Hence it is deleted as an erroneous insertion from 6:10 (*BH*, Hal.). On the mythological interpretation given the phrase, when emended, in 6:10, see the Commentary there. On that view the phrase must be deleted here. Several alternatives may be suggested. The phrase may possibly be regarded as an error for אֲיֻמָּה בְּמִגְדָּלוֹת, "awe-inspiring with its towers," and it would be a description of Jerusalem. (See the Introduction on this stylistic trait of describing the simile.) This would, however, necessitate deleting the phrase in 6:10. We prefer to interpret כִּנִדְגָּלוֹת from the Akkadian *dagâlu*, "look upon"; cf. דָּגֻל, דְּגוּל, "seen, distinguished" (5:10). The MT may then be rendered: "(She is) awe-inspiring like these cynosures, great sights," literally, "things looked upon." The reference is to the cities of Tirzah and Jerusalem, just mentioned, hence the feminine plural. Thus no change in the text is required, and the same meaning is appropriate also in 6:10. The demonstrative nuance "these" inheres in the definite article, as in הַיּוֹם, "this day," כָּעֵת, "at this time," etc. Jastrow's insertion of 6:10 before 6:4, like the removal of v. 5a after v. 10 (*BH*, Hal.), is uncalled for.

The interpretation of *nigdālōt* (in this verse and in 6:10) advanced in the Comm. and embodied in the Translation, "objects seen, things looked upon," was based on the Akkadian root *dagâlu*, "look upon, behold." It may be further supported from Akkadian usage. The root *dagâlu* carries the special nuance, "look with astonishment," as in *i-dag-ga-lu*, "they looked astounded" (as in the *Nimrud Epic*, ed. P. Haupt, p. 456, apud Muss-Arnolt, *A Concise Dictionary of the Assyrian Language*, vol. 1, p. 24), or "look with admiration," as in *bita šatin ana tabrâti ušepišma ana da-ga-lum kiššat nisē*, "I had that temple built as a structure to be looked at with admiration by all people" (*Vorderasiatische Bibliothek*, 4, 118, II, 53, cited in *The Assyrian Dictionary of the Oriental Institute of the University of Chicago*, Vol. III, pp. 21-24). This is precisely what our passages require. Hence, *nigdālōt* in both Biblical passages means "astonishing, admirable sights," and the phrase is to be rendered, "these great sights," as set forth in the Translation and in the body of the Commentary. Cf. our paper in *JBL*, vol. 88, 1969, pp. 203-4.

6:5. הִרְהִיבֻנִי, "have frightened me" (Arabic *rahiba*, "be frightened"; Syrian *rʿheb*, "tremble"). The same root seems to have, elsewhere in Hebrew, the connotation of "pride, arrogance" (Ps. 138:3; *Rahab*, the primordial beast in Isa. 30:7; 51:9). This may be an example of '*aḍdād*, "words of like and opposite meaning." On this common phenomenon in Semitic languages, cf. Th. Noeldeke, *Beiträge zur semitischen Sprachwissenschaft* (Strassburg, 1904); Gordis, "Words of Contrasted Meaning," in *JQR*, vol. 27, 1936, pp. 33–58. For an effort to explain its origin, see *idem*, "Some Effects of Primitive Thought on Language," in *AJSL*, vol. 55, 1938, pp. 270–84. There is no need to emend to הִלְהִיבֻנִי (Ehr.), "they have enflamed me." On 6:5-7, see the Commentary on 4:1–3.

6:6. The LXX adds the first two stichs of 4:3 here, another instance of "leveling" the text.

6:8. שִׁשִּׁים הֵמָּה. The pronoun emphasizes the general statement, "There are sixty queens." הֵמָּה has been emended to לִשְׁלֹמה (Budde, Hal.). But since the emphasis is on the contrast between Solomon and the speaker, the word-order we should have expected is שִׁשִּׁים שִׁשִּׁים לִשְׁלֹמֹה מְלָכוֹת (cf. 8:11) or לִשְׁלֹמה שִׁשִּׁים מְלָכוֹת, not מְלָכוֹת לִשְׁלֹמֹה שִׁשִּׁים. "Twenty" is a basic number in our passage, like the English "score," so that 60 and 80, which are three and four score, respectively, represent the "ascending numeration," common in Biblical and Semitic poetry for designating a large and indefinite quantity; cf. Amos 1:3, 6, 9, 11, 13; Prov. 30:15, 18, 21, 24, 29; Job 5:19. It is therefore impossible to delete "eighty concubines" (against Jast.).

6:9. בָּרָה, not "pure" or "lustrous," but "chosen," from בור, a Mediae Vav root for the more common geminate ברר, "choose, select"; on the former, cf. Eccl. 3:18; 9:1; on the latter, see the common Mishnaic ברר. There is no need, accordingly, to invent a word בָּרָה (against *BH*). The beloved is so outstanding that her mother prefers her to all her other children, so that she is, so to speak, "one" to her mother.

6:10. אֲיֻמָּה כַּנִּדְגָּלוֹת is deleted by *BH* as an insertion from 6:4. Here again the traditional interpretation, "striking awe as a bannered host" (Jast.), is irrelevant. Dalman has suggested reading אֲיֻמָּה כְּנֵרְגַל, "awe-inspiring like Nergal, the red star of Mars." The phrase would then be parallel with the other comparisons of the beloved to the dawn, the moon, and the sun. Even if we accept this attractive suggestion, as does Hal., it would be no evidence for the cultic use of the Song, but simply a mythological reference like those to be found in Isaiah, Psalms and Job. Several considerations, however, militate against this view: 1) It is not appropriate to 6:4, where the phrase must accordingly be deleted. 2) Not only does it require several changes in the text, but it creates a *hapax legomenon* in Hebrew. 3) While comparing one's beloved to the dawn, the sun, and the moon is understandable, to speak of her as the red star of Mars is rather strange. We accordingly prefer to interpret the phrase here exactly as in 6:4, with no change in the MT: "awe-inspiring like these great sights," literally, "these things looked upon," a participle passive of the Niphal of דגל, "gaze upon." The reference here is to the heavenly bodies mentioned before (לבנה, חמה), hence the feminine plural. See also the Commentary on 6:4.

6:11. בְּאִבֵּי הַנָּחַל, "the fresh shoots of the valley"; cf. Job 8:12.

6:12. This verse is completely incomprehensible as it stands, and as it is usually rendered, e. g. in JPS: "Before I was aware, my soul

set me upon the chariots of my princely people." The LXX, V, and
20 Hebrew mss. read עַמִּינָדָב, which Budde interprets as the name of the
lover or the groom. Jastrow solves the problem by regarding the verse
as containing three distinct glosses, while Haupt sees in לֹא יָדַעְתִּי נַפְשִׁי
the confession of a reader, "I don't understand it." But if these
words are deleted as the sentiment of a reader, there is nothing left
not to understand! Among the emendations proposed have been:
1) שַׂמְתַּנִי מַרְכְּבוֹת עַמִּינָדָב, "You have placed me in the chariots of Ammina-
dab." 2) Graetz, followed by Hal., reads שַׂמְתַּנִי מֹרֶךְ בַּת עַמִּי נָדִיב, "You
have made me fearful (literally, you have set me in fear), O nobleman's
daughter." 3) Tur-Sinai brilliantly proposes to emend the phrase
(and link the last three words to the next verse) to read: שָׁם תְּנִי מֹרֶךְ ‖
בַּת עַמִּי נָדִיב שׁוּבִי ‖ שׁוּבִי הַשּׁוּלַמִּית. However, attaching the two verses
disrupts the rhythm of 7:1, which is normal, and is not really required.
With the revocalization of our verse, as proposed by Tur-Sinai, as a
basis, the passage is to be rendered: "I am beside myself with joy,
for there (i. e. in the garden, v. 11) thou wilt give me thy myrrh
(cf. 7:13), O nobleman's daughter." The idiom לֹא יָדַעְתִּי נַפְשִׁי apparently means "lose one's balance, normal composure," whether through
great joy, as here, or through sorrow, as in Job 9:21 (Prov. 19:2 is
unclear). On the reference to the beloved as "daughter of a noble
kinsman" (בת עמי נדיב), or, more briefly (7:2), as "nobleman's daughter" (בת נדיב), cf. "The Dance of the Bride," in G. Dalman, *Palestinischer Diwan* (Leipzig, 1901, p. 256): "The daughter of the noble
dances with two candles. Rise up, mount to the palace. By the
light of thy father, precious." (Translated by Helen B. Jastrow)
Arabs refer to a girl as *bint el akbar*, "Nobleman's daughter."

   7:1. שׁוּבִי, either "turn" or "halt" (Ehr.). There is no need to
emend to סֹבִי (against *BH*). מַה־תֶּחֱזוּ — "What will you see?" — is
probably her modest reply, "What is there to see in me?", to which
the company responds. In that event, כִּמְחֹלַת הַמַּחֲנַיִם would be their
answer: "Indeed, the double — or counter dance." On the asseverative Kaph, see the Commentary on 1:7 and the references there. It is
therefore unnecessary to emend the phrase to בִּמְחֹלַת הַמַּחֲנַיִם, "in the
dance of two companies." It may be a reference to the sword-dance
still practised by Arab brides on their wedding day. To incorporate a
"military" reference in the "sword-dance," Jast. and Hal. read
הַמַּחֲנִים, "camps," but this is unnecessary. הַשּׁוּלַמִּית is not a reference
to the goddess Ištar (Wittekindt), nor need it be taken as the feminine
of שְׁלֹמֹה, hence "Solomon's woman" (Rowley, *AJSL*, 1939, pp. 15 f.),
or as the goddess Salmeiat or Shulmanitu, a Canaanite goddess of war

(cf. Gaster, *loc. cit.*). Aside from the intrinsic improbability of these suggestions, the definite article indicates that the word must be a gentilic or geographical substantive; the traditional interpretation is incomparably the best: "the girl of Shulem or Shunem" (cf. Josh. 19:18; I Kings 1:3).

7:2. The spectators describe the girl, who is either naked or clothed in diaphanous veils, so that her entire person can be seen. The attention of the company is first directed to the lightning rapidity of her dancing feet and then upwards. Haupt, who inverts the order of the verses, accordingly misses the point. Ibn Ezra struggles to explain away the details of the frank description, while Kuhn interprets it as a dream. On בַּת־נָדִיב, see the Commentary on 6:12. חַמּוּקֵי, "roundings, turns"; cf. Jer. 31:21; Song 5:6 for the root. חֲלָאִים, "links in a chain"; cf. Hos. 2:15; Prov. 25:12.

7:3. שָׁרְרֵךְ, "navel." אַגַּן הַסַּהַר, "bowl in the shape of a half-moon." אַל־יֶחְסַר הַמָּזֶג continues the figure of the wine goblet, "in which the mixture is not missing." See the Introduction for this stylistic usage. It is not a reference to the sperm (against Hal.).

7:5. כְּמִגְדַּל הַשֵּׁן, "like an ivory tower," because of the whiteness of the neck. Some read הַבָּשָׁן, to parallel the other geographical names in the verse, of which Heshbon is also in Transjordan. מִגְדַּל הַלְּבָנוֹן, "the tower of Lebanon," may not refer to a tower on the mountain or facing it, but to the Lebanon peak itself (Haupt, Jast.). On the standard of beauty implied, see the Introduction. צוֹפָה, "facing toward"; cf. נִשְׁקָפָה, Num. 21:20.

7:6. כַּרְמֶל, properly "the purple land," becomes a proper noun, "the Carmel mountain"; cf. the Commentary on שָׁרוֹן (2:1). Here it is used as a common noun, like כַּרְמִיל, "crimson" (cf. II Chron. 2:6, 13; 3:14). דַּלַּת רֹאשֵׁךְ, "hair of thy head," is not compared to אַרְגָּמָן in color, but in its shining quality. Jast. points out that also in Greek love-poetry, "purple" is used to denote the rich dark color of thick hair. רְהָטִים is interpreted *ad hoc* as meaning "tresses." Its use in Ex. 2:16 as "troughs" is obviously inappropriate here, nor does Song 1:17 help us here. The root is apparently רהט (Aramaic "run"), and implies the flowing character of the long hair. Cf. 4:1; 6:5 for the figure. מֶלֶךְ = "the bridegroom"; evidence that this song describes a wedding dance.

7:7. אַהֲבָה, "love," may be a metonomy for "loved one," and there is no need to emend to אֲהוּבָה (Dal., Hal.). It is, however, best taken as an apostrophe to the love-experience itself (so Jast.). The verse elicits this enthusiastic comment from Ibn Ezra: אין בעולם תענוג לנפש

ולא דבר יפה ונעים כמו החשק, "In all the world there is no such delight for the spirit and nothing as fair and pleasant as love."

7:9. סַנְסִנָּיו, "branches," from the Akkadian *sinsinnu*, "the topmost branches of the palm." A variant, with Lamed instead of Nun, occurs in Jer. 6:9, סַלְסִלּוֹת.

7:10. A very difficult verse. Stich a is obviously addressed to the beloved (וְחִכֵּךְ), while stich b would seem to be addressed by the maiden to the lover (לְדוֹדִי). The usual rendering "smoothly," for לְמֵישָׁרִים, is both unjustified and inept. For the difficult last stich LXX reads: ἱκανούμενος χείλεσί μου καὶ ὀδοῦσιν, "sufficient for my lips and teeth," which represents רַב בִּשְׂפָתַי וְשִׁנָּי (on the Greek-Hebrew equivalence, cf. the LXX on Num. 16:7). This probably is an erroneous rendering of a Hebrew text דּוֹבֵב שְׂפָתַי וְשִׁנָּי, a reading preferred by some commentators. Thus Hal. reads: כְּלֵיחַ שָׁרוֹן דּוֹבֵב שְׂפָתַי וְשִׁנָּי, "Like the juice of Sharon, flowing over my lips and teeth." Tur-Sinai cites the Akkadian love-charm, *ana shudbubi*, "to make the lover speak, i. e., think, of his beloved," and interprets דּוֹבֵב as a euphemism for sexual activity. The Hebrew text itself, however, needs no change. On the use of מֵישָׁרִים, in connection with wine and on its connotation of "strength, vigor," see the Commentary on 1:4. Stichs b and c, which follow the words כְּיֵין הַטּוֹב, are to be taken as descriptive of the power of wine to stimulate the strength of lovers' desire. If לְדוֹדִי is recognized as an apocopated plural for לְדוֹדִים, "for lovers" (cf., for example, Isa. 5:1, שִׁירַת דּוֹדִי, for שִׁירַת דּוֹדִים, "a love song"; Cant. 8:2, עֲסִיס רִמֹּנִי, "juice of pomegranates"; Ps. 144:2, הָרֹדֵד עַמִּי תַחְתָּי), there is no abrupt shift of speakers and the entire verse is spoken by the lover. The verse is to be rendered: "Thy palate is like good wine, giving vigor to lovers, stirring the lips of the sleepers (with desire)." לְדוֹדִים in the plural is parallel to יְשֵׁנִים.

Another possibility may also be suggested. The word למישרים, "for strength," may be a toast used in drinking wine, both in our passage and in Prov. 23:31, like the modern Hebrew *Leḥayyîm*, "for life," Swedish *skoal*, English "to your health," etc. Such a toast, we believe, is to be found in the Biblical יְחִי לְבַבְכֶם לָעַד, "May your hearts be alive forever" (Ps. 22:27), and דֹּרְשֵׁי אֱלֹהִים וִיחִי לְבַבְכֶם (Ps. 69:33), "Those who seek God *say*, 'May your hearts be alive!'" Our passage would then be rendered: "Thy palate is like good wine, going down for lovers with the toast 'for strength.'" The first interpretation suggested is preferable.

7:11. A reminiscence of Gen. 3:16, but radically different in spirit. There Eve is punished by being made subservient to her husband: "To thy husband will be thy desire, but he will rule over thee"; here, virtually the same words are used to express the joyous desire of the lovers for each other. On the similar use of classical Biblical texts for new ideas and attitudes in Ecclesiastes, cf. *KMW*, pp. 43 ff.

7:12. בִּכְפָרִים, either "among the henna flowers" (Ewald, Jast., Ehr.), or "among the villages." There is no need to emend to בֻּפָנִים (Jast.).

7:14. הַדּוּדָאִים, "mandrakes," are not only highly fragrant, but were regarded as aphrodisiacs (cf. Gen. 30:14), hence their name, derived from *dōd*, "lover." For דוֹדִי, "O my beloved," it seems better to revocalize דּוֹדִי, "My love, which I have saved for thee," taking up the theme from the end of v. 13. Verse 14a, b, c thus constitutes a parenthesis.

8:1. כְּאָח, not "like my brother," for that would not meet her problem, which is her desire to kiss her lover unashamedly in public. Nor need the Kaph be deleted (against Hal.). The Kaph is asseverative: "indeed my brother — my very brother." On this usage, cf. the Commentary on 1:7 and the references there. גַּם is adversative, "yet"; cf. Ps. 129:2, גַּם לֹא־יָכְלוּ לִי.

8:2. אֶל־בֵּית אִמִּי תְּלַמְּדֵנִי is difficult. The verb has been rendered: "that thou mightest instruct me" (JPS), but this is irrelevant here. Linking it with אַשְׁקְךָ, "she (i. e. my mother) would teach me how to make you drink," creates a harsh construction, and the meaning is dubious. The MT is explained most simply, but not quite satisfactorily, as: "to the house of my mother, who taught me." The LXX and P disregard the verb entirely and render: "to the room of her who bore me," following 3:4 (so also Dal., Hal.). It is possible that תְּלַמְּדֵנִי came into our text from a scribe, who misinterpreted וְאֶל חֶדֶר הוֹרָתִי, as in 3:4, from הוֹרָה, "teach," the Hiphil of ירה, rather than from הָרָה, "conceive," and then incorporated his erroneous synonym into the text.

Pomegranate-wine is made in lands as far apart as Persia and Mexico. רִמּוֹנִי is an apocopated plural for רִמּוֹנִים, which is actually the reading of some mss. and the rendering of the Targum. Cf. the Commentary on 7:10.

8:3–4. Cf. the Commentary on 2:6 f. and 3:5 and the Introductory Comment on Song XI for the interpretation of these verses and for their appropriateness here.

8:5. מִתְרַפֶּקֶת, "leaning" (JPS), "clinging" (Ibn Ezra, who cites the Arabic). חִבְּלָה, not "was in travail" (JPS), but, better, "gave birth to thee"; cf. Ps. 7:15 for the verb חָבַל and Job 39:3 for the noun

חֶבֶל, "offspring." Dal. and Hal. change all the suffixes in the verse to
the feminine, so as to make the entire verse an address to the beloved.
While this may well be justified, it is a hazardous procedure, in view
of the fragmentary and unclear nature of the passage as a whole. As
it stands, it is a duet. See the Introductory Comment and the
Translation.

8:6. Seals were worn on the hand (cf. Gen. 41:42; Jer. 22:24)
or on a chain around the neck (Prov. 3:3; Gen. 38:18); cf. Herodotus'
description of the Babylonians (I, 196). Thus they would be easily
accessible, when needed for signatures on documents. In this spirit,
the Torah enjoins that God's words be written "upon thy hand and
between thine eyes" (Deut. 6:8), and the phylacteries worn in Jewish
worship as the fulfillment of the Biblical injunction thus constitute
a commentary in action on the mutual love-relationship of God and
Israel. Changing the second כְּחוֹתָם to כַּצָּמִיד weakens the power of
the passage (against Hal.). Nor need רִשְׁפֵּי אֵשׁ be emended to רִשְׁפֵּי אֵל
(Hal.). קִנְאָה, not "jealousy," but "zeal, hence, passion," described
as unyielding, never being satisfied, and hence showing no pity, like
Sheol (cf. Prov. 30:15; Hab. 2:5). On שַׁלְהֶבֶתְיָה, "flame of God," as a
Hebraic mode of expressing the superlative, see the Introduction and
note 90, and see Gen. 10:9; Jer. 2:31; Ps. 80:11; Ps. 118:5.

8:7. The rhythm of this verse is difficult (Hal., Tur-Sinai), but
it is not on that account to be regarded as prose. A verse which in
isolation might well be taken for prose is to be scanned as verse if it
occurs in a poetic unit. Cf., for example, Ps. 2:6, 7, the metric character of which emerges only when read in conjunction with vv. 6 and 8:

וַאֲנִי נָסַכְתִּי מַלְכִּי ‖ עַל־צִיּוֹן הַר־קָדְשִׁי
אֲסַפְּרָה אֶל חֹק ‖ ה' אָמַר אֵלַי,
בְּנִי אַתָּה ‖ אֲנִי הַיּוֹם יְלִדְתִּיךָ

Our verse may perhaps be scanned as follows:

מַיִם רַבִּים לֹא יוּכְלוּ ‖ לְכַבּוֹת אֶת־הָאַהֲבָה ‖ וּנְהָרוֹת לֹא יִשְׁטְפוּהָ
אִם יִתֵּן אִישׁ ‖ אֶת־כָּל־הוֹן בֵּיתוֹ בָּאַהֲבָה ‖ בּוֹז יָבוּזוּ לוֹ

Because of the length of the stichs לכבות את האהבה and ישטפוה
ונהרות לא and the exigencies of the meter, each receives three beats. Similarly,
אם and לו receive a beat. The meter is therefore 3:3:3 ‖ 3:3:3. Cf.
the Introductory Commentary on 5:2 above, and the references there
on the metrical principles involved.

8:8. The use of the same first person plural, both in the question
in this verse (מַה־נַּעֲשֶׂה) and in the answer in v. 9 (נִבְנֶה, נָצוּר), disproves

the usual view of the passage that v. 8 is spoken by the girl's brothers
and v. 9 by the suitors. Actually, the suitors are putting the question
and answering it (so also Tur-Sinai). On "sister" for "beloved," cf.
the Introduction and 4:9 ff. Gebhardt finds two sisters here, which
might perhaps prove more satisfactory to suitors, but not to the
exegesis. וְשָׁדַיִם אֵין לָהּ ="not ripe for love"; cf. Ezek. 16:7–8. שֶׁיְדֻבַּר
בָּהּ = "be spoken for in marriage"; cf. I Sam. 25:39. The suitors complain, on the basis of her coldness, that she is not yet mature and ready
for love and marriage.

8:9. The formula employed by the suitors follows the structure
of the Oriental magic-charms (so Tur-Sinai; see the Introduction),
but is purely literary here. It bears the same relationship to the
genuine magical rite that a mythological reference in the Bible or in
Milton bears to pagan religion. The passage is usually taken to express
a contrast between the alternatives of the chastity of the maiden
("if she be a wall") and her looseness ("but if she be a door, etc.").
As Tur-Sinai demonstrates, no such contrast is intended, חוֹמָה and
דֶּלֶת being parallel; cf. the Akkadian יִדְל, "close." (The Hebrew דֶּלֶת
is the infinitive of this root; cf. לָדָת, רֶשֶׁת, from ילד, ירשׁ, respectively.)
Note the Hebrew idioms דְּלָתַיִם וּבְרִיחַ (חוֹמוֹת) חוֹמָה (Deut. 3:5; I Sam.
23:7) and (בְּרִיחִים) דְּלָתַיִם וּבְרִיחַ (Jer. 49:31; Job 38:10; II Chron. 8:5;
14:6). The parallelism of חוֹמה and דלת in our passage is well illustrated
by Ezek. 38:11: וברִיח ודלתים אין להם ‖ כלם ישבים באין חומה, and is clearly
exhibited in the Assyrian love-charm cited in the Introduction.
Accordingly, the board of cedar is not a punishment for unchastity.
The board (lūaḥ), like the turret (ṭīrāh), is a figure drawn from military
operations connected with a siege. The use of "cedar" and "silver"
may hint at the gifts with which the suitors hope to overcome her
resistance.

8:10. The maiden's reply. Though she be a wall against her
unwelcome suitors, her breasts are כַּמִּגְדָּלוֹת, "like towers." The simile
does double duty. It implies that she remains impregnable to them,
while her breasts are well-developed, so that she is ready for love, but
only with her lover. Her constancy brings her his favor. אָז, "therefore"; cf. Jer. 22:15. כְּמוֹצְאֵת שָׁלוֹם is very difficult. It has been rendered:
1) "as a fountain of well-being." 2) "as one that has found peace"
(Ibn Ezra, JPS). 3) "as one to whom good fortune comes" (Hal.).
Perhaps the best rendering is 4) "as one finding grace or favor"
(so Jastrow); it would then be synonymous with מָצָא חֵן. That בְּעֵינָיו
refers to the would-be assailant of her virtue (Bet.) is not likely, if
only because her suitors have only the honorable intention of marriage;
cf. שֶׁיְדֻבַּר בָּהּ, v. 8, and see the Commentary *ad loc*.

For the difficult *mōṣ'ēth šālōm,* four interpretations are advanced in the Comm., the last of which is adopted with reservations: "As one already finding favor." We now prefer the first approach listed and suggest that *mōṣ'ēth* be construed as a feminine by-form for the masculine noun *mōṣā* "lit., place of going forth," one meaning of which is "source of water, spring" (II Ki. 2:21; Isa. 41:18; 58:11; Ps. 107:33, 35; II Chr. 32:30). The feminine noun *mōṣā'āh* actually occurs in the plural, being used metaphorically in Mic. 5:1, *umōṣā'ōthāv,* "and his place of origin, his source." Cf. the same sense for *māqōr* (Jer. 51:36 and Hos. 13:15) parallel to *ma'ªyān.* In Pr. 5:18, *māqōr* refers to a wife as a source of joy; cf. vv. 15, 16; the young man is urged "drink water only out of your own well, so that your fountain may be blessed."

In our passage, the maiden, proclaiming her resistance to the overtures of all other lovers (8:10a), declares that therefore she is a fountain of well-being and joy for her lover (stich b). For the phrase "a fountain of peace" cf. *m^eqōr ḥayyim,* "a fountain of life" (Ps. 36:10; Pr. 10:11; 13:14; 14:27; 16:22), and *kanāhār šālōm,* "peace like a river" (Isa. 48:18; 66:12). The Kaph in *k^emōṣ'ēth* is asseverative, as in 1:7 and 8:1 (see the Comm. *ad loc.*). The noun is to be vocalized *k^emōṣā'at.*

Stich b is therefore to be rendered, "therefore am I in my lover's eyes truly a fountain of well-being." This interpretation has been incorporated into the Translation.

8:11. Though otherwise unknown, Baal Hamon (Baal Lamon in the LXX) need not be emended to Baal Hermon (Judg. 3:3). Many actual place-names do not occur in the Bible and sometimes appear in an inscription. On the other hand, it may be an imaginary locale, created to express the meaning "master of wealth." On הָמוֹן = wealth, cf. Isa. 60:5; Ps. 37:16; Eccl. 5:9; I Chron. 29:16.

While Baal Hamon may have been chosen because it suggests the idea "owner of wealth" (see the Comm.), the locale is probably not imaginary. The apocryphal Book of Judith (8:3) mentions *Balamon* as a place not far from Dothan. Abel (*Géographie,* vol. 2, p. 357) refers to Tel Belame, 2 kilometers south of Jenin. A vineyard which would yield produce worth a thousand pieces of silver would have a thousand vines (cf. Isa. 7:23). In Talmudic times, a tenant-farmer tilling a field received a half, a third, or a fourth of the crops as his share (B. B. 110a; Giṭ. 74b). Here the vine-tenders, נֹטְרִים (literally, "keepers"), receive only a fifth or a sixth (200 out of 1,000 or out of 1,200) for their labor. Conditions in pre-Exilic Palestine may have differed from those in Talmudic Babylonia, or, as seems more likely, farmers tilling a field would receive a greater percentage than vintners, because the work was more difficult than the tending or guarding of a vineyard. אִישׁ יָבִיא is impersonal: "any one would give"; cf. 8:7.

8:13. In accordance with the rhythm (2:2:2) and against the accents, לְקוֹלֵךְ is to be construed as the direct object of הַשְׁמִיעִנִי. On the Lamed accusative, cf. Lev. 19:18, and see the Commentary on Song 2:15.

8:14. The verse is best taken as a quotation of what the lover wants to hear (so Ibn Ezra and Hal.). Hence it is not necessary to assume a series of disjointed fragments (against Jast.). For the symbolism, cf. 2:17.

BIBLIOGRAPHY

A. TEXTS AND VERSIONS

I. *The Hebrew Text*
   S. BAER and FR. DELITZSCH, Quinque Volumina (Leipzig, 1886)
   C. D. GINSBURG, Masoretic Bible (London, 1st ed., 1894; 2nd ed., 1926)
   R. KITTEL, Biblia Hebraica, 4th ed. (Stuttgart, 1937), edited by A. Alt and O. Eissfeldt (Masoretic notes by P. Kahle; *Canticles* edited by F. Horst)

II. *The Septuagint*
   H. B. SWETE, The Old Testament in Greek (Cambridge, 1887-94)
   A. RAHLFS, Septuaginta, 2 vols. (Stuttgart, 1935)

III. *Aquila, Symmachus, Theodotion*
   F. FIELD, Origenis Hexaplorum quae Supersunt (Oxford, 1875)

IV. *The Vulgate*
   R. STIER and K. G. W. THEILE, Polyglotten-Bibel, 4th ed. (Bielefeld-Leipzig, 1875)

V. *The Peshitta*
   Kethabe Kadishe, ed. S. LEE (London, 1823)

VI. *Targum*
   Mikraoth Gedoloth, Pentateuch and Megilloth (Vilna, 1912, and often reprinted)

B. SOURCES

The Hebrew Bible
The Apocrypha and Pseudepigrapha of the Old Testament (ed. (R. H. Charles, Oxford, 1913)
The New Testament—Authorized Version
Josephus, Works (Loeb Classics)
Mekilta de Rabbi Ishmael, ed. J. Z. Lauterbach (Philadelphia, 1933)

103

Sifre de be Rab, ed. M. Friedmann (Vienna, 1864)

The Mishnah (ed. Vilna), frequently reprinted

Tosefta, ed. M. S. Zuckermandel, 2nd ed. (Jerusalem, 1938)

Aboth de Rabbi Nathan, ed. S. Schechter, 2nd printing (New York, 1945)

Babylonian Talmud (Vilna, 1928), frequently reprinted

Jerusalem Talmud (Krotoshin, 1866)

Midrash Rabbot on the Torah and the Megillot (ed. Vilna, 1938), frequently reprinted

Pesikta de Rab Kahana, ed. S. Buber, 2nd ed. (Vilna, 1925)

Midrash Tehillim, ed. S. Buber (Vilna, 1891)

Pirke de Rabbi Eliezer Hagadol (Warsaw, 1862)

Tractate Sopherim, ed. M. Higger (New York, 1937)

C. COMMENTARIES

Jonah Abulwalid Ibn Janah (d. 1040), Rashi (d. 1105), Abraham Ibn Ezra (d. 1167), David Kimhi (d. 1235), E. W. Hengstenberg (Berlin, 1853), F. Hitzig (Leipzig, 1855), C. D. Ginsburg (London, 1857), G. H. A. Ewald (Göttingen, 1867), Heinrich Graetz (Vienna, 1871), Franz Delitzsch (Leipzig, 1875; English trans., Edinburgh, 1877), C. Siegfried (Göttingen, 1898), Karl Budde (Freiburg, 1898), A. Harper (Cambridge, 1907), P. Haupt (Leipzig, 1907), V. Zapletal (Freiburg, 1907), A. B. Ehrlich (Leipzig, 1918), M. Jastrow (Philadelphia, 1921), R. Breuer (Frankfort, 1923), G. Kuhn (Leipzig, 1926), G. Ricciotti (Turin, 1928), C. Gebhardt (Berlin, 1931), W. Pouget and J. Guitton (Paris, 1934; English version, New York, 1948), M. Haller (Tuebingen, 1940), A. Cohen (London, 1946), L. Waterman (Ann Arbor, 1948), Israel Bettan (Cincinnati, 1950), D. Buzy (Paris, 1950).

D. GENERAL BIBLIOGRAPHY

ALBRIGHT, W. F., From the Stone Age to Christianity (Baltimore, 1940)

———, "Palestinian Inscriptions," in J. B. Pritchard, Ancient Near Eastern Texts Relating to the Old Testament (Princeton, 1950)

———, "The Biblical Period," in The Jews—Their History,

Culture and Religion, ed. Louis Finkelstein, 2 vols. (New York, 1949)

————, "The Role of the Canaanites in the History of Civilization," in Studies in the History of Culture in Honor of W. G. Leland (Menasha, Wis., 1942)

BALLA, E., Das Ich der Psalmen (Goettingen, 1913)

BARON, SALO W., A Social and Religious History of the Jews (2nd ed.), vols. 1 and 2 (New York, 1952)

BEN JEHUDAH, ELIEZER, Thesaurus Totius Hebraitatis et Veteris et Recentioris, 14 vols. (Jerusalem, 1918-)

BRIGGS, C. A., The Psalms (International Critical Commentary), 2 vols. (New York, 1906)

BROWN, F., DRIVER, S. R., and BRIGGS, C. A., A Hebrew and English Lexicon to the Old Testament (Edinburgh, 1892)

BUHL, F., Canon and Text of the Old Testament (Edinburgh, 1892)

BUTTENWIESER, MOSES, The Psalms (Chicago, 1938)

CHEYNE, T. K., The Book of Psalms (London, 1888)

COBB, W. H., A Criticism of Systems of Hebrew Meter (Oxford, 1905)

COHON, SAMUEL S., "The Name of God, a Study in Rabbinic Theology," in *HUCA*, vol. 23 (1950-51), Part 1

CORNILL, C. H., Einleitung in das Alte Testament, 7th ed. (Freiburg, 1913)

CRAWLEY, E., The Mystic Rose (London, 1902)

DALMAN, GUSTAF H., Palestinischer Diwan (Leipzig, 1901)

————, "The Old Hebrew Calendar Inscription from Gezer," in PEFQS (1909)

DESNOYERS, L., Histoire du peuple hébreu des juges à la captivité, 3 vols. (Paris, 1922-30)

DIRINGER, D., Le iscrizioni anticho-ebraiche Palestinesi (Florence, 1934)

DORNSEIFF, F., "Aegyptische Liebeslieder, Hohes Lied, Sappho, Theokrit," in *ZDMG*, 1936

DRIVER, S. R., Introduction to the Literature of the Old Testament (12th ed., New York, 1906)

EBELING, E., "Aus den Keilschrifttexten," in *MDOG*, vol. 58 (1917)

————, "Liebeszauber im alten Orient," in *MAOG*, vol. 1 (1925)

————, "Aus dem Tagewerk eines assyrischen Zauberpriesters," in *MAOG,* vol. 5 (1931)

EHRLICH, A. B., Kommentar zu Psalmen (Berlin, 1905)

EISSFELDT, O., Einleitung in das Alte Testament (Tuebingen, 1934)

ENZYKLOPEDIA MIQRAIT, vol. 1, ed. by E. L. Sukenik and M. D. Cassuto (Jerusalem, 1950)

ERBT, W., Der Sternhimmel im Alten Testament (Leipzig, 1912)

ERMAN, A., The Literature of the Ancient Egyptians, trans. A. M. Blackman (New York, 1927)

FÉVRIER, J. G., "Remarques sur le Calendrier de Gezer," in *Semitica,* vol. 1 (1948)

FINKELSTEIN, L. (ed.), The Jews — Their History, Culture and Religion, 2 vols. (New York, 1949)

FRAZER, J. G., The Golden Bough (New York, 1928)

GALLING, K., Biblisches Reallexikon (Tuebingen, 1937)

GASTER, THEODORE H., "The Song of Songs," in *Commentary,* vol. 13 (April, 1952)

GESENIUS, W., and KAUTZSCH, E., Hebräische Grammatik (25th ed.) (Leipzig, 1889)

GOLDBERG, B. Z., The Sacred Fire (New York, 1930)

GOLDMAN, SOLOMON, The Book of Human Destiny (New York, 1948)

GORDIS, ROBERT, "Studies in Hebrew Roots of Contrasted Meanings," in *JQR,* vol. 27 (1936)

————, The Biblical Text in the Making (Philadelphia, 1937)

————, "Some Effects of Primitive Thought on Language," in *AJSL,* vol. 55 (1938)

————, "The Asseverative Kaph in Hebrew and Ugaritic," in *JAOS,* vol. 63 (1943)

————, "Studies in the Relationship of Biblical and Rabbinic Hebrew," in Louis Ginzberg Jubilee Volumes (New York, 1943)

————, "Al Mibneh Hashirah Haivrit Haqedumah," in *Sefer Hashanah Lihude Amerikah* 5705 (New York, 1944)

————, "A Wedding Song For Solomon," in *JBL,* vol. 63 (1944)

————, "The Bible as a Cultural Monument," in The Jews— Their History, Culture and Religion, ed. Louis Finkelstein, 2 vols. (New York, 1949)

————, "Quotations As a Literary Usage in Biblical, Rabbinic and Oriental Literature," in *HUCA,* vol. 22 (1949)

————, Koheleth—The Man and His World (New York, 1951)

————, (ed.), Max Leopold Margolis—Scholar and Teacher (Philadelphia, 1952)

GORDON, C. H., "Phoenician Inscriptions from Karatepe," in *JQR*, vol. 38 (1948)

————, "Azitawadd's Phoenician Inscription," in *JNES*, vol. 8 (1949)

GRAHAM, W. C., and MAY H. G., Culture and Conscience (Chicago, 1936)

GRANQUIST, H. N., Marriage Conditions in a Palestinian Village (Helsingfors, 1931-35)

HEMPEL, J., Die althebraeische Literatur und ihr hellenistisch-juedisches Nachleben (Wildpark-Potsdam, 1930)

HOELSCHER, G., Geschichte der israelitischen und juedischen Religion (Giessen, 1922)

HORNELL, J., "Naval Activity in the Days of Solomon and Rameses III," in *Antiquity*, vol. 21 (1947)

HUMBERT, P., Le problème du livre de Nahoum," in *RHPR*, vol. 12 (1932)

————, "Essai d'analyse de Nahoum 1:2-2:3," in *ZATW*, vol. 3 (1926)

JACOB, G., Das Hohe Lied auf Grund arabischer und anderer Parallelen neu untersucht (Berlin, 1902)

JOHNSON, BURGESS, The Lost Art of Profanity (New York,1948)

JOUON, P., Le Cantique des Cantiques (1909)

KAUTZSCH, EMIL, Die Poesie und die poetischen Bücher des Alten Testaments (Tuebingen-Leipzig, 1902)

KITTEL, R., ed., Biblia Hebraica, 4th ed. (Stuttgart, 1937)

KOEHLER, L., and BAUMGARTNER, W., Lexicon in Veteris Testamenti Libros (Leiden, 1948-)

KOEHLER, L., Theologie des Alten Testaments (Tuebingen, 1936)

KRAMER, S. N., "Sumerian Love Songs," in J. B. Pritchard, Ancient Near Eastern Texts Relating to the Old Testament (Princeton, 1950)

LESLIE, E. A., The Psalms (New York, 1949)

LIDDELL, H. G., and SCOTT, R., A Greek-English Lexicon (New York, 1883)

LIEBERMAN, S., Greek in Jewish Palestine (New York, 1942)

————, Hellenism in Jewish Palestine (New York, 1950)

LÖW, I., Die Flora der Juden, 4 vols. (Vienna-Leipzig, 1924-34)

MARGOLIS, MAX L., The Hebrew Scriptures in the Making (Philadelphia, 1922)

MAY, H. G., "The Fertility Cult in Hosea," in *AJSL*, vol. 48 (1930)

MEEK, THEOPHILE J., "Canticles and the Tammuz Cult," in *AJSL*, vol. 39 (1922)

———, "Babylonian Parallels to the Song of Songs," in *JBL*, vol. 43 (1923)

———, "The Song of Songs and the Fertility Cult," in The Song of Songs—A Symposium, ed. by W. H. Schoff (Philadelphia, 1924)

MOSCATI, SABBATINO, L'epigrafia ebraica antica 1935-50 (Rome, 1951)

MOWINCKEL, S., Psalmenstudien, Nos. 1-6 (Christiania, 1921-24)

NEUSCHATZ DE JASSY, O., Le Cantique des Cantiques et le mythe d'Osiris-Hetep (1914)

NICHOLSON, R. A., Studies in Islamic Mysticism (Cambridge, 1921)

NOELDEKE, THEODOR, Beiträge zur semitischen Sprachwissenschaft (Strassburg, 1904)

———, Neue Beiträge zur semitischen Sprachwissenschaft (Strassburg, 1910)

NOTH, MARTIN, Ueberlieferungsgeschichtliche Studien (Halle, 1943)

OESTERLEY. W. O. E., and ROBINSON, T. H., History of Israel (Oxford, 1932)

OLMSTEAD, A. T., A History of Palestine and Syria to the Macedonian Conquest (New York, 1931)

PFEIFFER, R. H., Introduction to the Old Testament (New York, 1941)

POWIS-SMITH, J. M., and GOODSPEED, E. J., The Complete Bible —An American Translation (Chicago, 1943)

PRITCHARD, J. B., Ancient Near Eastern Texts Relating to the Old Testament (Princeton, 1950)

ROBERT, A., "Le genre littéraire du Cantique des Cantiques," in *Revue Biblique*, vol. 52 (1943-44)

ROWLEY, H. H., "The Interpretation of the Song of Songs," in *JThS*, vol. 38 (1937)

———, "The Song of Songs—An Examination of Recent Theory," in *JRAS* (1938)

———, "The Meaning of the Shulammite," in *AJSL,* vol. 56 (1939)

———, The Servant of the Lord and Other Essays on the Old Testament (London, 1952)

RYLE, H. E., Canon of the Old Testament (2nd ed., London, 1909) '

SALFELD, S., Das Hohelied Salomos bei den juedischen Erklärern des Mittelalters (Berlin, 1879)

SCHMIDT, N., "Is Canticles an Adonis Liturgy?", in *JAOS,* vol. 46 (1926)

SCHOFF, W. H., ed., The Song of Songs—A Symposium (Philadelphia, 1924)

SCHOTT, S., Altaegyptische Liebeslieder (Zurich, 1950)

SCHOLEM, G., Major Trends in Jewish Mysticism (New York, 1941)

SELLIN, E., Israelitische und juedische Religionsgeschichte (Leipzig, 1933)

———, Einleitung in das Alte Testament (8th ed., Heidelberg, 1950)

SPEISER, E. A., "The Contribution of M. L. Margolis to Semitic Linguistics," in Max Leopold Margolis—Scholar and Teacher, ed. by Robert Gordis (Philadelphia, 1952)

STAPLES, W. E., "The Book of Ruth," in *AJSL,* vol. 53 (1939)

STEPHAN, ST. H., Modern Palestinian Parallels to the Song of Songs (Jerusalem, 1926)

STICKEL, J. G., Das Hohelied in seiner Einheit und dramatischen Gliederung (Berlin, 1888)

TOBAC, E., Les cinq livres de Salomon (1926)

TUR-SINAI, N. H., "Shir Hashirim Asher Lishelomo," in *Halashon Vehasefer,* vol. 2 (Jerusalem, 1951)

———, "Hakethobheth Hakena 'anith Hagedolah Mi-Karatepe," in *Leshonenu,* vol. 17

VACCARI, A., I Libri Poetici della Bibbia (1925)

VON RAD, G., Das Geschichtsbild des chronistischen Werkes (Stuttgart, 1930)

VRIEZEN, TH. C., and HOSPERS, J. H., Palestine Inscriptions (Leiden, 1951)

WATERMAN, L., "The Role of Solomon in the Song of Songs," in *JBL,* vol. 56 (1936)

———, The Song of Songs Interpreted As a Dramatic Poem (Ann Arbor, 1948)

WEIR, M., A Lexicon of Accadian Prayers (London, 1934)

WETZSTEIN, J. G., "Die syrische Dreschtafel," in *Zeitschrift für Ethnologie,* vol. 5 (1873)

———, "Bemerkungen zum Hohenliede," in F. Delitzsch, Biblischer Commentar über die poetischen Bücher des Alten Testaments (Leipzig, 1875)

WITTEKINDT, W., Das Hohe-Lied und seine Beziehung zum Istarkult (Hannover, 1925)

WRIGHT, G. E., and FILSON, F. V., A Historical Atlas to the Bible (Philadelphia, 1945)

ZEITLIN, S., "An Historical Study of the Canonization of Hebrew Scriptures," in *PAAJR,* vol. 3 (1932)

INDEX OF ABBREVIATIONS

ad loc.=ad locum (to the passage)
ag.=against
AJSL=American Journal of Semitic Languages
Am.=Amos
AV=the Authorized Version (of the Old and New Testaments)

B.=the Babylonian Talmud
BASOR=Bulletins of the American Society for Oriental Research
B.C.E.=Before the Common (or Christian) Era
Bet.=Bettan
BH=R. Kittel ed., Biblia Hebraica, 4th ed.
B. S.=Ben Sira (Ecclesiasticus)

c.=circa
Cant.=Canticles (Song of Songs)
C.E.=Common (or Christian) Era
cent.=century
cf.=compare
chap.=chapter
chaps.=chapters
Comm.=The Commentary

d.=died
Dal.=Dalman
Dan.=Daniel
Del.=Delitzsch
Deut.=Deuteronomy

Ecc.=Ecclesiastes
ed.=edited, edited by, or edition
e. g.=for example
Ehr.=Ehrlich
Erub.=the tractate Erubin
Est.=Esther
Ex.=Exodus
Ezek.=Ezekiel

f., ff.=following (i.e. and the following verse [verses] or page [pages])

Gen.=Genesis

Hab.=Habakkuk
Hag.=the tractate Hagigah
Hal.=Haller
HUCA=Hebrew Union College Annual

I Chron.=I Chronicles
II Chron.=II Chronicles
1 Sam.=I Samuel
II Sam.=II Samuel
ibid.=in the same place, in the same work
ICC=the International Critical Commentary
i.e.=id est (that is)
Isa.=Isaiah

JAOS=Journal of the American Oriental Society
JBL=Journal of Biblical Literature
Jer.=Jeremiah
JNES=Journal of Near-Eastern Studies
Josh.=Joshua
JPS=The Jewish Publication Society of America Version (of the Bible)
JQR=Jewish Quarterly Review
JRAS=Journal of the Royal Asiatic Society
JThS=Journal of Theological Studies (Oxford)
Judg.=Judges

KMW=Gordis, Robert, Koheleth—The Man and His World (New York, 1951)

Lam.=Lamentations
Lev.=Leviticus
lit.=literally
LXX=the Septuagint

M.=the Mishnah
MAOG=Mittheilungen der alt-orientalischen Gesellschaft
Matt.=Matthew

MDMG=Mittheilungen der deutschen morgenländischen Gesellschaft
MDOG=Mittheilungen der deutschen orientalischen Gesellschaft
M. Hag.=Mishnah Hagigah
Mid.=the Midrash
ms.=manuscript
mss.=manuscripts
MT=the Masoretic text (of the Hebrew Bible)

Neh.=Nehemiah
No.=Number
Nos.=Numbers
N. T.=the New Testament
Num.=Numbers (Biblical book)

op. cit.=opere citato (in the above-cited work)
O. T.=the Old Testament

p.=page
P=the Peshitta
PAAJR=Proceedings of the American Academy for Jewish Research
PEFQS=Palestine Exploration Fund Quarterly Statement
Pes.=the tractate Pesahim
pp.=pages
Prov.=Proverbs

Ps.=Psalm

RHPR=Revue de l'Histoire et de la Philosophie des Religions
RV=the Revised Version (of the Old and New Testaments)

Sanh.=the tractate Sanhedrin
sec.=section
Shab.=the tractate Shabbath
Sym.=Symmachus

Tan.=Midrash Tanhuma
Tar.=the Targum
Tos.=the Tosefta
trans.=translated by, translation

v.=verse
V=the Vulgate
vol.=volume
vols.=volumes
vv.=verses

Wit.=Wittekindt

Yad.=the tractate Yadayim

ZATW=Zeitschrift für die alttestamentliche Wissenschaft
ZDMG=Zeitschrift der deutschen morgenländischen Gesellschaft
Zech.=Zechariah
Zeph.=Zephaniah

LAMENTATIONS

TABLE OF CONTENTS

(Lamentations)

INTRODUCTION

THE BOOK OF LAMENTATIONS (*Ekhāh* or *Kīnōth*) is placed in
our Bibles among the Five Megillot read during the year in
the synagogue. In its literary character, it resembles the
Psalms and *Song of Songs*, being a collection of independent
lyrical compositions.

The book consists of five elegies, three of which (Chaps.
1, 2, 4) are laments on the burning of the Temple and
the destruction of Jerusalem by the Babylonians, as well
as on the national devastation that followed the calamities of 587 B.C.E. Chapter 3 is basically an individual
psalm dealing with the tribulations of an individual who has
suffered illness, indignity, and scorn at the hands of his
fellow-men (vv. 1-39). By a process of psychological identification, the complaint of the individual passes over into the
lament of the community with which he identifies himself
(vv. 40-48), and then reverts once more to his own personal
tragedy with which echoes of the national disaster are com-
mingled (vv. 49-66). Chapter 5 is a liturgical composition, a
penitential prayer confessing the sins of the people and
praying for a restoration of God's favor.

Poetic form. The book of *Lamentations* exhibits all the major
traits of Biblical poetry.[1] It possesses also some distinctive

---

[1] On Biblical poetry, see *inter alia*, G. B. Gray, *The Forms of Hebrew
Poetry* (London, 1915); T. H. Robinson, *The Poetry of the O.T.*
(London, 1947); R. Gordis, *ʿAl Mibneh Haśīrāh Ha ʿivrīth Haqedumah* ("On the Structure of Ancient Hebrew Poetry") in
Sefer Haśanah Liyehudei Amerikah (New York, 5745=1944), referred
to below as AMHH, where several principles of Hebrew metrics, not
adequately recognized heretofore, are set forth. The study is now available in English, "The Structure of Biblical Poetry," in Gordis, *Poets,
Prophets and Sages* (Bloomington, Indiana, 1971), pp. 61-94. The volume is cited as *PPS*.

characteristics. The first is the *Kinah* meter, so called because it is frequent in elegies, and was first recognized in *Lamentations*. [2] It is, however, by no means restricted to elegiac poetry, occuring also in love lyrics, and in religious hymns. [3] The rhythm possesses a particular haunting quality appropriate to the expression of grief. Basically, the *Kinah* meter consists of two stichs, the first of which is longer than the second. Since the 3: 3 meter is the most common pattern in Biblical poetry, the usual *Kinah* rhythm is 3: 2. There are, however, many variations upon this basic pattern, such as 4: 3‖4: 2; and more elaborate combinations, such as 4: 4: 2‖ 3: 2; 3: 3‖3: 2.

For a full discussion of the various aspects of Biblical prosody, the reader is referred to the literature on the subject, some of which is listed in Note 1 above and in the Bibliography.

1. Basic to Biblical poetry is *the principle of one beat for each thought-unit*. Generally, this means that every important word will receive one stress. There are, however, several important modifications that need to be set forth, in order to establish the meter in our book.

2. For metrical purposes, *one word, especially a long one, may at times receive two stresses instead of one*, the test lying in the meter-pattern of the passage as a whole.

Hence, stichs consisting of two words, especially when they are *important in meaning and contain a larger number of syllables than their parallels,* receive three beats. The recognition of this prosodic principle of three beats for two words solves the problem commentators have encountered with the metrics of various passages (cf., e. g., Hillers on 1 :9). The desired result of three beats for two longer words is achieved by giving to one of the words two beats and to the other word only one stress.

A few instances of this principle in practice, including some of the ramifications involved, may be set down in order to make matters clear.

In 3:6, stich a consists of 7 full syllables and 2 half syllables (*hatēph* or *śewā*); stich b of 4 full syllables and one half-syllable.

---

[2] It was first noted by K. Budde, in "Das hebräische Klagelied" in *ZATW*, 1882, who restricted the term to the 3: 2 meter.

[3] *Cf.* e.g., *Song of Songs* 1: 15 ff.; 5: 9 ff.; *Ps.* 19: 8-15; Chaps. 27 and 42, as well as *Isa.* 1: 20 f.; *Jer.* 15: 5-9.

In 4:5, stich a consists of 6 full syllables and 3 half-syllables; stich b of 6 full syllables only. It is also clear that in biblical times half-syllables were pronounced more fully than in the Masoretic system, so that the difference in length was even more marked.

In 1:17, the first four stichs exhibit the basic *Qinah* pattern 3:2 ‖ 3:2. The two closing stichs consist of two words each. In stich e, *hāyethāh Yerūšālayim* is to be given three stresses, and the meter for the verse emerges as 3:2 ‖ 3:2 ‖ 3:2.

A more complex form of the *Qinah* rhythm occurs in 1:8, where stichs a and b each receive three stresses and stichs d, e, and f receive two each. By giving to either of the two long words in stich c, *mekhabbedehā hizzilūhā*, two stresses, the meter of the verse emerges as 3:3 ‖ 3:2 ‖ 2:2.

In 4:14d, the long word *bilebhušĕhen* receives two beats, thus establishing a 3:2 rhythm.

In 1:13, stich e consisting of two long and important words, *nethānannī šōmēmāh,* they must receive three stresses, by endowing either of these two vocables with two beats, thus paralleling the 3:2 meter of stichs c and d.

The first two stichs in this verse must obviously possess the same 3:2 meter as the four following. In this instance, the 3:2 meter pattern may be achieved in one of two ways: (1) by following the implication of the *Maqqeph* which links *sālah 'ēs* and giving the short combination one stress, like the word preceding and following them. In that event, *vayyirdennāh* constitutes stich b and receives two stresses because of its length and importance. (2) The other and preferable method is to place the poetic caesura after *'ēs,* thus diverging from the logical caesura which comes after *beʿasmōtāy.* Thus each one of the five words in the two stichs receives one accent, and the meter of the verse as a whole is 3:2 ‖ 3:2 ‖ 3:2. In addition to the examples cited above, other instances are 1:17e; 1:19a, c; 2:2c; 2:4b; 2:12a; 2:19e; 2:20; 2:21a, c; 3:56; 4:5; 4:17.

3. When *two words, particularly short ones,* express one idea, they *may,* if the meter requires it, *receive one stress.* Cf. Ps. 114:1b, where *mēʿam lōʿēz,* which corresponds to *mimmisrayim,* in stich a, receives only one stress.

Thus in 1:12 f., *ḥᵃrōn appō* receives one beat, giving the verse a 3:2 pattern. In 2:3e, the two words *kᵉ'ēš lᵉhābhāh*, "flaming fire," receive only one stress, especially since they represent one idea, thus preserving the 3:2 pattern.

In 2:12b, *'ayyēh dāgān vāyayin* receives only two stresses, giving a 3:2 meter.

In 3:24b, *'āmᵉrāh naphšī* receives only one beat, in accordance with the 3:2 pattern of the verse. It is equivalent to *'āmartī*.

4. On the other hand, *two short words,* that would ordinarily receive one stress, *may receive two beats for metric reasons.*

Thus in 1:6a, b, the two short words *mibbat șiōn* receive two beats and, similarly, *kol hadārāh,* thus giving stichs c and d a 3:2 meter.

In 3:31a, each word, *kī lō' yiznaḥ,* including the two short ones, receives a stress, thus creating the 3:2 meter for the verse. Cf. Micah 6:8; Ps. 27:5 (*kī*) and Ps. 5:6 (*lō'*) for other instances.

5. The determination of the meter pattern of a given verse or passage in Lamentations often depends on a stylistic usage that has not been sufficiently noted. Not infrequently, *the poetic caesura will diverge from the logical caesura,* that is to say, the thought will continue beyond the pause imposed by the meter pattern. Readers of traditional Western poetry are familiar with the phenomenon of the thought flowing beyond the end of a line. This can be illustrated in countless instances in Shakespeare, Wordsworth, Browning, and Tennyson, and other poets.

This tendency for the poetic and the logical caesura to diverge occurs sporadically elsewhere in Biblical poetry as well, as, e. g., Job 4:8; 31:13 (see our Comm. *ad loc.*). In Lamentations, this divergence is so common that it may fairly be regarded as a special characteristic of the poet. Conceivably, it may inhere in the *Qinah* meter, where the brevity of the poetic line compels the writer to go beyond the metric caesura in order to complete his thought.

Examples of this usage are to be found in 1:7e, 10c, 14e, 22b; 2:4a, 9e; 3:3a, 5a, 27a, 31a, 32a, 50a; 4:14c. Recognition of this feature obviates difficulties which scholars have found in the scansion of these poems (cf., e. g., Hillers on 1:10, 13; 2:14; 3:31).

6. It is a methodological error to propose deletions or transpositions in the Masoretic Text on the basis of metric considerations alone. When there are, however, additional grounds for textual criticism, the meter is a useful adjunct in helping to establish the original text. One caveat is in order—it is important that all the various possibilities of scansion be adequately taken into account.

7. The metric pattern is particularly useful in discovering cases of *conflation* where two variant readings may have been incorporated into the received text (e. g., 1:7; 2:7, 21; 4:18; see Comm. *ad loc.*).

8. *Repetition of identical roots in parallelism*

It has long been maintained that the principle of parallelism precludes the repetition of the same root in adjacent stichs. It has, therefore, been taken as virtually axiomatic that whenever the same root occurs in parallel stichs in MT, it is the result of a scribal error and yeoman efforts have been expended to discover the "original" reading. M. D. Cassuto was the first to point out that Ugaritic verse employs at times the same verb, though in different tenses or in varying voices (active or passive) (*Tarbiṣ,* vol. 14, 1942, pp. 9 ff.; *The Goddess Anath.* Jerusalem, 1953, pp. 37 ff., English trans. I. Abrahams, Jerusalem, 1971, pp. 46 ff.). In addition to Ugaritic examples, he cited some biblical instances, such as Jer. 17:14; 31:4; Ps. 69:50. Subsequently, M. Held added some Ugaritic examples and Jer. 31:18 and Ps. 24:7 (*JBL,* vol. 84, 1965, pp. 272-82). Recently, S. Gevirtz has discussed the phenomenon and sought to adduce instances of this usage from Tel-el-Amarna (*JNES,* vol. 32, 1973, pp. 99-104).

On the basis of independent research in *Job,* I arrived at some wider conclusions. I found that the repetition of the same root in parallel stichs may occur without a variation in tense or voice (e.g. Job 8:3). Moreover, it is not limited to verbs, but includes substantives as well. Finally, the practice is especially characteristic of some writers, such as the author of

Job (40 examples) and the author of *Lamentations,* chap. 2 (4 instances).

With regard to the principle of the repetition of identical verbs enunciated by Cassuto, analysis reveals that the practice falls into two categories, both in Ugaritic and in Hebrew:

(A) The use of the same verb in two different tenses or voices, *in two separate and parallel stichs.* Hence the meaning is identical, as it would have been if synonyms had been employed. Ugaritic examples are UT 51 VI, lines 34-35, 38-40; 67 I, lines 16-17; *AQHT,* lines 114-115; *ANAT,* II, lines 40-41. Biblical examples include Deut. 33:12; Isa. 60:16; Jer. 31.4; Ps. 24:7; 38:12; 69:15; Pr. 11:7.

(B) The use of the two verbs *within the same stich and in a special manner* so that they are *not* identical in meaning. These instances constitute a "plea-and-response" formula. The first verb is invariably in the imperative second person and the second verb is in the imperfect first person singular or plural, with a special nuance indicated below.

Thus Jer. 17:14 *r^{e}phā 'ēnī w^e 'ēraphē . . . hōši 'ēnī w^{e}iwwāšē 'a* is to be rendered "Heal me O Lord and I shall really be healed, save me and I shall truly be saved."

Jer. 31:17c *h^{a}šībhēnī w^e'āšūbhāh,* is to be rendered "restore me and I shall really be restored."

The identical construction and meaning occurs in Lam. 5:21: "Turn us to Yourself O God and we will return." See Comm. *ad loc.*

(C) Similar in character to Category B is a variant that may be called the "action-and-result" formula. Here, too, the verbal root is used twice in the same stich, but in different persons. Its repetition is designed here also to give a special nuance to the second verb. Thus Jer. 31:4 *'ōd 'ebhnēkh w^{e}nibhnēth.* "I shall yet rebuild you and you will be truly (i.e. permanently) rebuilt." So, too, Jer. 14:17 *yissartani wa'iwwāsēr,* "You chastised me and I was really chastised, like an untrained calf, etc."

9. An interesting rhetorical usage encountered in our book is *talḥin,* the choice of a particular word because it not only carries a primary significance appropriate to the context, but also a secondary meaning. Unlike paronomasia, where only one

meaning is intended, in *talḥin* both are present in the consciousness of the poet and the reader. While this usage is by no means limited to Lamentations (cf. our discussion in *Sepher Moshe Seidel*, Jerusalem, 5722 = 1962, pp. 255-67), our book offers one of the most felicitous instances in 2:13. Other possible instances are 1:8 and 2:22 (see the Comm.).

10. A very important and widespread rhetorical usage which occurs in Lamentations as well as throughout Biblical, Oriental, and rabbinic literature, is that of *virtual quotations*. That is to say, the speech or thought of the author or of another character, which modern writers would introduce by using a verb of speaking or thinking ("he said, I thought, etc.") and by inserting quotation marks, is presented without a *verbum dicendi* or *cogitandi*, and, it need not be added, without quotation marks. The reader is counted upon to recognize the intent of the passage. On this highly important feature of Biblical and Oriental literature, see the detailed analysis and documentation in *PPS*, pp. 104-59 and in *BGM*, pp. 169-189.

An obvious example of a "virtual quotation" occurs in 1:11e, f, which introduces Zion's words without an explicit verb of speaking. Another instance follows 1:17, the balance of the passage in the first person being the sentiments thought or expressed by Zion (vv. 18-22).

Another example occurs in chapter 3. In v. 39, the poet has declared that a living man should not complain about his suffering, for which there surely is a reason to be found in his sins. Instead, a man should spur himself and his fellow men to scrutinize their actions and repent sincerely. V. 40, therefore, requires understanding a phrase such as "A man should rather say." See the Special Introduction to Chapter 3 and the Comm. *ad loc*.

The second special characteristic of Lamentations is that its first four chapters are written in an alphabetical acrostic, each verse beginning with a letter of the alphabet in succession. [4] Chapter 3 is a triple acrostic, each letter of the alphabet

[4] In chapters 2, 3, and 4, the *Pe* precedes the *Ayin*, an alternate order of the alphabet. The same sequence originally existed in *Psalm 34*, as the context there makes clear. There is therefore no need to emend 34:18, as is frequently proposed, only to reverse the order of vv. 16 and 17.

being represented by three verses. Chapter 5, which is not an acrostic, contains twenty-two verses, the precise number of letters in the Hebrew alphabet, which may be purely a coincidence.

It is doubtful whether the use of the acrostic arose as a magical formula, though the alphabet played an important part in medieval incantations. Undoubtedly it served as a mnemonic device, but this is scarcely its origin. The use of the full alphabet may have symbolized an expression of the full gamut of emotion, [5] as in our phrase "from A to Z." Whatever its origin, the restrictions of a self-imposed literary form became a convention which the poet delighted to transcend. Witness the enduring popularity of the fourteen line sonnet, with its traditional division into an octet and a sestet.

Authorship and Unity. The tradition which ascribes Lamentations to the prophet Jeremiah is very ancient. It occurs in the superscription of our book in the Septuagint, as well as in the opening verses of the Aramaic *Targum* and the Syriac *Pešīta*. The starting-point for the tradition may even be older, going back to II Chronicles 35: 25: "And Jeremiah lamented for Josiah; and all the singing men and singing women spoke of Josiah in their lamentations, unto this day; and they made them an ordinance in Israel; and, behold, they are written in the lamentations." The *locus classicus* in the Talmud, (B. Batra 15a) informs us that "Jeremiah wrote his book, the book of Kings and *Kinoth*."

The tragic career of Jeremiah, who was a contemporary of the destruction of the Judean state, naturally suggested his authorship of these elegies. The resemblances go further. We find in both Jeremiah and Lamentations the same sensitive temper, and the same deep conviction that the national sin is the cause of national disaster. Similar figures of speech exist in both books, such as the references "to the virgin daughter of Zion," "tears," "destruction," and the striking phrase, *māgōr missābhībh*, "terror all about." [6]

---

[5] Cf. N. K. Gottwald, *Studies in the Book of Lamentations*, (Chicago, 1954).

[6] This phrase, which occurs in *Lam.* 2: 22 is a favorite of the prophet. Cf. *Jer.* 6: 25; 20: 3, 10; 46: 5.

On the other hand, linguistic parallels are notoriously hazardous to invoke. There are, too, many terms, such as *'ānī; šōmēm, 'ōlēl*, which are not to be found in *Jeremiah*, while similarities in phraseology with Ezekiel, Deutero-Isaiah, and Psalms are not lacking. [7]

More decisive evidence with reference to authorship may be found in several significant differences of standpoint between Lamentations and *Jeremiah*: Jeremiah had condemned the Temple as "a den of robbers" (7: 11), while throughout Lamentations, the Temple is the sacred seat of God (e.g., 2: 1, 6 and *passim*), with no blot upon its escutcheon. While the prophet was vigorously opposed to any alliance with Egypt, the poet treats the invoking of aid from Egypt favorably, or at least neutrally (5: 6). The adulatory references to the King as "the breath of our nostrils, the anointed of God" (4: 20), [8] stands in stark contrast to Jeremiah's condemnation of the royal house (chap. 22). Nor can chapter 3, which deals with the agony of an individual, be regarded as a picture of Jeremiah's condition. The troubles that overwhelm the poet here are those of a private citizen, not a public figure.

The differences between Lamentations and Jeremiah are real, but they do not tell the whole story. There are important similarities to be considered. The basic prophetic insight that national sin is at the root of national disaster is accepted wholeheartedly by the poet. Nonetheless, he has not surrendered the traditional doctrine of the Torah concerning group solidarity, as expressed in the idea of the fathers' sins being visited upon the children, to which Jeremiah, like Ezekiel, strongly objected. [9] The poet shares the prophets' attitude toward prophecy. Jeremiah and the other great prophets had condemned the "respectable" seers of the day for their failure to fulfill their duty "to declare to Jacob his transgression and to Israel his sin." [10] Similarly, the poet charges

[7] *Cf.* S. R. Driver, *Introduction to the Literature of the O.T.* (New York) p. 463, note; M. Haller, *Die fünf Megilloth* (Tübingen 1940), p. 91.

[8] Conscious of this contradiction, the Targum refers the verse to Josiah, who died at Megiddo in 609 B.C.E. and cannot of course, be referred to here.

[9] *Cf. Ex.* 20: 5 and *Lam.* 5: 7 as contrasted with *Jer.* 31: 28 f.; *Ez.* chap. 18.

[10] Cf. *inter alia, Mic.* 3: 5-8; *Jer.* chap. 28.

the prophets with betraying their trust and thus being responsible for the destruction of Jerusalem (2: 14). Together with the prophet and the people, the poet shares a conviction in the righteousness and power of God, a trust in the saving virtue of repentance, and a faith that God's love will bring forgiveness and restoration.

Both the similarities and the differences suggest that these elegies, like the bulk of the book of *Psalms*, reflect the faith of the average Jew, who was influenced strongly by prophetic thought, but did not identify himself completely with it.

Date. The differences in theme and in standpoint make it clear that the various elegies do not emanate from a single author. [11] Though the effort has frequently been made, it is impossible to date these poems exactly, since it is of the nature of lyric poetry that they rarely refer to precise events, but reflect permanent states of mind and feeling. Chapters 2 and 4 give a graphic picture of the fall of Jerusalem and probably emanate from an eyewitness of the destruction. They may therefore be dated within the two decades following the destruction of the Temple, *circa* 570-560 B.C.E. Chapter 1 views the destruction of Jerusalem as further in the background. The active period of warfare and destruction is over and the long, disheartening era of desolation is at hand: "The roads of Zion are in mourning, with no one assembling for the festival." The second half of the sixth century, *circa* 530 B.C.E., would therefore be an appropriate date. Chapter 3, which expresses a universal human condition, would be entirely undatable, were it not for the central section in which the poet identifies himself with the suffering people (3: 39-48). Here the poet gives a vivid description of the people's alienation from God because of its sin (vv. 43-44), the contempt of the nations (vv. 44-45), and the fear engendered by the wholesale destruction (v. 47). Its more vivid recollection of the national tragedy would suggest a date midway between

[11] The differences are recognized by virtually all scholars (Thenius, Gunkel, Pfeiffer, Meek, Haller). I find myself unable to accept the view of Y. Kaufmann, *Tōledōt Ha' emūnāh Hayisre' ēlīt* (Tel Aviv 1937-56) vol. 7, pp. 584-601, that "the five poems constitute a poetic unit (*masekhet piyyutith 'aḥath*).

the other chapters, hence *circa* 550-540 B.C.E. [12] Chapter 5, being a liturgy, is typological rather than specific, yet it seems to reflect an extended period of national subjection and Zion's desolation. It is therefore best dated *circa* 530 B.C.E.

If these proposed dates are sound, there may be some significance in the structure of the book, which seems to consist of three concentric sections. Chapter 3, which is an individual elegy with collective overtones, constitutes the "core," surrounded by a "layer," chapters 2 and 4, which are contemporary *Kinot* on the national catastrophe. The outermost "layer" consists of the latest chapters (1 and 5), which reflect the indignities of national subjection. The prayer (chap. 5) is placed at the end in order to make the collection suitable for liturgical use. [13]

The theory of Sumerian influence. In recent years, the distinguished Sumerologist, S. N. Kramer, has published the extant Sumerian laments over destroyed cities *(Studia Biblica et Orientalia III: Oriens Antiquus,* Analecta Biblica, Vol. 12, Rome, 1959; *idem, Eretz-Israel,* No. 9, 1969). He has maintained the view that the Biblical book was directly influenced by Sumerian models, a position adopted by C. J. Gadd and H. J. Kraus, but rejected by T. S. McDaniel and D. R. Hillers. While the parallels that Kramer has adduced are interesting, none are verbally exact or even sufficiently close to demonstrate dependence by the Biblical poet. In fact, in order to create what is described as "a genuine parallel" (AB, p. xxx), the Biblical text of 1:20c, which is thoroughly unexceptionable and appropriate, is emended and a nonexistent *hapax legomenon* is created in the passage, while the bearing of Biblical parallels, like Deut. 32:25b, c, is discounted.

It is obvious—or should be—that similar circumstances will lead to similar descriptions of conditions and similar expressions of mood. Unless some strikingly unique feature is to be found in two documents, the theory of dependence must be regarded as unproved.

---

[12] See the special Introduction which prefaces our Commentary to Chapter 3, which is unique in this collection of *kinot* and the meaning of which has been misunderstood because of faulty exegesis.

Moreover, there still remains the main problem of establishing channels of transmission between Sumer in Mesopotamia in the early second millennium B. C. E. and Judah 1,500 years later in the sixth century. We have repeatedly called attention to these methodological issues which are, unfortunately, all too often ignored *(Louis Ginzberg Jubilee Volumes,* English Volume, New York, 1945, pp. 173-75; *JQR,* Vol. 61, 1970, pp. 102 f.; *Proceedings of the American Academy of Jewish Research,* 1972, in process of publication).

The theme of the five *Kinot* may be expressed in these titles:

Chapter 1   The Desolation of Zion
Chapter 2   God's Wrath and Zion's Ruin
Chapter 3   Man's Yoke of Suffering
Chapter 4   The Agony of the Holy City
Chapter 5   O Lord, Remember Us and Forgive

Chapter 1—THE DESOLATION OF ZION

Zion, once a populous city, now sits in isolation like a leper, weeping in the night. Betrayed by her erstwhile lovers, she finds no rest. The land is desolate, and the highways are deserted, with no pilgrims flocking to the Holy City at festival times. Once honored by the nations, Zion is now despised. God has looked on unconcerned as pagans have penetrated and desecrated the Temple courts. Zion has deserved her fate because she has sinned and defied her God. But the enemies who have conquered her and now despise her deserve no better fate.

In structure, the elegy falls into two principal parts: the first section describes the physical devastation of Jerusalem (vv. 1-11). It ends with a cry by Zion (1. 11 e,f) which introduces Zion's lament over her spiritual desolation, the result of her sins (vv. 12-16). In v. 17, Zion stretches out her hand in a prayer for forgiveness, in which she calls for the punishment of her cruel and contemptuous foes (vv. 18-22).

1.   How she sits an outcast,
        the city once filled with people!
    She has become a widow,
        once great among the nations.
    A princess among provinces
        she is now in forced labor.

2.   Bitterly she weeps at night,
        a tear on her cheek.
    She has no comforter
        from among all her lovers.
    All her friends have betrayed her,
        they have become her foes.

3.   Judah is in exile,
        in poverty and oppression.
    She dwells among the nations,
        finding no rest.
    All her pursuers have overtaken her
        in the narrow straits.

4.   Zion's roads are in mourning,
        with no festival pilgrims.
    All her gates are desolate,
        her priests are groaning.
    Her virgins are sad
        and she—bitter is her lot!

5.   Her enemies have grown great,
        her foes are at ease,
    for the Lord has punished her
        for her many sins.
    Her infants have gone captive
        before the enemy.

6.   Departed from daughter Zion
        is all her glory.
    Her princes have been like rams
        that find no pasture,
    fleeing without strength
        before the pursuer.

7.   Jerusalem remembers, in the days of her poverty
        and wandering,
        all the delights she had in days of yore.
    Now when her people has fallen into enemy hands
        with none to help her,
    her foes have seen her
        and laughed at her destruction.

8.   Greatly has Jerusalem sinned,
        therefore she is scorned.
    All who honored her now despise her,
        for they have seen her nakedness.

She herself groans,
    feeling herself defeated.

9.   Uncleanness clings to her skirts;
    she is not even mindful of her children.
She has come astoundingly low,
    with none to comfort her,
"O Lord, see my affliction,
    for the enemy has triumphed."

10.   The foe has stretched his hand
    over all her treasures,
for You looked on as pagans
    came into her sanctuary,
concerning whom You had commanded,
    "They must not enter your assembly!"

11.   All her people groan,
    seeking bread.
They have given up their treasures for food
    merely to keep alive.
"Look, O Lord, and see
    that I have become worthless!"

12.   May no such fate be yours!
    All you passersby, look and see—
Is there any pain like the pain
    that has befallen me,
with which the Lord has afflicted me
    in the day of His wrath.

13.   From above He has sent fire
    into my bones and crushed them.
He has spread a net for my feet,
    hurling me backward.
He has made me desolate,
    in pain all day.

14.   He watches over my sins;
    in His hand they are interwoven.

Clambering up my neck
    they destroy my strength.
The Lord has given me into the hands
    of those I cannot resist.

15.   The Lord has spurned
    all the mighty ones in my midst.
He has proclaimed an open season
    for destroying my young men.
The Lord has trampled as in a winepress
    the virgin Judah.

16.   At this I weep,
    my eye runs with water,
for He has removed any comforter from me
    who might sustain my life.
My children are desolate
    for the foe has prevailed.

17.   Zion spreads out her hands,
    she has no comforter.
The Lord has marshalled against Jacob
    His foes roundabout.
Jerusalem has become
    a thing unclean among them.

18.   Righteous is the Lord
    for I have defied His word.
Listen to me, all you nations,
    and behold my pain—
my young men and women
    have gone into captivity.

19.   I called out to my lovers,
    they played me false.
My priests and my elders
    perished in the city,
as they sought food for themselves
    to sustain their lives.

20.   See, O Lord, that I am in anguish,
             my bowels are heated up;
        my heart is turned with me
             for I have been defiant.
        Outside, the sword destroys,
             within, it is the plague.

21.   Hear me as I groan;
             there is none to comfort me.
        All my foes heard of my disaster,
             rejoicing because You did it.
        Bring on the day You proclaimed
             and let them be like me!

22.   May all their wickedness come before You
             and do to them
        as You did to me,
             for all my transgressions,
        for my groans are many
             and my heart is sick.

Chapter 2—GOD'S WRATH AND ZION'S RUIN

UNLIKE chapter 1, which describes the desolation of the land years after the burning of the Temple and the destruction of Jerusalem, this elegy bears the earmarks of having been written by an eyewitness of the last agonies of the Holy City. The poet sees Jerusalem falling and the flames licking the Temple walls. He hears the last outcries of the dying and the moaning of the starving children, whose helpless mothers finally devour their offspring, as they wander among the corpses. The king and lords are now deprived of the Law they had previously flouted, and the prophets are now bereft of the word of God they had formerly violated. The neighboring enemies gloat over the catastrophe which has befallen Israel.

It is, however, not their prowess which has brought the disaster upon Israel, but the will of God. For He had announced Israel's inevitable doom if the people persisted in sin, unchecked by the prophets, who had offered honeyed words and soothing messages, instead of stern denunciation of evil. Now all is lost—Zion can only rise in the night, weep bitterly, and implore mercy for her dying children.

1. How the Lord has beclouded in his wrath
       the daughter of Zion!
   He has cast from heaven to earth
       the glory of Israel,
   and has not remembered his footstool
       in the day of his anger.

2. The Lord has destroyed without mercy
       all the dwellings of Jacob.
   He has torn down in his wrath
       the fortresses of Judah.
   He has brought down to the ground and profaned
       the kingdom and its princes.

134

3.   He has hewn down in his indignation
           the whole glory of Israel.
       He has withdrawn his right hand
           before the enemy,
       and He has burnt in Jacob like a flame
           devouring all about.

4.   He bends his bow like an enemy,
               poised like a foe.
       His right hand has slain
               all our handsome men.
       On the tent of daughter Zion
           He has poured his fury like fire.

5.   The Lord has become the enemy;
           He has devoured Israel.
       He has devoured all its palaces,
           destroyed its fortresses.
       He has multiplied in Judah
           mourning and lamentation.

6.   He has stripped his booth like a garden,
           destroyed his tent of meeting.
       The Lord has blotted out in Zion
           all memory of festival and Sabbath.
       In his bitter wrath He has despised
           king and priest.

7.   The Lord found his altar odious,
           He spurned his temple.
       He gave into the enemy's hands
           the walls of her palaces.
       They made a noise in the Lord's house
           as though it were a festival day.

8.   The Lord was determined to destroy
           the wall of Zion.
       He measured out the line,
               not drawing back from destruction.
       Rampart and wall were in mourning,
           languishing altogether.

9. Her gates sank into the ground;
    He smashed their bars.
  Her king and princes are among the nations
    with no law to guide them.
  Her prophets, too, do not find
    any vision from the Lord.

10. They sit on the ground in silence,
    the elders of Zion.
  They place dust upon their heads;
    they are girded in sackcloth.
  They lower their heads to the ground,
    the maidens of Jerusalem.

11. My eyes are worn out with tears,
    my spirit is in ferment.
  My heart is poured out to the ground
    because of the breaking of my people,
  when infant and suckling grow faint
    in the streets of the city.

12. To their mothers they cry,
    "Where is corn and wine?"
  as they grow faint, like dying men,
    in the streets of the city,
  when they breathe their last
    in their mother's bosom.

13. How can I strengthen you, to what compare you,
    O daughter Jerusalem?
  To what can I liken you and comfort you,
    O virgin Zion?
  For your break is great as the sea;
    who can heal you?

14. Your prophets saw for you
    false visions and plastered lies.
  They did not lay bare your sin
    to restore your former state.
  But they saw for you
    oracles false and misleading.

15.   All who pass along the way
        clap their hands in derision.
They hiss and shake their heads
        at daughter Jerusalem.
"Is this the city, the perfection of beauty,
        the joy of all the earth?"

16.   They open their mouths against you,
        all your enemies;
they hiss and gnash their teeth
        saying "We have devoured her!
Indeed, here is the day we hoped for;
        we have found it and seen it!"

17.   The Lord has done what He intended,
        He has fulfilled his word.
What He commanded in ancient days
        He has now torn down without pity,
He is letting the enemy gloat over you,
        exalting the might of your foes.

18.   Pour out your heart to the Lord,
        O wall of Zion!
Let your tears flow like a stream
        day and night.
Give yourself no rest,
        your eyes, no respite.

19.   Arise, cry out in the night
        at the beginning of each watch,
Pour out your heart like water
        in the presence of the Lord,
lift up your hands to him
        for the lives of your children,
who grow faint through hunger
        at the corner of each street.

20.   "Look, O Lord, and see;
        to whom have You done this?
Must women eat their offspring,
        the children they tenderly nurtured?

Must there be killed in the Lord's sanctuary
     priest and prophet?

21.   They lie on the ground in the streets,
          the young and the old.
       My maidens and young men
          have fallen by the sword.
       You killed them in the day of Your anger,
          slaughtering without pity.

22.   You gathered as for a feast day
          my hostile neighbors roundabout.
       In the day of the Lord's wrath
          no one escaped or survived.
       Those I had nurtured and raised
          my enemy has destroyed."

Chapter 3—MAN'S YOKE OF SUFFERING

Chapter 3 differs markedly in structure, theme, and mood from the two preceding elegies, though sharing with them the acrostic pattern and the *Qinah* rhythm. In the two preceding chapters, the successive letters of the alphabet appear at the opening of each verse, each of which contains three distichs (or six cola). In chapter 3, each letter of the alphabet appears at the beginning of three successive verses, each of which consists of only one distich (or two cola).

The subject of the first two chapters is collective, dealing with the national catastrophe which befell Judah in the conquest of Jerusalem and the burning of the Temple. While Zion is called upon to implore God's mercy, the predominant mood in these two *Qinot* is one of despair, and the only hope being voiced is that the enemies may suffer the same fate.

In chapter 3, the primary, overriding theme is the suffering of the individual, while the tragic destiny of the people is secondary. The poet begins with a vivid portrayal of his personal suffering, then passes to the tragic lot of his people, reverts once more to his own tragic situation, and concludes with a prayer for the punishment of his nation's enemies. This interplay of personal and collective factors is rooted in the fundamental Biblical concept of "fluid personality," on which see the Special Introduction to this chapter.

The mood of the chapter also differs from chapters 1 and 2. While it repeats the call for retribution on Israel's foes, it expresses a more positive faith in the triumph of righteousness, rooted in the conviction that God cannot be the source of evil in the world. It is not enough for men to lament their fate and complain of their sufferings. They may hope for regeneration and the restoration of a right relationship with God, if they recognize their sins and repent of their wrongdoing. This outlook is basic to biblical religion in all its manifestations. It underlies the call to repentance expressed in the Torah and emphasized by the Prophets, and is fundamental to the teaching of the Wisdom writers. This approach by traditional religion to the agonizing issue of suffering is expounded in detail by Eliphaz, the oldest of Job's friends (Job, chap. 4-5), who contends that man, not God, is responsible for the evil in the world (Job 5:6, 7).

To be sure, denying that God is responsible for suffering leaves unanswered the ontological question as to the source and origin of evil in the world. Yet the contrary view, which attributes both good and evil directly to God, is, obviously, not free from grave theological problems of its own. It must wrestle with the contradiction between the existence of evil and the goodness of an omnipotent God.

In any event, the poet is concerned here, not with metaphysical abstractions, but with the painful, concrete realities of human misery. He finds an anodyne for the agony that both he and his people have undergone in the conviction that a good God cannot be charged with the pain and suffering in the world, and that there is, therefore, hope for man. To all the suffering and heavy-hearted, the poet offers not a meticulously reasoned theology, but a deeply emotional expression of faith in man's potential for regeneration, through the mercy of God.

A.

1.   I am the man who has seen affliction
        through the rod of God's wrath.

2.   He has guided and led me
        into darkness, with no light,

3.   Against me has He constantly turned
        his hand all day.

4.   He has worn out my flesh and my skin,
        He has broken my bones.

5.   He has besieged and surrounded me
         with poverty and travail.

6.   He has made me dwell in darkness
         like those long dead.

7.   He has fenced me in, so that I cannot escape;
         He has put me in heavy chains.

8.   Even when I shout and cry out
         He has shut out my prayer.

9.   He has fenced my paths with hewn stone,
         He has twisted my way.

10. He is a bear in ambush to me,
         a lion in hiding.

11. My paths He has hedged in and torn me apart,
         He has made me desolate.

12. He has aimed his bow and set me up
         as a target for his arrow.

13. He has driven into my heart
         the arrows of his quiver.

14. I have been a mockery to all my people,
         their taunt-song all day.

15. He has filled me with bitterness,
         He has sated me with wormwood.

16. He has ground down my teeth with gravel;
         He has pressed me into the ashes.

17. Peace has forsaken me;
         I have forgotten all joy.

18. And I thought, "My vital spark is gone,
         and any hope from the Lord."

19. O remember my poverty and my wandering,
         the wormwood and gall,

20. for I surely remember
         and my spirit is brought low.

B.

21. But this, too, I recall
    and therefore have hope—

22. God's kindnesses have not ceased;
    His mercies have not ended,

23. new are they each morning,
    great is God's faithfulness.

24. "My portion is the Lord," I declare,
    "therefore I trust in Him."

25. The Lord is good to those who wait for Him,
    to every one who seeks Him.

26. It is good that men wait patiently
    for the Lord's deliverance.

27. It is good for a man to bear
    the yoke in his youth,

28. to sit silent and alone,
    when it is thrust upon him,

29. to place his mouth in the dust
    —there may yet be hope—

30. to turn his cheek to the smiter,
    to take his fill of shame.

C.

31. For the Lord does not
    forsake forever.

32. Even if He afflicts, yet He has mercy
    according to his great love.

33. For He does not afflict men willingly,
    nor bring grief to the sons of men.

34. To crush underfoot
    all the prisoners of the earth,

35.   to pervert a man's just case
            is against the desire of the Most High.

36.   To subvert a man in his cause—
            this the Lord does not approve.

37.   Who has commanded that it come to pass—
            The Lord has not ordained it!

38.   Not from the mouth of the Most High is it
                decreed
            to do harm to a good man!

D.

39.   Why should a man alive complain,
            any man, about his punishment?

40.   Rather he should say,
            "Let us search and examine our ways
                and return to the Lord!"

41.   Let us raise our hearts—and not merely our hands—
            to God in Heaven, *saying,*

42.   "We have transgressed and rebelled;
            You have not forgiven

43.   You have wrapped yourself in anger and pursued us,
            killing us without mercy.

44.   You have wrapped yourself with a cloud
            so that no prayer can penetrate.

45.   Filth and refuse have you made us
            among the peoples.

46.   They open their mouths against us,
            all our enemies.

47.   A terror and a trap has been our lot,
            wrack and ruin."

E.

48.   Streams of tears flow from my eyes
        because of my people's calamity.

49.   My eyes flow without ceasing,
        without any pause,

50.   Until the Lord looks down from Heaven
        and sees us.

51.   What I see causes me anguish,
        at the fate of the maidens of my city.

52.   I have been hunted like a bird
        by my foes without cause.

53.   They pressed me into the pit,
        having cast rocks upon me.

54.   Waters flowed over my head.
        I said, "I am cut off."

55.   I have called Your name, O Lord
        from the bottommost pit,

56.   "Hear my voice, do not hide your ear
        from my groaning and my cry,

57.   Be near on the day I call You;
        tell me, 'Do not fear.' "

58.   Plead my cause, O God,
        redeem my life.

59.   Lord, see the injustice I suffer,
        fight my cause.

60.   See the vengeance they plan,
        all their schemes against me.

61.   Hear how they disgrace me,
        all their schemes against me.

62.   The lips of my foes and their thoughts
        are against me all day.

63.   See them at leisure and at labor;
        I am always the butt of their taunt-song.

64.   Render them their just deserts
        according to the work of their hands.

65.   Empty their hearts of all understanding;
        Your curse be upon them!

66.   May You pursue them in Your anger and destroy them
        from beneath the heavens of the Lord!

Chapter 4—THE AGONY OF THE HOLY CITY

This lament contains the most vivid description in the book of the siege of Jerusalem and of the intense suffering it caused among the people. Even the most high-born inhabitants of the capital are brought to degradation and hunger. Mothers become cruel to their own children, who cry out in vain for food and drink. The punishment that God had visited upon Sodom and Gomorrah, that for centuries had served as symbols of total destruction, is not as horrible as the catastrophe that has befallen Jerusalem. Quick death by the sword was preferable to the slow agony of hunger which drove mothers to eat the bodies of their offspring.

The blame for this disaster is to be placed at the door of the prophets and the priests who, either by their acts of commission or of omission, were responsible for the murder of innocent men. On the principle of "measure for measure," the enemy now shows no compassion for priests or elders. The people, seeking to flee, are pursued and captured by the victors. The king himself, once the shining hope and glory of the people, is caught in a trap like a common criminal.

The final indignity is the rejoicing of Judah's foes over her fall. Today Judah is in ruins and Edom gloats over the catastrophe. But soon, Edom will be forced to drink the same bitter cup, while Zion will be forgiven and restored.

1. How the gold is tarnished,
       the purest gold transformed;
   the holy jewels are scattered
       at the corner of every street!

2. Zion's precious children,
       worth their weight in fine gold,
   how are they treated like clay jugs,
       the handiwork of any potter!

146

3. Even jackals press their breast
        to suckle their young;
    the daughter of my people has turned cruel,
        like ostriches in the desert.

4. The infant's tongue cleaves
        to his palate in thirst;
    children plead for bread,
        but no one gives it to them.

5. Those who feasted on dainties
        now are desolate in the streets;
    those reared in scarlet
        now embrace ash-heaps.

6. The punishment of my people has been greater
        than the penalty of Sodom,
    which was overturned in a moment,
        with no human hand involved.

7. Her princes were whiter than snow,
        purer than milk;
    their bodies ruddier than corals;
        their frames, like sapphire.

8. Now blacker than soot is their image;
        they cannot be recognized in the streets.
    Their skin has shrunk upon their bones;
        it has become dry as wood.

9. Happier were the victims of the sword
        than the victims of hunger;
    the stabbed, whose blood flowed,
        than those perishing for lack of food.

10. The hands of merciful women
        cooked their own children;
    they became their food
        during the destruction of my people.

11. The Lord vented his full anger;
        He poured out his wrath.

He kindled a fire in Zion
   which devoured her foundations.

12.   The kings of the earth could not believe it,
      nor all the inhabitants of the world,
   that the foe and enemy could enter
      the gates of Jerusalem.

13.   Because of the sins of her prophets,
      the transgressions of her priests,
   who poured out in her midst
      the blood of the righteous,

14.   the prophets now wandered blind in the streets;
      the priests were defiled by blood,
   so that no one dared touch
      their filthy garments.

15.   "Turn away, you are unclean,"
      men called to them,
   "Turn away, turn away,
      do not touch us!
   Indeed, they have wandered far away," men said,
      "Among the nations they can live no longer.

16.   God himself has scattered them,
      He will regard them no more."
   Hence the priests were shown no deference;
      the elders, no mercy.

17.   Our eyes were still filled with longing
      for help—in vain.
   Anxiously we kept on watching
      for a nation—that could not save.

18.   Our steps grew narrow,
      so we could not walk in our streets.
   Our end drew near, our days were over,
      for our end was at hand.

19.   Swifter were our foes
        than the vultures in the sky.
    Over the mountains they chased us;
        in the desert, they lay in ambush.

20.   The breath of our nostrils, the Lord's anointed,
        was caught in their trap,
    of whom we had said,
        "In his shadow we shall live among the nations."

21.   Rejoice and be glad, daughter Edom,
        dweller in the land of Uz!
    But to you too the cup will pass!
        You will get drunk and strip yourself naked.

22.   Your punishment is fulfilled, daughter Zion;
        God will exile you no longer.
    He will punish your iniquity, daughter Edom,
        He will lay bare your sins.

Chapter 5—O LORD, REMEMBER US AND FORGIVE

The closing chapter of Lamentations differs from the preceding in several significant respects. It does not contain the alphabetic acrostic, though, whether by design or accident, the verses number 22, as in the Hebrew alphabet. The chapter is not a lament upon the fall of Jerusalem, but a penitential psalm confessing the sins which have led to the disaster and invoking God's forgiveness.

It may well have been composed for a special ritual of commemoration and penitence, probably at the anniversary of the destruction of the Temple. Placed at the end, it makes possible the use of the entire book for liturgical purposes.

In order not to conclude with an unpalatable phrase, synagogue practice ordains the repetition of verse 21 at the public chanting of Lamentations.

1. Remember, O Lord, what has happened to us;
    look and see our disgrace!

2. Our inheritance has been turned over to strangers;
    our homes, to aliens.

3. We have become orphans without a father,
    our mothers are widows.

4. Our own water that we drink we must pay for,
    our own wood we get only for a price.

5. Our pursuers are hot upon our necks;
    we are exhausted and have no rest.

6. With Egypt we had made a pact,
    with Assyria, to have enough bread.

7. Our fathers sinned and they are gone,
    now we suffer for their transgressions.

150

8.   Slaves rule over us;
       a deliverer there is none.

9.   At the risk of our lives we get our bread,
       exposed to the heat of the wilderness.

10.   Our skin is burnt black like an oven
       through the burning ravages of famine.

11.   Women are raped in Zion;
       virgins, in the cities of Judah.

12.   Princes are hanged by their hands;
       elders are not spared.

13.   Young men must carry the millstone
       and youths stagger under its bar.

14.   The elders have quit the gates;
       the young men, their music.

15.   Ended is the joy of our heart;
       our dance is turned to mourning.

16.   The crown of our head is fallen!
       Woe to us, for we have sinned!

17.   For this our heart is sick;
       for this, our eyes grow dark,

18.   for Mount Zion now desolate,
       jackals prowling about.

19.   You, O Lord, are enthroned forever,
       Your seat endures for all generations.

20.   Why have You forgotten us for an eternity,
       forsaken us for so long?

21.   Turn us to Yourself, O God, and we will return;
       renew our days as of old,

22.   even though You had greatly despised us
       and had been very angry with us!

Lamentations

איכה

1:1 אֵיכָה is the longer and more poetical form of the adverb אֵיךְ "how," the hallmark of the Hebrew elegy. Both forms are used to express the incredulity and grief of the poet at the disaster he is bewailing (cf. e.g. *Isa.* 1: 21 and *Jer.* 2: 21). The usage also occurs in prose, as in Koheleth's outburst at the same fate befalling the sage and the fool (*Ecc.* 2: 16). The emotion of grief may be genuine, as is generally the case, or it may be feigned, so that it becomes a mock-elegy expressing *Schadenfreude* vis-à-vis an enemy as in *Obad.* 1: 5.

1:2 רֵעֶיהָ = not "her friends," but "her lovers," as is clear from the parallelism. For the meaning, cf. Jer. 3: 1, 20; *Song of Songs* 5: 1, 16.

1:3 נָּלְתָה יְהוּדָה מֵעֹנִי וּמֵרֹב עֲבוֹדָה. As Meek correctly recognizes, the verse cannot mean "she has gone into exile *because of* poverty." His rendering "with the result that she suffers poverty" is logically acceptable but is not borne out by the text. The *Mem* is best taken as the "*Mem* of condition" which occurs in Rabbinic Hebrew, as e.g. *Abot* 4: 9: כל המקיים את התורה מעוני סופה לקיימה מעושר "whoever fulfills the Torah in a condition of poverty will ultimately fulfill the Torah in a condition of wealth." The same usage occurs in the phrases מֵעוֹמֵד and מִיוֹשֵׁב "from a sitting position,"

153

"from a standing position" (cf. *B. Shab.* 113b and elsewhere), generally misvocalized as *me ʿummad* and *meyūššābh*. It is also to be found in Biblical Hebrew as in *Hos.* 9: 11, 12 [14] מֵרֶחֶם 11 מִבֶּטֶן אִמִּי and *Job* 3: 11 מֵרֶחֶם; *Ps.* 22: 11 מִלֵּדָה מִבֶּטֶן וּמֵהָרָיוֹן

The parallelism in our verse (a, b|| a¹ b¹) also makes it clear that the verse describes Judah's present condition and not its cause:

"Judah is in exile, in a state of poverty and oppression,
    She dwells among the nations, she has found no rest."

1: 7   Most scholars delete in part either stich b יְמֵי עָנְיָהּ

וּמְרוּדֶיהָ or stich c כָּל מַחֲמַדֶיהָ ··· מִימֵי קֶדֶם, in order to reduce the verse to the three-stich pattern which characterizes the entire elegy. It is possible that MT represents a conflate, the two phrases being variant objects of *zākherāh,* both being incorporated into our text.

Another approach is, however, possible. When stich b is recognized (with Ibn Ezra) as an adverbial accusative of time (cf. *Gen.* 2:3 *sēseth yāmīm*), it is clear that substantively both clauses are necessary to the context.

Deletions solely on metric grounds are increasingly recognized as methodologically unsound. The Kinah rhythm does not consist exclusively of the 3: 2 meter, which is, to be sure, the basic pattern. Its haunting effect is achieved by having a longer stich followed by a shorter. This can be achieved either by giving stich a a greater number of stressed words or thought-units than stich b, or by having stich a contain longer words than stich b. [15] The verse is therefore to be scanned: 4: 3 || 3: 2 || 3: 2

זכרה ירושלים ימי עניה ומרודיה // כל מחמריה אשר היו מימי קדם
בנפל עמה ביד־צר //   ואין עוזר־לה
ראו צרים שחקו //   על משבתה

The poetic caesura in the third distich does not correspond

---

[13] *Cf.* such liturgical additions at the end of *Psalms,* as 2: 12; 14: 7=53: 7; 51: 20 f.; 125: 5c.

[14] Cf. R. Gordis, "Lešōn Hamiqrāʾ Leʾōr Lešōn Ḥakhāmīm" in *Sepher Tur-Sinai* (Jerusalem, 5721 = 1960), pp. 167 ff. for a discussion of this syntactic usage.

[15] Cf. *idem,* "Al Mibneh Hašīrāh Haʿivrit Haqedummāh" in *Sepher Hašānāh Liyehudei Amerika,* 5745=1944, pp. 136-59.

with the logical pause, an exceptional but by no means
rare phenomenon.

On מרודיה cf. 3: 19. It is generally derived either from
māradh "rebellious, bitter" (cf. *Isa.* 58: 7) or from *rādadh*
"oppress," Arabic ﻍ, (so Meek). Better from *rūdh* "wander"
(cf. *Jer.* 2: 3; *Hos.* 12: 1). Cf. *meṣūgāh* from *šūg* and *mesukhah*
from *sūkh*, metaplastic forms of the more familiar geminate
roots *šāgag* "err" and *sākhakh* "hedge, fence in."

1: 8 נידה is usually regarded as a plene spelling for נִדָּה
"unclean," or interpreted as "wandering" from *nūdh, nīdh.*
On the other hand, it may be an elliptical phrase for מְנוֹד רֹאשׁ
"an object of shaking of the head, of scorn." See *Ps.* 44: 14, 15,
and the parallels there, and הִזִּילוּהָ "have held her in contempt" in our passage. It may be that both meanings, "unclean" and "object of scorn" are intended by the poet.
This would be an instance of *talḥin*, a rhetorical figure where
a word is consciously chosen because in addition to its dominant sense it carries another meaning on a secondaɪy level.
This rhetorical device occurs elsewhere in our book in 2: 13
gādōl kayam šibhrekh. "Thy break is great as the sea." [16]

1: 9 While the root *zākhar* means not only "remember the
past," but also "to be mindful of the present" (as in *Ex.* 20: 9;
cf. *Mal.* 3: 22; also *Ecc.* 5: 19, "for not long will he remember
the days of his life"), it can scarcely mean "to be mindful of
the future." Rashi is conscious of this difficulty which he
seeks to avoid by interpreting, *"when they were sinning,*
they did not consider what would be their end." However, the
entire passage is describing her present condition in exile,
not the sins which occasioned it. אַחֲרִיתָהּ here possesses the
special meaning "offspring, children" (cf. *Jer.* 31: 16; *Ez.*
23: 25; *Am.* 4: 2; *Ps.* 37: 38 f.; 109: 13). Zion's children are
also subtly referred to in the parallel phrase אֵין מְנַחֵם לָהּ.
Normally a mother cannot forget her young (cf. *Isa.* 49: 14 ff.),
and it is the duty of children to support their parents and
comfort them (cf. *Isa.* 51: 18, 19 and the explanation for
the naming of Noah, *Gen.* 6: 29, "he will comfort us from our

---

[16] On *talḥin* in the Bible, cf. Gordis, "Lisegūlōt Hameliṣāh Bekhith-
bei Haqōdeš" in *Sepher Seidel* (Jerusalem 5722=1962), pp. 255-261.

labor and the toil of our hands"). It is the ultimate disaster when a mother consumes her young (*Deut.* 28: 53; *Lam.* 4: 3, 10). Here Zion is so degraded that "she does not remember her children." And her children fail in their filial duty to comfort their mother. The closing stich of the verse is a virtual quotation without a *verbum dicendi*, "saying, 'Behold my affliction, O Lord.' "

1: 10 כִּי־רָאָתָה does not follow logically upon stich a, since it does not supply the reason for the enemy's stretching out his hand upon all her precious things. We suggest that MT be vocalized as a 2nd per. masc. רָאִתָה and rendered "for You saw it as proper, regarded it as right." This use of *rā'ah* is common in Rabbinic Hebrew. Cf. *M. Eduyot* 6: 3: אמרו לו לרבי אליעזר מה ראית לטמא כזית בשר וגו' "They said to R. Eliezer, 'How is it that you have regarded it right to declare unclean an olive's bulk of flesh severed from a member of a living being?' "; אמרו לו לרבי אליעזר מה ראית לחלק מדותיך "They said to R. Eliezer, 'How is it that you regard it proper to follow different rules?' "; *B. Bat.* 123a מה ראה יעקב שנטל בכורה מראובן ונתנה ליוסף "Why did Jacob regard it proper to take the birth-right from Reuben and give it to Joseph?" Cf. also *M. Ned.* 9: 9; *B. Pesahim* 53b and often, as well as the common Mishnic adjective רָאוּי "worthy, proper." The same meaning also occurs in *Lam.* 3: 36. The closing stich refers to the prohibition in *Deut.* 23: 4, 8 against the admission of pagans into the "community of the Lord." With regard to the revocalization proposed, the exact orthography of רָאתָה without *Yod* and with *He* occurs in *Ps.* 10: 14 and the final *He* in the 2nd per. masc. is common (*Num.* 27: 13; *II Sam.* 18: 21; *Ps.* 35: 22; *Lam.* 3: 59f.). The verse is to be rendered:

"His hand the foe has stretched out || upon all that she loved, For You found it proper for Gentiles || to enter her sanctuary Of whom You had commanded, 'They shall not enter your community.' "
Note the poetic caesura once more as distinct from the logical caesura.

1:11   Hillers makes out a strong case for referring *maḥᵃ-maddēhem (Qere)*, "precious things," not to possessions, as in v. 10, but to "children, objects of love," as in Hos. 9:16; cf. also Ezek. 24:16; Lam. 2:4. This interpretation gives greater poignancy to the passage.

The substantive *zōlēlāh* was rendered by the older interpreters as "gluttonous," on the basis of such passages as Deut. 21:20; Pr. 23:20 (Tar., Ibn Ezra). Most moderns prefer the meaning "despised, worthless," the opposite of *yāqār*, "precious," as in Jer. 15:19. It is possible that we have here an instance of *talḥin* with both meanings present in the consciousness of the poet and his readers.

1:12   לֹא אֲלֵיכֶם is not to be mended to לוּ אַתֶּם הַבִּיטוּ (Rudolph, Haller) or to the inept לְכוּ לָכֶם. Now can the MT be rendered, "Is it nothing to you?" (AV, RV). The phrase is an apotropaic prayer, "Let not this fate come to you!" Cf. *Job* 21:16; 22:18 עֲצַת רְשָׁעִים רָחֲקָה מֶנִּי, "Far be from me the counsel of the wicked!," and the modern Hebrew idiom להבדיל "to separate A from B."

These two opening words, being an interjection, are an anacrusis, a phrase outside the meter pattern, and thus serving for greater emphasis. Cf. the two opening words of Ps. 1, *'ašrēy hā'īš*. The remainder of the v. scans as 3:2 ǁ 3:2 ǁ 3:2.

The two final words in the v., *ḥarōn 'appō*, receive one beat, since they express a single idea.

1:13   In וירדנה the suffix is best construed as third person plural and taken to refer to בעצמתי. There is no need to revocalize with LXX as וַיֹּרִדֶנָּה. The root *rādāh*, which occurs in *Joel* 4:13 בֹּאוּ רְדוּ, *Arab* rādāy, "tread, trample down" (so Hal.), is parallel to *rādad* in Mishnic Hebrew, as e.g. *Tos. M. Kat.* 1:4 וּמִרְדָּד הָאֲדָמָה, "tramples down the earth." On Lamed Yodh and geminate roots, cf. *šāgāh* ǁ *šāgag* (cf. *Job* 12:16); *ḥāqaq*, *ḥāqāh*, "engrave" (cf. *Isa.* 10:1; *Job* 13:27, etc.). Translate, "From above he has sent his fire into my bones and crushed them."

1:14   No appropriate meaning or etymology for נִשְׂקַד is

available. Perles' emendation נִשְׁקַד עַל פְּשָׁעַי, "he guards my steps," leaves ישתרגו without an appropriate subject. Read נִשְׁקַד עַל פְּשָׁעַי "he watches over my sins." Cf. *Job* 14:16 *Jer.* 5:6 לא תשמר על חטאתי נמר שקד על־עריהם On *sārag* = "interlace, interweave", cf. מסרגין את המיטות *M. Katan* 1:8; *Y. Ber* III 5d, a.e. כל שמסרגין. The sins are pictured as weaving themselves into a thick net-like pattern which then rises and chokes its victim. One is reminded of the classical myth of the Trojan priest Laocoön and his sons being choked to death by the serpents rising from the sea.

There is no need to emend עָלוּ into עָלוּ with *Pes*. It may be preferable (though not absolutely necessary) to revocalize הִכְשִׁיל as a plural הִכְשִׁילוּ, so that *pešā'ay*, rather than God, is its subject. The verse is to be rendered:

He stands guard over my sins,
   In his hand they are woven together,
They climb up my neck,
   They destroy my strength.

1:15   The verb *sillah*, which occurs in a similar context in Ps. 119:118 (though in the Qal), is generally given an *ad hoc* meaning. The medieval commentators render "trampled," on the basis of Isa. 62:10 (so Rashi, Ibn Ezra); the moderns prefer "flouted, made light of" (BDB, Perles, RSV), for which the Aramaic and Syriac *selā'*, "despise," is adduced. Yet it is noteworthy that the Syriac Pešita renders "he trampled down," and the Aramaic Targum *kenas*, "he gathered in." The verb is also treated as a metaplastic form or as an error for *sillēl* and given the meaning of "heaping up" on the basis of Jer. 50:26 (so Hillers).

The noun *mō'ēdh* is either "an assembly of foes" or "the proper season." "Trampling the vintage" is a vivid figure for pouring out blood (Isa. 63:1 ff.; Joel 4:13).

1:17   In בידיה, the Beth of means is used, an alternate usage to the direct accusative in 1:15. Note *Isa.* 5:14 *pā'arāh phīhā* "She opened her mouth" as against *Job*16:10, *pā'arū 'ālai bephīhem; tāphas* "seize" with both usages (*Ez.* 30:21; *Am.* 2:15), and the rabbinic use of הרכנתי את

ראשי "I bowed my head' with the acc. (*Num. R.* 10: 7), but also with the Beth of means הרכין בראשו (*B. Horayot* 3b).

1: 19 בָּעִיר need not be emended to בְּרָעָב (ag., Budde, Hal.). The phrase emphasizes that in the city, where the priests and elders previously occupied honored positions they will now starve to death, and is thus equivalent to "publicly, before all." The same meaning inheres in Amos' prediction to the priest Amaziah, אשתך בעיר תזנה "your wife will play the harlot in the city" (*Am.* 7: 17). The Piel participle of *'ahabh* carries the overtone of "those pretending to be my lovers."

1: 16 Many commentators have deleted one of the two occurrences of *'einī* as a dittography, maintaining that it improves the rhythm. The repetition of the noun adds poignancy to the line and has a striking parallel in Jer. 4: 19; *mē'ay mē'ay 'ōḥīlāh*. The meter, too, is unexceptionable, representing a legitimate variation of the *Qinah* meter. With each word in stich a receiving a stress, the pattern is 4: 4 ‖ 3: 2 ‖ 3: 2.

1: 20 The verb *ḥ*ᵃ*marmārū* has been derived from two Arabic roots: (1) *ḥamara* II (undotted *ḥa*) "become red," and (2) *ḥamara* (dotted *ḥa*) "ferment," hence "broil, foam up." The use of the root with "face" in Job 16: 16 permits either meaning or etymology, but the references in our book to bowels make only the second possible. It is hardly likely that this rare verb should occur as two distinct homonyms. Hence the meaning "boil, ferment, heat up" is to be assigned to all three passages, Job 16: 16; Lam. 1: 20; and 2: 11.

Kammāweth is not to be rendered "like death" nor is the *Kaph* to be elided. The *asseverative Kaph* (*Kāph ha'amitūth*) was clearly recognized by the medieval Jewish commentators but unaccountably ignored by the moderns. It generally occurs in the predicate. It is now attested by Ugaritic as well as by a substantial number of Biblical passages, as we have pointed out elsewhere. [17] For Biblical examples, *inter alia*, cf. *Num.* 11: 1; *Hos.* 5: 10; *Obad.* 1: 11; *Neh.* 7: 2. Render our passage: "Without, the sword bereaved; within, there was death."

The emendation of *kammāweth* into a presently nonexistent

noun *kaphnūt*, "hunger," on the basis of a Sumerian "parallel"
(Hillers) is unnecessary.

1:21   The opening verb *šām'ū* is to be revocalized as an
imperative, either in the plural *šim'ʰū*, addressed to the nations
(cf. v. 18), so LXX, or preferably in the singular *šʰmā'*, addressed to God (so Pešita).

1: 21   הֵבֵ֫אתָ need not be emended to הָבֵא אֵת, nor was it
read otherwise by the Vss., who rendered it as an imperative.
In Biblical Hebrew, the perfect tense focuses attention upon
an act as completed. It is therefore admirably suited to convey
intense desire (hence the precative perfect) or intense assurance
that the event will come to pass (whence the perfect of prophetic certitude). For one instance out of many of the precative
perfect, cf. *Ps.* 6: 10 *šama'* ‖ *yiqqāḥ.* For the perfect of
prophetic certitude cf. *Isa.* 5: 13; *Hos.* 4: 6 *nidmū.* [18]

1: 21f.   Budde followed by Hal. rearranges vv. 21 and 22
by a) placing על כל פשעי (from v. 22) after יום קראת (in v. 21);
b) placing ויהיו כמני (from v. 21) after תבא כל־רעתם לפניך in
(v. 22); c) reversing stichs b and c in v. 22 and d) deleting the
Vav of ועולל to read כאשר עוללת לי עולל למו. This extensive
rearrangement is unnecessary, if we recall the principle in
prosody already referred to on 1: 7, that at times a thought
may be carried over from one stich to another. Hence the
poetic and logical caesuras do not always coincide. The
Masoretic accentuation, which places the secondary pause at
lāmō (*zākeph kātān*) and the primary pause (*'athnāh*) at
pʰšā'āy, is therefore correct. V. 22 is to be scanned and
rendered as follows:

May all their evil come before you   and do to them,
  As you have done to me   because of my sin,
For my groans are many   and my heart is faint.

For another example where the poetic caesura does not
coincide with logical pause, cf. 2: 2c ממלכה ‖ הגיע לארץ חלל
ושריה.

---

[17] See R. Gordis, "Asseverative Kaph in Hebrew and Ugaritic"
(*JAOS*, 1943, vol. 63), pp. 176-78.
[18] *Cf.* S. R. Driver, *Hebrew Tenses* (Oxford, 1892), chap. 2, esp.
pp. 18 ff.

2 : 1   The verb *yā'ībh* in MT is generally derived from the noun, *'ābh* "cloud," and given the meaning "becloud, set under a cloud" (so RSV). The word has been related to an Arabic root *'aba* "blame, revile" (Ehr.), or emended to *yō'ībh* from an assumed root *ya'wb* "abominate" (McDaniel, *Biblica*, vol. 49, 1968, p. 34 f., followed by Hillers), on the ground that the imagery suggested by MT is unparalleled elsewhere. It is over-looked that a gifted poet may express himself in a strikingly original manner; indeed, this is the essence of poetic genius. For another instance, cf. the Comm. on 2 : 18.

2 : 2   The phrase, ולא חמל (Kethib being asyndetonic) is adverbial: "The Lord has destroyed mercilessly all the dwell-ings of Jacob." For the asyndeton of the Kethib *cf. Job* 6 : 10, לא יחמול "I shall tremble in a terror that is merciless."

2 : 4   The difficulty of stich b, נצב ימינו כצר is not solved by giving the verb a transitive meaning (so Pes and LXX), either by emending to הָצִּיב or revocalizing as a Piel נִצֵּב (so Perles), since the verb "stand up" is inappropriate to "right hand." It would be better to regard the stich as a *casus pendens*, "He stands—with his right hand like an enemy" (my former student, Rabbi Edward Gershfield).

However, the verse has another problem—it contains only five stichs. Transposing כְּצָר וַיַּהֲרֹג to read וַיַּהֲרֹג כְּצָר (so Meek) aggravates the difficulty with stich b and does not help the metric structure of the verse. We propose placing יְמִינוֹ after וַיַּהֲרֹג. While יָמִין is usually feminine, it occurs as a masculine in *Ex.* 15 : 6. Or *y'mīnō* is to be construed as an accusative of means and the phrase rendered "He has killed with his right hand." For metric reasons, the stich ויהרג ומינו, which has two long words will receive three beats. *Cf.* 2 : 12 לְאִמּוֹתָם יֹאמְרוּ, The entire verse scans in *Kinah* rhythm as 3 : 2‖ 3 : 2 ‖ 3 : 2:

נצב כצר	דרך קשתו כאויב
כל־מחמדי־עין	ויהרג ימינו
כאש חמתו	באהל בת־ציון שפך

In the third distich the poetic caesura comes after *šāphakh*, though again it is not the logical pause. See note on 1: 22.

2: 5 כַּאוֹיֵב is not "like an enemy" but "the Lord has indeed become the enemy." The Kaph is asseverative. *Cf.* note on 1: 20.

2: 7 זָנַח in its usual meaning "leave, forsake," is too weak for the context. We prefer to derive it from Arabic *zanaḥ* II "smell bad." The root occurs in Hebrew intransitively in *Isa.* 19: 6, וְהֶאֱזְנִיחוּ נְהָרוֹת. It is used, we believe figuratively, in *Hos.* 8: 2, זָנַח יִשְׂרָאֵל טוֹב "Israel has sinned greatly, lit. smells very bad"; and *Hos.* 8: 5 זָנַח עֶגְלֵךְ. Cf. the Biblical באש (*Ex.* 5: 21; *Gen.* 34: 30) and the rabbinic סרח, (*Keth.* 45a and often) meaning "stink, sin." In our passage, the verb is used declaratively, "the Lord finds His altar odious, i.e., He hates His altar."

2: 9 Stich b אִבַּד וְשִׁבַּר בְּרִיחֶיהָ is not only metrically too long but is logically contradictory or redundant. Nor can the second verb be regarded as a gloss to the first. The two verbs are a conflate, representing variants of manuscripts which were both preserved in a very early stage of Proto-masoretic activity, evidence for which is to be found in the Biblical texts of Qumran. [19] The early guardians of the text were unwilling to choose between variants which they found in old, reliable manuscripts that they collated. They therefore preserved them both by incorporating them side by side into

---

[19] *Cf.* R. Gordis, *The Biblical Text in the Making—A Study of the Kethib-Qere*, (Phila. 1937) where this theory of early Masoretic activity before the destruction of the Second Temple (70 C.E.) was set forth, on the basis of inner Biblical material and Rabbinic sources (pp. 29-54). The implications of the Qumran Biblical texts for the history of the Masorah were explored in קדמותה של המסורה לאור ספרות חז״ל והמגילות הגנוזות "The Origins of the Masorah in the Light of Rabbinic Literature and the Dead Sea Scrolls," (*Tarbiz*, 5718=1958, vol. 27), pp. 444-69. Since it was first proposed, nearly three decades ago, this insight into the history of the MT has been adopted, though without acknowledgement, by several scholars, to whom, nevertheless, thanks are due for giving it wider currency. For a *catena* of examples of Masoretic conflation, see *The Biblical Text in the Making* (pp. 41-43, amplified in *Qadmuthah*, pp. 467-69, now available in the second augmented edition of the book [New York, 1971]).

the accepted text. We called attention to this stage in the technique of the Masorah as long ago as 1937. [20]

In our passage the two texts conflated were a) אבד בריחיה and b) שבר בריחיה. The Vav was added when both variants were combined in the text.

2:12 כְּחָלָל here can scarcely have its usual meaning of "corpse" (lit. "bored, pierced," Arabic خل). Nor is there any evidence for the interpretation advanced *ad hoc*, "one perishing from hunger." The noun here is to be related to חלל III "pollute, defile," Arabic حل X). It occurs in *Lev.* 21:7, 14, (חֲלָלָה), where it is juxtaposed with זֹנָה and means "profaned, defiled." Since a corpse was regarded as unclean (e.g., Num. 19:11, etc.), the term could be applied to a corpse or, by prolepsis, to a person dying; cf. *bᵉmōth hammēth*, lit. "the death of a dead (i.e. dying) man" (*Ezek.* 18:32). In our passage, the word would mean "like a dying man." It may possibly have the nuance of "outcast." The poignancy is heightened by the reference to the streets of the city. Cf. the Note on 1:19.

In the stich אַיֵּה דָגָן וָיַיִן, there is no need to delete וָיַיִן on metric grounds (ag. Haller). In each case the opening stich, בְּהִתְעַטְּפָם כֶּחָלָל, לְאִמֹּתָם יֹאמְרוּ and בְּהִשְׁתַּפֵּךְ נַפְשָׁם, consists of two long words and therefore receives three beats, while the succeeding stich contains two or three short words, בִּרְחֹבוֹת עִיר אַיֵּה דָגָן וָיַיִן and אֶל־חֵיק אִמֹּתָם and therefore' receives only two beats. This is one of the occasional divergences from the basic principle of Biblical metrics of "one thought unit—one stress." [21]

---

[20] Obviously only one of the variants is original and the other arose as a scribal error. The process is easy to reconstruct. The *Beth* is common to both verbs, and *Reš* and *Daledh* are virtually indistinguishable in all stages of the Hebrew script. *Aleph* and *Šin* are very similar in the square "Aramaic" script. See the "Table of Alphabets" in the Hebrew *Encyclopedia Miqraʿ ith* (Jerusalem, 1950) vol. 1, col. 409-410, referred to below as EM. Both readings *ʾibbad* and *šibbar* are appropriate to the context; the latter verb, however, is used elsewhere in connection with *berīḥîm* (*Am.* 1:5) as is the synonym *giddēʿa* (*Isa.* 45:2; *Ps.* 107:16).

[21] *Cf.* AMHHH, pp. 140 ff.

2: 13 מָה אֲעִידֵךְ (Qere) has been interpreted, "whom shall I call as a witness for you" (Perles) but that would have been expressed by מָה אָעִיד לָךְ. The rendering "whom shall I make similar to you?" is based on regarding the verb as a derivative from the adverb עוֹד "still, yet." There is, however, no evidence for such a verb. The key to the understanding of the passage lies in recognizing the chiasmus of the four verbs: the first and fourth (אֲעִידֵךְ and אֲנַחֲמֵךְ) are parallel to each other, as are the second and the fourth (אֲדַמֶּה and אַשְׁוֶה). [22] The root means "strengthen." It occurs in Biblical Hebrew in the Polel (*Ps.* 146: 9) מְעוֹדֵד and in the Hithpael (*Ps.* 20: 9) נִתְעוֹדָד. In *Ben Sira* 4: 11 the root occurs in the same meaning in the Hiphil: חכמות למדה בניה ותעיד לכל מבינים בה exactly as in our verse[23]. On the equivalence of Hiphil and Polel, *cf. Ps.* 23: 3 נַפְשִׁי יְשׁוֹבֵב and *Ps.* 19: 8 מְשִׁיבַת נָפֶשׁ.

For *ʾaʿidēkh*, the reading *ʾeʿerōkh*, "can I compare," was proposed by J. Meinhold (*ZAW*, vol. 15, 1895, p. 286) and adopted by Hillers. It is, however, an impossibility in the context; in view of the other suffixes, it would need to be *ʾeʿerkhēkh*. This aside from the fact that the emendation ignores the chiastic structure of the verbs.

The repetition of the interrogative *māh* gives great power to the passage in Hebrew, which cannot be captured in translation, where the interrogative needs to be translated variously as "what" and "how." For a similar instance of the use of *māh* in a variety of meanings, *cf.* Gen. 44: 16: מַה נֹּאמַר מַה־נְּדַבֵּר וּמַה נִּצְטַדָּק "What shall we say, how shall we speak, how shall we justify ourselves?"

The stich גָּדוֹל כַּיָּם שִׁבְרֵךְ is a superb example of the Semitic rhetorical figure *talḥin*, which is to be distinguished from paronomasia. In this latter and more familiar rhetorical

---

[22] On this passage, see "A Note on Lamentations II 13" in *Journal of Theological Studies* (Oxford, 1933), vol. 34, pp. 162 f.

[23] So Israel Lévi, *The Hebrew Text of the Book of Ecclesiasticus*, (Leiden, 1904) p. 3, n. 1 and Glossary, p. 82, who renders the verb as "fortify," and M. H. Segal, *Sefer Ben Sira Hašālēm* (Jerusalem 5713 = 1953), p. 25.

figure, the writer chooses a word possessing one meaning
because it is similar in sound to another word. In *talḥin* the
author's choice of a particular word instead of a synonym is
dictated by his desire to suggest both meanings simultaneously
to the consciousness of the reader. The one serves as the
primary or dominant meaning, and the other as the secondary
concept, thus enriching the thought or emotion of the reader.
In our passage the poet has chosen the noun שֶׁבֶר for "destruction, calamity" out of many available synonyms because it
suggests the noun מִשְׁבָּר (*Jon.* 2: 4; *Ps.* 42: 8 a.e.) "breaker,
wave," which is particularly appropriate in this comparison
to the sea.

Generally, instances of *talḥin*, like most figures of speech,
are not translatable. Here it is possible to capture something
of the aura of the passage because of the existence in English
of the noun, "breaker, wave," by rendering the stich as:
"Thy break is great as the sea." For another instance, see note
on 1: 8 and reference there.

Our verse is therefore to be rendered:

> How shall I fortify you
> What shall I compare with you,
>> O daughter of Jerusalem?
> What shall I liken to you
>> And comfort you,
>> O virgin daughter of Zion?
> For thy break is great as the sea,
>> Who can heal you?

2: 15   For metrical reasons Haller deletes הָעִיר שֶׁיֹּאמְרוּ. The
passage is obviously a reminiscence of *Ps.* 48: 2, 3, on the basis
of which הָעִיר, which is needed for the sense, should be retained
and only the prosaic-שֶׁיֹּאמְרוּ deleted. The final distich is in
4: 2 (or 4: 3) meter, a basic form of the *kinah* rhythm:

הֲזֹאת הָעִיר כְּלִילַת יֹפִי // מָשׂוֹשׂ לְכָל־הָאָרֶץ

2: 17   אֲשֶׁר צִוָּה מִימֵי־קֶדֶם does not refer back to אִמְרָתוֹ
The passage is to be rendered:

> "That which he has commanded from of old,
> He has destroyed without pity."

The reference is to the Temple, the building of which God commanded. For the inverted word order, *cf.* 2:22:
אֲשֶׁר־טִפַּחְתִּי וְרִבִּיתִי אֹיְבִי כִלָּם

2:18　The opening stich צָעַק לִבָּם is extremely difficult. The suffix of *libbām* has no antecedent. It obviously cannot refer to the previously mentioned foes. The perfect *ṣā'aq* is not parallel to the other verbs that are in the imperative (*hōrīdiy*, etc.). Hence a variety of emendations have been proposed which are either graphically distant or unidiomatic or both: צַעֲקִי עֲלֵיהֶם (Ehrlich), צַעֲקִי לָךְ (Haller), צְעִי לִבֵּךְ = "turn your heart," on the basis of *Jer.* 48:12 (Perles), הֵמִי (Meek). [24]

We propose the reading צְקִי לִבֵּךְ אֶל אֲדֹנָי "pour out your heart to the Lord," which is an excellent parallel to stich c הוֹרִידִי כַנַּחַל דִּמְעָה. The error was induced because the author used the rarer synonym *yāṣaq* "pour" for the familiar *šāphakh*, which occurs in v. 19, שִׁפְכִי כַמַּיִם לִבֵּךְ. The imperative of the root *yaṣaq* צֹק occurs in *II Ki.* 4:41, the figurative use in *Isa.* 44:3. It may occur also in the enigmatic phrase צָקוּן לַחַשׁ in *Isa.* 26:16, generally rendered: "They poured out a silent prayer." [25]

The final *Kaph* of לִבֵּךְ was misread as a *Mem* since *Mem* and *Kaph* were graphically similar in both the early Hebrew-Canaanite alphabet and in the later square "Aramaic"

---

[24] Max Haller, *Die Fünf Megilloth Handbuch zum A. T.* (Tübingen, 1940), pp. 92-113; Th. J. Meek, "Commentary on Lamentations" in *Interpreters' Bible*, vol. 6 (New York-Nashville, 1956), pp. 3-40, *ad loc.*

[25] So most commentators, who see in it an apocopated form of יִצְקוּן, Another such *primae Yod* form occurs in רַד (*Jud.* 19:11). *Cf.* also other examples of aphaeresis such as תַּתָּה (*II Sam.* 22:41) for נָתַתָּה, קַח (*Ez.* 17:5) for לָקַח and קְחָם (*Hos.* 11:3) for לְקָחָם (so Kimhi). In favor of the view that these apocopated forms are remnants of popular speech, which tends to contract and slur over sounds (so König) rather than scribal errors (so Gesenius-Kautzsch, *Hebräische Grammatik*, 20th ed., Leipzig, 1889, sec. 18, 3a), is the existence of similar forms in medieval Payyetanic Hebrew, as e.g. גָּשׁ for נִגַּשׁ, קָץ for וַיִּיקַץ, etc.

script. [26] A familiar example occurs in *Ezek*. 3: 12 where, as Luzzatto pointed out long ago, בָּרוּךְ כְּבוֹד is an error for בְּרוּם. [27] When the unusual phrase צְקִי לִבֵּךְ (or צק לבם) went unrecognized, a scribe could easily insert an *Ayin* after the Ṣade. This could occur in one of two ways. It might be an unconscious scribal error, a virtual dittography, because of the similarity of these two letters in the square script. [28] The *MT* presents a clear-cut instance of the confusion of Ṣade and *Ayin* in *II Kings* 20: 4: העיר Kethib; חָצֵר Qere. [29] Or a scribe may have regarded צק as exhibiting an instance of the syncope of *Ayin*, which he proceeded to "restore." [30]

The poet apostrophizes the walls, and personifies the city, so that stich b is virtually an appositional genitive, "the wall, namely, Zion." Our verse now has a clear and unforced meaning:

Pour out your heart to the Lord	O wall of Zion!
Let flow your tears like a stream,	day and night!
Give yourself no rest,	your eyes, no respite!

The penchant for parallel-hunting, characteristic of contemporary scholarship, has impelled some scholars to delete the noun *homāth* on the ground that the figure of speech does not occur elsewhere; the principle of *difficilior lectio*, which supports the authenticity of MT, is ignored.

[26] Cf. the Tables of Alphabets in EM, col. 403-410, for the Mesha and Siloam inscriptions, the Samaria ostraca and the Lachi'h Letters for the earlier script and the Nash Papyrus, Nabatean, and 3rd century synagogical inscriptions for the later.

[27] Cf. *Ezek*. 10: 4 *vayārom kebhōdh Adonay mēʿal hakkerūbhīm*. For other instances of errors between *Mem* and *Kaph* and between *Mem* and the phonetically related *Beth*, see F. Delitzsch, *Lese und Schreibfehler im A. T.* (Berlin-Leipzig, 1920, pp. 114).

[28] *Cf. EM,.*col. 409-410, cited in note 13.

[29] For other instances, which must, however, be scrutinized critically, *cf.* Delitzsch, *op. cit.*, p. 110; A. S. Kennedy, *An Aid to the Textual Amendment of the O.T.*, (Edinburgh, 1924), p. 104.

[30] Examples of the elision of *Ayin* are preserved in *MT* in *Am.* 8: 8 ונשקה Kethib, וְנִשְׁקְעָה Qere; in *Josh.* 19: 3 f. בָּלָה for בַּעֲלָה (15: 29). *Cf.* also בְּי "please," for which the etymology proposed by the medievals = בְּעִי is still the most acceptable, and the proper name רוּת as equivalent to רְעוּת = "desire, willingness" (so in Pešita) as against עָרְפָּה "lit, turn the back, reject."

Perhaps to meet this objection, it has been suggested that the word in the text should be corrected to the Niphal of the root *nāḥam* and read *niḥemeth*, "repentant, remorseful" (so Hillers).

Actually, the bold figure in MT has its parallel in a moving passage in the Midrash, which, be it noted, is not a reminiscence of our passage. Commenting on Lam. 2:1, *Midrash Ekhah Rabbati* (and parallels) says: "Why does the verse read 'she weeps at night'? Because when a man weeps at night the very walls of the house *(kothlei habbayit)* and the planets in heaven weep with him." That a gifted writer will create original and striking modes of expression should be, but unfortunately often is not, a self-evident principle in Biblical exegesis. Cf. the Comm. on 3:41; 5:5 for other instances.

2:19 The noun *'ašmūrōth*, "watches," is distributive; hence, render the phrase not "at the beginning of the watches" (RSV), but "at the beginning of each watch (when the crier announces the time)." On this distributive use of the plural, cf. Jud. 12:7, 'he was buried *(beʿārēi)* in one of the cities of Gilead"; Isa. 50:4; Job 3:16; 40:29, and see Ges.-Kautzsch, sec. 124.

The verse exceptionally contains eight stichs instead of the usual six. Perhaps the two closing stichs are to be deleted as a seribal expansion, based upon 2:12.

2:21 שָׁכְבוּ לָאָרֶץ חוּצוֹת is difficult. The rendering "they lay in the dust of the streets" *(RSV)* is not possible even if we revoclize to read לָאָרֶץ. The metric pattern suggests also that לָאָרֶץ and חוּצוֹת are best regarded as a conflate of two readings. a) שָׁכְבוּ לָאָרֶץ and b) שָׁכְבוּ (בַּ)חוּצוֹת. In the two first distichs the opening stich receives three stresses because it consists of two longer words and the closing stich receives only two. Thus the verse exhibits the normal kinah rhythm 3:2 ‖ 3:2 ‖ 3:2:

שכבו לארץ ‖ נער וזקן
(חוצות)
בתולתי ובחורי ‖ נפלו בחרב
הרגת ביום אפך ‖ טבחת לא חמלת

2:22 The verb תקרא has the connotation of "gather."

Cf. *Pr.* 27: 16; [31] וְשֶׁמֶן יְמִינוֹ יִקְרָא "like one who seeks to gather
up in his right hand"; so also *Amos* 5: 8; 9: 6. The phrase
מְגוּרַי מִסָּבִיב is an excellent example of *talḥin*. The term
מְגוּרַי has been chosen rather than any of the synonyms for
"neighbors" or "my foes" such as שֹׂנְאַי אֹיְבַי, שְׁכֵנַי, because it
suggests the secondary meaning of "terrors," a meaning which
occurs in the identical phrase five times in *Jeremiah* (6: 25;
20: 3, 10; 46: 5; 48: 29) and once in *Psalms* (31: 12). The
opening distich of our verse is therefore to be rendered:
"You gather, as on a festival day, my neighbors (terrors)
round about." The aesthetic impact of the double sense of
the *talḥin* here is, of course, lost in translation.

[31] This interpretation of *qārā* was proposed by I. Eitan, *A Contribution to Hebrew Lexicography*, (New York, 1924).

INTRODUCTION — CHAPTER 3

Man's Yoke of Suffering

AS HAS ALREADY BEEN noted, this moving *kinah* differs radically from the *kinot* in chaps. 1, 2 and 4, both in form and in content. While the other elegies consist of a single alphabetic acrostic of three distichs, chapter 3 contains a triple alphabetic acrostic, each line consisting of a single distich. Even more important is the difference in theme. The other *kinot* in the book are concerned with the calamities of national destruction and exile, and are naturally couched in the plural in order to refer to the group. Chapter 3 begins in the singular, "I am the man who has seen affliction, under the rod of His wrath," and the singular predominates throughout the *kinah*. Accordingly, most scholars maintain that the chapter is the elegy of an individual. [19] On the other hand, substantial sections of the *kinah* here are written in the first person plural (vv. 40-48 and other passages), and are of such cosmic sweep as to suggest national foes rather than personal enemies:

> May You pursue them in wrath and destroy them
> from beneath the heavens of the Lord. (3: 66)

The concern in this *kinah* with the destiny of the nation bulks too large, quantitatively and qualitatively, to be ignored or excised as an interpolation.

In order to harmonize the singular and the plural passages, the effort has been made to interpret the singular collectively,

---

* See, *The Seventy-Fifth Anniversary Volume of The Jewish Quarterly Review*, pp. 267-286.

[19] So Haller, *Die Fünf Megilloth* (Tübingen, 1940), Smend.

as representing a personification of Zion or Judah [20]. This procedure cannot, however, do justice to several sections where the references unmistakably point to an individual human being, e.g., v. 27, "It is good for a man to bear a yoke in his youth" (see also vv. 35-36). As Hillers has acutely noted, the speaker in this section is a man, and not Mother Zion. Hence, other scholars maintain the view that this poem is concerned with an individual (so Stade, Budde). Not a few interpreters identify the man with a historical figure. Thus N. W. Porteous argues that "the man" is King Jehoiachin *(Rudolph Festschrift*, Túbingen, 1961, pp. 244 f.). Many more identify "the man" with Jeremiah (so Stade, Löhr, Budde, Rudolph, apparently also Meek and Hillers). However, this individualist interpretation cannot explain the plural passages in the poem. Nor is the integrity of the poem advanced by Kraus's view, followed by Hillers, that the "I" of vv. 52-66 is not the same as the "I" at the beginning of the poem.

Moreover, the time-honored critical procedure of atomizing the text and separating it into two distinct poems fails us completely here. Dividing the chapter into singular and plural sections would destroy the acrostic structure. Even more important, the singular and plural sections are closely articulated into one another, and the poet shifts from one to the other with no discernible pause. Thus, after a vivid picture of illness (v. 4) and perhaps imprisonment (v. 7), vv. 20-39 raise the question of God's goodness and man's suffering in terms of the individual. In v. 40 the answer, while still concerned with the individual, is couched in the plural: "Let us search and try our ways, and return to the Lord." It thus leads almost imperceptibly to the note of national sin and punishment in vv. 42-48 (note, "in the midst of the nations," v. 45; "the calamity of the daughter of my people," v. 48).

Finally, to describe the chapter as a *Mischgattung*, "a mixture of types," [21] simply indicates the existence of a problem but offers no clue to its solution.

[20] So Smend, Ehrlich, Eissfeldt *(Einleitung in das A. T.,* p. 547), Gottwald, Albrektsen.

[21] *Cf.* Gunkel-Begrich, *Einleitung in die Psalmen,* p. 400; W. Rudolph, *Die Klagelieder des Jeremias,* 2nd ed., (Göttingen, 1906) p. 45; also Haller, *op. cit.,* p. 105.

Two factors have hindered the full understanding of the content and the structure of this *kinah*. The first has been the failure to apply to our poem the concept of "fluid personality" which is basic to Biblical thought. The second has been the faulty exegesis of the crucial passage vv. 33-40, which has been made to yield a sense diametrically opposite to the poet's meaning. On the second factor, see the Commentary below.

With regard to the first, H. W. Robinson and O. Eissfeldt independently called attention to the phenomenon of "fluid personality" in dealing with the problem of the identity of "the Servant of the Lord" in Deutero-Isaiah.[22] The Servant songs have long proved difficult, since they contain some features that obviously refer to the people collectively and others that mirror individual traits. Hence neither the collective interpretation, which refers the poems to Israel, nor the various theories, which refer it to one or another individual [23], do justice to every detail in the Servant Songs. The point of departure is the Prophet's role as a teacher of the Exilic community, serving as the messenger of the God of Israel to his co-religionists. This position he identifies with the function which Israel as a people is destined to play among the nations. Hence the descriptions of the Servant contain both individual and collective features, with now one and now the other predominating. Rowley concludes a brief discussion on the identity of the Servant with this sound judgment: "It seems wiser, therefore, to adopt no simple individual or collective view. It is probable that the Servant is in part the personification of the mission of Israel, and in part the delineation of one who should embody its mission in himself ... the servant is both the community and the individual who

[22] *Cf.* H. W. Robinson, *The Cross of the Servant—A Study in Deutero-Isaiah* (London, 1926) and "The Hebrew Concept of Corporate Personality" in *Werden und Wesen des A.T.*, ed. J. Hempel, 1936, pp. 49 ff.; O. Eissfeldt, *Der Gottesknecht bei Deuterojesaia* (Halle, 1933); H. H. Rowley, *The Servant of the Lord and other Essays* (London 1952), esp. pp. 33 ff.; 38f.

[23]) Those suggested as prototypes for "the Servant of the Lord" include Zerubbabel, or some other scion of the Davidic house, Moses, Uzziah, Ezekiel, the martyr Eleazar of the Maccabean period, Cyrus, an anonymous contemporary of the prophet, whom he regarded as the Messiah, and the prophet himself.

represents it." [24] In North's summary, "the ebb and flow of Deutero-Isaiah's thought was from Israel to his own prophetic consciousness and back to Israel." [25]

The concept of "fluid personality" is generally assumed to be based on the idea of primitive psychology as propounded by Lévy-Brühl [26] and E. Durkheim. [27] In early thought the highly defined individualism characteristic of modern man had not yet emerged. Hence the individual is both representative of his group and merges and disappears within it. The source of this concept of "fluid personality" may perhaps be found in the psychological phenomenon of "identification" which psychoanalytical theory has highlighted in our time. This is defined as "the self-definition of the Ego in terms of some other person, initially the father or the mother . . . Identification is the mechanism underlying grouping . . . Each member of the group identifies himself with the others, via the prior identification of himself with the leader, who thus replaces the parent of the family group." [28]

Whatever the precise mechanism underlying "fluid personality," the existence of the phenomenon in biblical thought is beyond question. It is the key to such various aspects as the self-identification of the prophet with his God, so that he speaks of God now in the first person, and now in the third, according as he identifies or dissociates his personality from God. It explains the frequent shifting in the *Prophets* and the *Psalms* from the singular to the plural in referring to the people as a whole. It is particularly fruitful in dealing with the long-standing issue of the "I" in the *Psalms*, which scholars were wont to identify either with an individual or with the people, collectively viewed. For the Psalmist often speaks now in his own name as a distinct individual, then identifies himself with his party or group, and finally with the people

[24] *Cf.* his "Meaning of Sacrifice in O.T." in *Bulletin of John Rylands Library*, vol. 33, 1950, pp. 108 f.

[25] *Cf.* C. R. North, *The suffering Servant in Deutero-Isaiah* (Oxford, 1948), pp. 215 f.

[26] In his *How Natives Think* (1926).

[27] In his *Elementary Forms of the Religious Life* (1915).

[28] *Encyclopedia of the Social Sciences* (New York, 1946), vol. 11, p. 584 b.

of Israel. The movement from one position to the other cannot always be pinpointed with certainty. When "fluid personality" is taken into account, the division of psalms into brief fragments is seen to be unnecessary and methodologically unsound. This concept also explains the career and message of the prophet Hosea, whose personal experience in marriage is identified with the relationship of God and Israel.[29] This insight serves also to illumine such varied phenomena as the patriarchal history of Genesis [30] and the rhetoric of medieval Hebrew poetry.[31]

The concept of "fluid personality" supplies the key to the understanding of our *kinah*, which may well be described as a" Job lament." Here the poet begins with the contemplation of his personal lot and then wrestles with the problem of man's suffering. He then moves on to the tragic destiny of his people. Again he turns to his own sad condition, and finally ends with a prayer for retribution on his nation's foes. It is of the essence of "fluid personality" that it is often impossible to find the line of demarcation between the individual and the nation, since both aspects of the poet's concern are blended together.[32]

The *kinah* falls into five major sections:

A. *The poet's description of his troubles* (vv. 1-20). He has been stricken with illness (vv. 1-4) and may have suffered imprisonment (vv. 6-7). His neighbors have mocked him in his misery (v. 13). The source of all his suffering is the cause of all causes, namely God. The poet is brought to the threshold of despair. But like Job in his opening lament (chap. 3), the poet does not explicitly charge God with his suffering at the outset. Not until v. 18 is God's name mentioned.

---

[29] We have applied this idea to the problems of Hosea, chaps. 1-3 in "Hosea's Marriage and Message," *HUCA*, vol. 25, 1954, pp. 9-35, where the relevance of the concept to Biblical thought in general is also discussed at greater length.

[30] *Cf.* W. G. Dougherty, "The World of the Hebrew Prophets" in *Scriptures*, vol. 3, 1948, p. 98, cited in Gordis, *op. cit.*, *supra*, p. 18.

[31] *Cf.* Gordis, *op. cit.*, p. 19 for a striking instance from the *Diwan* of Todros Halevi Abulafia.

[32] A telling case in point is to be found in *Hos.* 2: 4, on which see the paper cited in note 29 above, pp. 12 f.

B. *The rebirth of faith* (vv. 21-30). Though weighted down by his misery, the poet recalls God's unceasing mercy. Man may undergo suffering for a brief period. Particularly in youth, when the power of temptation is strongest, a man's troubles help to chastise and discipline his spirit (vv. 27-28), but God does not permanently or willingly afflict His creatures (vv. 29-31).

C. *Man's suffering is not God's will* (vv. 31-38). Not God, but man, is the source of evil in the world. The poet's standpoint is very similar to that of Eliphaz (*Job* 5: 6, 7), who affirms that suffering is not rooted in the universe, but is the result of man's sinful actions:

> Evil does not grow out of the earth,
>   nor suffering sprout from the ground.
> It is man who gives birth to trouble
>   as the sparks fly upward.[33]

Since evil is not part of the cosmic order, and therefore neither inevitable nor eternal, man may hope to emerge from its toils. On the meaning of v. 38, which is crucial to the understanding of the passage, see the Commentary below.

D. *Return and regeneration* (vv. 39-47). Man may hope to escape from his troubles if he scrutinizes his actions, repents his sins, and returns to God. The theme of *t°shūbhāh* is basic to Biblical and post-Biblical thought. To cite two passages out of hundreds, from the prophets, "Take words with you and return to God";[34] and from the Rabbis: "If a man sees troubles coming upon him, let him scrutinize his actions."[35]

The same conception underlies the rabbinic term *yissūrīm*, "sufferings," lit. "chastisement, instruction." From the contemplation of his own personal misery, the poet imperceptibly passes over to the tragic condition of his people, which is the consequence of its rebelliousness against God (vv. 41-42). The people have been persecuted and murdered

---

[33] Reading with many moderns *yōlīd* for *yūlād*.
[34] *Hos.* 14:2.
[35] *Ber.* 5a: אם רואה אדם יסורים באים עליו יפשפש במעשיו

without mercy (vv. 43-44) and have become a subject of
scorn to all nations (vv. 45-46).

E. *A prayer for restoration* (vv. 48-64). The poet entreats
God for salvation. His basic concern here seems to be the
national disaster, yet there are some phrases that suggest
the individual (vv. 51, 53-54) rather than the group.

It is noteworthy that the various sections of the *kinah* do
not coincide with the introduction of new letters in the acrostic,
so that any effort to separate the individual-passages from
the group-passages is impossible. The two themes are closely
interwoven, particularly in vv. 20-21, 31-32, 39-40 and 48-49.

The unity of the *kinah* is psychological rather than logical.
The poet begins with a complaint, moves on to the recognition
of his sins as the cause of his troubles, and reaches the climax
of faith in his prayer for God's redemption. These themes of
suffering, sin and salvation are brought to bear both on his
individual situation and on the lot of his people with whom he
identifies himself as a faithful son.

3:5   Haller dismisses MT as hopeless. He emends the verse
to read, the acrostic notwithstanding כָּבֵד עָלַי עֻלּוֹ וַיָּנַקֵף רֹאשִׁי
and deletes וּתְלָאָה. Perles reads וַיַּקֵּף רֹאשִׁי תְלָאָה. The difficulty
resides in the combination of רֹאשׁ וּתְלָאָה, which is generally
rendered "gall and travail". We suggest that רֹאשׁ is to be
rendered "poverty"; cf. וְרִישׁ *Pr.* 28:19; 31:7; רֵישׁ *Pr.* 6:11;
10:15; 13:18; 24:34. The MT need not be revocalized, but
is a phonetic variant of רָאשׁ *Pr.* 30:8. On the interchange of
Sere and *Ḥolem* cf. מְרֵרָה (*Job* 16:13) and מְרוֹרָה "bitterness,
poison" (*Deut.* 16:13; Job. 20:14).[36] The MT is therefore to
be rendered:

"He has built and surrounded me with poverty and trouble."

3:11   The verb *sōrēr* is generally rendered "he has turned
aside," but the figure is much too weak for the context. Since it
is the only instance of the Polel in Biblical Hebrew, it is better to
treat the verb as a denominative of the noun *sīrīm*, "thorns"

---

[36] This phonetic interchange is attested in the pronunciation of the
Ḥolem as a *Sere* by Lithuanian Jews.

(Isa. 34:13; Nah. 1:10; Ecc. 7:6), and render "he has hedged my way with thorns." For this vivid figure of a man oppressed and confined, cf. Hos. 2:8, *lākhēn hin^enī sākh 'et darkēkh bassīrīm,* "behold, I am hedging in your path with thorns," as well as Job 3:23 and, in our chapter, v. 7 above.

The Hebrew hapax legomenon *vayyephaš^ehēnī,* "He has torm me in pieces," is entirely appropriate to one ripped apart by thorns as he seeks to make his way through them.

Note the plethora of metaphors to describe the enmity of God; God is a bear and a lion (v. 10), He blocks his way (vv. 9 and 11), He aims His arrows at him (vv. 12 and 13). The heaping up of metaphors, including "mixed metaphors," is a characteristic of Biblical poetry, as Psalms 23 and 48, and "the Allegory of Old Age" in Ecclesiastes (11:9-12:8), demonstrate. For this rhetorical usage in Biblical and Western literature, see our discussion in *The Book of God and Man,* Chicago, 1965, pp. 202 f.

3:14 For *'ammī,* "my people," the Masorah registers a Sebir, *'ammim, "peoples."* On this Masoretic category of Sebirin, which is still widely misunderstood, see *The Biblical Text in the Making,* pp. 226 f. The purpose of the Masoretic notation is to warn the scribe against adopting a suggested reading which may appear attractive. In our passage, the Sebir reflects the attempt to interpret the entire poem as referring to the whole people. On the interplay of personal and collective motifs in the chapter, see the Special Introduction.

3:16 The verb *hikhpišanī* is a hapax legomenon. It is generally derived from the Arabic *kafisa,* "to have a bent or crooked foot," and hence is rendered "he has made me cower in the ashes." It may be better to regard the verb as a phonetic variant of the Hebrew *kābhaš,* the primary, concrete meaning of which is "press, tread down, squeeze" (so the Aram., Syr., and Mish. Heb.; cf. Arabic *kabasa,* "press, squeeze"). The more usual sense of the verb, "conquer," is the abstract, secondary meaning. For the concrete use of the verb, cf. Mic. 7:19; for the theme, cf. Job 16:15b; 40:13.

3:18 The noun *neṣah* has been rendered "glory" or "endurance," the latter on the basis of the fàmiliar noun meaning "eternity, perpetuity." In our passage, it has also been treated

as a hendiadys with *tōḥaltī* in stich b, so that "my enduring and
my hope" = "my enduring hope" (so Hillers). Attractive as
this suggestion appears, a hendiadys would require the reverse
order, cf., Gen. 3:16, "your pain and your conception" =
"the pain of your conception"; Isa. 53:8a, etc.; for this rhetorical figure, see Gordis, in *Sepher Moshe Seidel* (Jerusalem,
5722 = 1962, pp. 263-66).

The noun *neṣaḥ* is perhaps better related to Isa. 63:3, 6,
"juice of grapes, blood," on the basis of the Arabic and
Ethiopic cognate *naḍaḥa* (dotted dad, undotted ha). Its meaning would be "juice, blood," hence "vitality"; cf. *lēaḥ* lit."
moisture, natural force." (Deut. 34:7); see also Job 21:24.

3:19   The imperative in MT, *zᵉkhōr*, has been regarded as
a problem by many commentators. However, the suggestion to
read a noun *zekher* or to interpret the form in MT as an infinitive and render "the memory of my wandering is worm-
wood" is unattractive. On the basis of the translation in LXX,
"I remember," many emend the text to read either *zākhartī* or
zākhōr ᵃnī, the infinitive absolute followed by a personal pronoun, hence "I remember." While the last two procedures are
possible, they are not necessary. MT may express a contrast
between v. 19, which calls upon God to remember the sufferer's
plight, and v. 20, in which the poet says that he himself has not
forgotten. Note the emphatic use of the infinitive absolute in
v. 19, and see the Translation.

3:20   On the alleged *tiqqun sophᵉrim* in stich b, see the
excellent discussion in Hillers, pp. 55 f. Not only is this passage
not cited in the older lists of *tiqqunei sophᵉrim,* but its precise
form is unclear. If the original reading is presumed to have been
naphšekhā, the stich would need to be rendered "Your soul is
bowed down on my account." If the original reading was
ᶜālekhā, the stich would mean, "my soul is bowed down on
Your account." Three considerations militate against either
assumption: (1) The resulting phrase would be without parallel
in Hebrew usage, while MT is strongly supported by Ps. 42:6,
7; 43:5, as Hillers correctly notes. (2) All the *tiqqunei sophᵉrim*
are designed to obviate statements felt to be an affront to the
dignity of God. Neither of the two suggested "original" read-

ings would be regarded as "irreverent" and therefore requiring a change of text. The idea that God suffers when man is in agony, which is deepened in post-Biblical mystical literature, is already articulated in the Bible; cf. Isa. 63:9. The alternative idea, that man suffers on God's account, is also clearly enunciated, as in Ps. 44:23. (3) Neither idea is appropriate to the context at this point, while, on the contrary, MT is eminently in place.

3:22 כִּי is asseverative:"indeed"; cf. *Gen.* 18:20. It is not to be deleted on metric grounds (ag. Haller), the verse being in perfect *kinah* rhythm (3:2). תָמְנוּ is a conflate of תַּמוּ and נִגְמְנוּ, as Perles has suggested.[37] The parallelism makes it clear that the former is the original reading.

3:22 The particle *ki* is asseverative in both stichs. The Masoretic *tamnū* may perhaps be explained as an erroneous dissimilation for the double consonant in *tammū*, "are ended." For a clear instance of this phonetic phenomenos cf. Dan. 6:24, where *lᵉhansaqāh* is an erroneous dissimilation of the double consonant in *lᵉhassāqāh*.

3:24 Haller changes אָמְרָה נַפְשִׁי to אָמַרְתִּי on metric grounds. The change is unnecessary. The basic principle of Hebrew metrics—one beat per thought-unit—is strikingly exhibited

---

[37] Conflation generally takes the form of two distinct readings incorporated into the text side by side. See comment on 2:9 and references there. On the other hand, two forms may be combined to create a grammatical *forma mixta* as in הָתְפָּקְדוּ (*Num.* 1:47; 2:33; 26:62; *I Ki.* 20:27) which combines *Hophal* הָפְקְדוּ and *Hithpael* הִתְפָּקְדוּ. The phenomenon of conflation constitutes irrefragable evidence that the function of Masoretic (and proto-Masoretic) activity was the preservation of the received text and wherever possible, the retention of variations from ancient and well-regarded manuscripts, not the improvement or correction of the Biblical text. See Gordis, The Biblical Text in the Making (Phila, 1937), where the evidence for this fundamental conclusion was first presented. So too, the phonetic system of Biblical Hebrew was not an invention of the Masoretes of the Middle Ages, as Kahle and his school had maintained, but an embodiment of the traditional pronunciation and morphology of Hebrew in the form it reached the Masoretic schools. See the important paper of E. Y. Kutscher, "Contemporary Studies in North-West Semitic," in *Journal of Semitic Studies*, vol. X, 1965, pp. 21-51.

here. אָמְרָה נַפְשִׁי which corresponds in meaning to אָמַרְתִּי
receives one beat, so that the verse is in 3:2 rhythm.

3:26 While the general sense is clear, the plethora of
Vavs creates a syntactic problem. Perles reads טוּבוֹ יָחִיל
וְדָמַם "he awaits his goodness and is silent." Haller's emendation is preferable טוֹב וְיוֹחִילוּ דוּמָם. However his change of the
verb from *ḥīl, mediae Yod* to *yāḥal, primae Yod* is unnecessary.
The interchange of the two weak conjugations is common, cf.
נוּק and ינק; בוש and the Hiphil הוֹבִיש, etc. It is also well
attested in Mishnic Hebrew.[38] All that is needed is to move
the Vav of וְדוּמָם to the preceding vocable and read טוֹב וְיָחִילוּ
דוּמָם, "It is good that men wait expectantly for the Lord's
saving power." On the change of number in the passage, note
that v. 25a is in the plural, 25b in the singular, 26a is again
in the plural, and 27 again in the singular.

3:28 כִּי נָטַל עָלָיו is generally rendered, "when He has laid
it upon him," but both the subject and the object are un-
expressed. While the meaning "cast, place" occurs (*II Sam.*
24:12), this has been challenged by some scholars. On the
other hand, the significance "bear, carry" is better attested.
Cf. *Isa.* 40:5 and particularly *Isa.* 63:9 where it is parallel to
נָשָׂא. Read therefore with Pešita עָלוֹ and render, "when he
bears his yoke."

3:28 On the other hand, the passage may exhibit the
pathetic use of the preposition *'al* (cf. BDB, s.v. *'al*, II, l, d,
p. 753b) and the object may be understood, so that no change
in the text would be required: "when he carries it (i.e. the
yoke) upon himself."

---

[38] Cf. Ch. Yalon, *Mābhŏ' Leniqqūd Hamišnāh* (Jerusalem, 1964),
pp. 165-170.

The crucial passage following is to be rendered:

3:31 For the Lord will not reject forever.
   32 If He brings grief, He will have mercy
       according to the abundance of His love.
   33 For He does not afflict out of His own will
       nor bring grief to the sons of men.
   34 To crush beneath the earth
       all the prisoners of the earth,
   35 to pervert a man's case
       is against the desire of the Most High.
   36 To subvert a man in his cause
       the Lord does not think proper.
   37 Who has commanded that it came to pass—
       The Lord has not ordained it!
   38 Not from the mouth of the Most High has it issued
       to bring suffering to a good man.
   39 Why should a living man complain,
       a human being, about his punishment?
   40 *A man should rather say,*
       "Let us search and examine our ways
       and return to the Lord!"

3:34. Some commentators have found this v. and those following syntactically difficult. Thus Hillers believes that vv. 34-36 "do not make a sentence." He therefore attaches the infinitives to the verbs in v. 33, rendering them: "Because He does not . . . afflict them, by crushing . . . denying . . . twisting." In his discussion, he himself is constrained to describe the passage several times as "odd" (pp. 57 f.). A better approach is to treat vv. 34 and 35 as the object of *'adōnai lō' rā'āh* in 36b: "to crush . . . the Lord does not approve" (RSV), "The Lord does not mind it" (Rudolph). However, this interpretation has not been more widely adopted, because there still remain the minor problem of 35b and the major difficulty of v. 38, on which see the notes following.

3:35-37 This entire passage has been misunderstood, largely, but not entirely, because of the difficulties of v. 38. The basic theme has already been adumbrated in v. 33, where

מִלִּבּוֹ means "willingly, of his own volition," cf. *Num.* 16:28 מִלִּבִּי. The poet declares that man's suffering is not due to the will of God but to man's own wrong-doing. Scholars have generally failed to recognize that the three verses, 35-37 are parallel in structure as well as in content, the second stich in each being the predicate of the first. Thus נֶגֶד פְּנֵי עֶלְיוֹן (v. 35) is not be rendered "in the presence of the All High" but "is against the face, i.e., the desire of the All High." On the "face of God" as representing his favorable presence, cf. *inter alia Ex.* 33:15, אִם אֵין פָּנֶיךָ הֹלְכִים, etc. In v. 37, אֲדֹנָי לֹא רָאָה = "the Lord does not find proper, does not approve." On the meaning of the verb, cf. our note on 1:10. In v. 36 אֲדֹנָי לֹא צִוָּה is not a circumstantial clause meaning "unless the Lord commanded it," but like the verses preceding and following, the predicate of the opening stich. For our rendering of the entire passage, see the preceding page.

3:35   It is a truism that biblical Hebrew did not develop a technical theological vocabulary. The term *pānim* is functionally equivalent to the philosophic term "essence, nature." Thus in Ex. 33:20, "You cannot see My face, for no man can see Me and live," and *ibid.*, v. 23, "You may see My back parts, but My face may not be seen," the meaning is virtually equivalent to the theological formulation that God's attributes are accessible to man, but not His essence.

Hence stich b = "is against the nature, essence, of the All High." The thought is rendered more freely in the Translation by the word "desire." The stich, which is the predicate, is parallel, in meaning as well as in function, to 36b and 37b. For another possible instance of this meaning of *pānim*, cf. 4:16.

3:38   The usual rendering of this crucially difficult and important verse is: "From the mouth of the Most High has there not gone forth (or does there not go forth) evil and good?" (SRV, Haller, Perles) The difficulties of this interpretation are manifold:

1. While the reading of the entire verse as a question is not ruled out, it is rendered doubtful by the absence of any sign of the interrogative.

2. On this view, the poet would be emphasizing that God is the source of both good and evil. It is therefore scarcely congruent with v. 36, which declares that God does not approve the perversion of a good man's cause and the suffering which he necessarily sustains as a result.

3. In the larger context of the *kinah*, which emphasizes the mercy of God (vv. 22-25), one would not expect the stress upon God as the source of evil in the world, however valid the idea may be theologically in other settings.[39]

4. Most decisively, the combination of a feminine plural and a masculine singular, in הָרָעוֹת וְהַטּוֹב is impossible Hebrew. We should expect either רַע וָטוֹב or הָרָעוֹת וְהַטּוֹבוֹת.

The solution to the problem is to be found in Ehrlich's brilliant emendation: מִפִּי עֶלְיוֹן לֹא תֵצֵא הָרַע אֶת הַטּוֹב "Not from the mouth of the Most High issues (the decision) to bring suffering on the righteous man." For the use of the feminine verb, תֵצֵא with an infinitive as its subject, see *Jer.* 2:17: הֲלוֹא זֹאת תַּעֲשֶׂה לָּךְ עָזְבֵךְ אֶת ה׳ אֱלֹהַיִךְ. v. 38 now expresses the same idea as vv. 35, 36 and 37. In the face of his calamities (vv. 1-20) the poet reminds himself of God's mercy (vv. 21-32), because God does not willingly afflict His children, nor does He oppress men or pervert their judgment with Him. Strong in his faith, the suffering poet declares that man's troubles are to be laid at man's door and not to be imputed to his Maker. Cf. *Job* 5:6, 7, already referred to. The term *rībh*, like *mišpāt*, is forensic in origin and is used to refer to a legal contest of God with man (*Isa.* 3:13; *Am.* 7:4; *Mic.* 6:1, 2), and of man against God (*Job* 9:3; 10:2; 13:8, 19; 23:6; 33:13; 40:2).

3:39 The rendering, "Why should a living man murmur, a man because of his sins?" (so Gottwald) is not merely irrelevant to the context but essentially meaningless—to be unhappy about one's sins is the beginning of virtue and moral

---

[39] Thus in the saga of the Exodus, God "hardens the Pharaoh's heart," since He is the ultimate source of all events. *Deutero-Isaiah* categorically affirms that God "fashions light and creates darkness, makes peace and creates evil" (*Isa.* 45: 7), but this is part of the struggle against the dualism of Zoroastrianism.

restoration! Rudolph and Haller emend the text to read יְהִי גְבִיר עַל חֲטָאָיו, "Let man be master of his sins," but the emendation, which makes the verse a combination question-and-answer and destroys the parallelism, is unnecessary.

As Kimhi noted (followed by AV, SRV, Meek), חֵטְא means "the consequence of sin, i.e., punishment." We may compare the use of עָוֹן and חַטָּאת in 4:6, עָוֹן in *Gen.* 4:13, אַשְׁמָה and the verb אָשֵׁם (*Lev.* 4:3, 13, 22, 27; *Jer.* 2:1).[40] There is a profound philosophic and religious truth in the Hebrew semantic process, by which an act and its consequence are expressed by the same term. Cf. יָגַע יְגִיעַ "labor" (*Isa.* 55:2; *Job* 10:3; 39:11, 16), which, in fact, more often means "the result of labor, wage, reward." (*Isa.* 45:14; *Ez.* 23:29; *Hos.* 12:9; *Hag.* 1:11; *Ps.* 78:46; 128:2; 109:11; *Job* 20:18), and such nouns as חַיִל "strength, ability, cleverness" (e.g., *Gen.* 47:6; *Ex.* 18:21; *Pr.* 12:4; 31:10), which develops the meaning of "wealth, that which is acquired through strength or ability" (e.g., *Gen.* 34:29; *Isa.* 8:4; 10:14; 30:6; *Job* 5:5; 15:29) and פֹּעַל, פְּעֻלָּה "work, deed", which also means "recompense, wage, i.e., the result of labor" (*Lev.* 19:13; *Isa.* 49:4; 61:8; *Jer.* 22:13; *Pr.* 10:16; *Job* 7:2).

For a fuller discussion of the semantics involved in this identification of an act or quality with its consequence, with particular reference to the root *ʿāmāl* in Koheleth, cf. *KMW*, 3rd edition, Supplementary Note D, pp. 418-20.

---

[40] The traditional renderings of *ʾāšam* in *Lev.* chap. 4 as "sin," "be guilty," (AV, RV) are meaningless, since the offender is previously described as having done "all of the things that the Lord has command-ed not to be done." Nor is the rendering "incur blame" satisfactory. The entire chapter deals with sins committed unwittingly. Now how can the individual become aware that he has violated the will of God and must bring a sin-offering? In one of two ways: either he learns that he has sinned by becoming conscious of what he has done un-wittingly ("his sin is made known to him", vv. 14, 23, 28), or he experiences personal suffering which he sees as Divine punishment (vv. 13, 22, 27). He thus is led to examine his actions and discover his offence. In the case of "the anointed priest," his sins may bring punishment upon the entire people (*leʾašmath hāʿām*, v. 3). Note the use of *ʾō* in vv. 23 and 28; the *Vav* in v. 14 *venōdeʿāh* is to be rendered "or", as in *Ex.* 21:16, 17 and often, see BDB *Lexicon, s.v. Vav.* 1, d (p. 252 b).

3:40 This verse is the conclusion of the section. Since sin is human in origin, we have only to scrutinize our actions and return to God in order to be saved from suffering. The verse introduces a virtual quotation, hypothetical in character: *A man should rather say*, "Let us search and examine our ways, etc." [41]

The entire passage now presents a coherent view of life appropriate to a deeply afflicted soul, which, in spite of its troubles, has retained its steadfast faith in God's goodness, and thus is able to bear its trials with hope and courage.

3:41 נִשָּׂא לְבָבֵנוּ אֶל כַּפָּיִם is emended by Haller and Meek to עַל כַּפָּיִם on the basis of LXX, P, V, and rendered, "Let us lift up our hearts upon (or along with) our hands." Meek notes that this expression has no parallel in Hebrew. Actually, the figure is strange to the point of impossibility. Moreover, the consonantal change from 'el to 'al is unnecessary in view of *Joel* 2:13; 2:3 קִרְעוּ לְבַבְכֶם וְאַל בִּגְדֵיכֶם "Rend your hearts and not your garments." This striking parallel suggests that we read here נִשָּׂא לְבָבֵנוּ וְאַל כַּפֵּינוּ "Let us lift up our hearts. and not our hands, to God in heaven." On the scribal confusion of נו and final *Mem*, cf. *Josh.* 5:1, עברנו *Kethib*, עָבְרָם Qere and *Ps.* 12:8 where תִּצְּרֶנּוּ is parallel to תִּשְׁמְרֵם and obviously the same person is required in both suffixes.

3:51 The MT is extremely difficult, but it remains superior to all the proposed emendations, that may be studied in the Commentaries. The verse may perhaps be understood as follows: lit. "my eye (cf. vv. 48, 49) has acted severely to me, because of (the fate of) the daughters of my city." This may be rendered freely, "what I have seen has caused me anguish, because of the

---

[41] On the importance of quotations without a *verbum dicendi*, see R. Gordis, "Quotations as a Literary Usage in Biblical, Rabbinical and Oriental Literature," in *HUCA*, vol. 22, 1949, and see p. 194 for the hypothetical use of virtual quotations. For an instance in Biblical Hebrew, *cf. Ecc.* 4:8: וּלְמִי אֲנִי עָמֵל וּמְחַסֵּר אֶת נַפְשִׁי מִטּוֹבָה "*A man does not say*, 'For whom do I toil?'" For an apposite instance in Mishnic Hebrew, see *M. Kethuboth* 13:3 אמר אדמון מפני שאני זכר הפסדתי Admon said, "*A man might argue*, 'Because I am a male child, shall I lose.'"

lot of the maidens of my city." On *'ālal,* "act severely," cf. Lam. 1:22; Ex. 10:2; Nu. 22:29; Jud. 19:25, etc., and the noun *'ᵃlīlāh,* "evil deed" (Ezek. 14:23; 20:43, and often).

3:53 The verb *ṣāmᵉthū* is best interpreted here, not in its secondary, abstract meaning "put an end to, exterminate," but in its primary, concrete sense "compress, crush" which occurs in Mishnaic Hebrew, as, e. g., *ṣāmᵉthāh yādō,* "his hand was crushed" (B. Baba Kamma 85b).

By giving the verb in stich b, *vayyaddū,* a pluperfect meaning, we derive excellent sense for the v.: "They smashed me in the pit, having cast rocks upon me." Or the two stichs may be construed as a *hysteron proteron,* in which the chronological and logical order is reversed to put the later but more important act first. Cf. *na'ᵃseh wᵉnišmā'* (Ex. 24:7); *qiyyᵉmū wᵉqibbelū* (Est. 9:27), and see our treatment of this rhetorical figure in *Sepher Moshe Seidel* (Jerusalem, 1962).

3:56 שָׁמַעְתָּ is a clear example of the precative perfect, "You must surely hear our voice." In the second stich Perles emends לְשַׁוְעָתִי to לִישׁוּעָתִי, "My salvation", in order to bring it into harmony with לְרַוְחָתִי which occurs in *Ex.* 8:11, (הָרְוָחָה) in the meaning of "respite." However, this reading would create a very poor connection with "do not hide your ear" in stich a. While the Masoretic text is thoroughly in place. לְרַוְחָתִי is to be rendered "my groaning", lit. "my heavy breathing" Cf. the Syriac *rāḥ,* "breathe" and the Arabic and Ethiopic cognates. The verse is to be rendered:

"You must surely hear my voice

Do not hide your ear from my groaning, from my cry." The Lamedh is the Lamedh of reference, lit. "with respect to." [42]

3:57-62 Meek, who denies the existence of the precative perfect, renders קָרַבְתָּ frequentatively "you were wont to come near." He similarly gives a pluperfect sense to all the perfect verbs in vv. 57, 58, 61 and 62. Actually, there is no reason to reject a usage, which is in thorough harmony with

[42] *Cf.* the detailed treatment of the preposition in BDB *Lexicon, s.v. Lamedh* 5, e (p. 514, a, b).

the character of Hebrew tenses, and is well illustrated in other Semitic languages as well.[43] In v. 59b the imperative שָׁפְטָה is parallel to the perfect רָאִיתָה. The Septuagint reading "You judged," which Haller accepts, is an example of "levelling," an effort to bring an exceptional form into harmony with the rest of the passage. Moreover, it would be a striking disproportion to have a long description of God's mercies in the past (vv. 56-62) followed by a much briefer plea for His help in the agonizing present (vv. 63-66). The pluperfect rendering of the verbs is particularly far-fetched and cumbersome in vv. 60, 61, while rendering the verbs as imperatives gives a natural and unforced meaning to the passage.

This entire concluding section of the *kinah* is a characteristic psalmic plea for God's help, expressed through the precative perfect, because of the poet's strong faith that help will be forthcoming. The verbs are all to be rendered as imperatives or imperfects, "You will come near" or "come near," etc.

3:63 The two opening nouns, *šibhtām v*ᵉ*qīmātām*, are a merismus, equivalent to "all the time." Specifically, the terms refer to periods of inactivity and of labor. Cf. the familiar passage in Deut. 6:7, "when you sit in your house and when you walk on your way," and for a more exact parallel, Ps. 139:2, "You know my sitting down and my rising up." Note also the technical Mishnaic phrases *šēbh v*ᵉ*ʾal taʿaseh*, "lit., sit and do not do, i.e. refrain from action," and *qūm vaʿaśēh*, "rise up and act" (B. Ber. 20a; Erub. 100a). The poet complains that he has been the butt of their mockery both during their leisure time and in their working hours.

3:65 מְגִנַּת לֵב is an ancient crux. The root *gānan*, "protect," is of no help. The passage is frequently translated "oppression," an *ad hoc* rendering. Perles emends to מִיַּת לֵב, which he renders "weakness of the heart." Targum renders תבירות לבא "heartbreak." We believe that the phrase is to be

---

[43] We may adduce the traditional Islamic phrase used after the name of the prophet Mohammed, *ṣalla ʿallahu ʿalaihi wasallama*, "May God pray for him and give him peace," where both verbs are in the perfect.

interpreted in the light of the Arabic مجان the Syriac ܡܓܢ "empty, free." The word occurs in Biblical Hebrew in *Pr.* 6:11, where אִישׁ מָגֵן is parallel to מְהַלֵּךְ "wayfarer" and means "a beggar, a destitute person." מְגִנַּת לֵב would therefore mean "emptiness of heart, lack of understanding." We may compare the common Wisdom phrase חֲסַר לֵב "lacking understanding" (*Pr.* 6:32; 7:7; 9:4; 10:13; 11:12; 12:11; 17:18; 28:16; also *Ecc.* 10:3). The Arabic parallel "derangement of the mind" which Meek cites has a similar meaning. Note also תִּמְהוֹן לֵבָב "bewilderment of the mind, madness," (*Deut.* 28:28) and תִּמָּהוֹן (*Zec.* 12:4), both parallel to שִׁגָּעוֹן "madness." The verse is to be translated: Give them derangement of the mind; your curse be upon them."

3:66 Perhaps the ultimate in moral blindness is the comment of Haller on this verse. Commenting upon this imprecation pronounced by the poet upon his foes, Haller says, constitutes *einen für der Christen beinahe unverträglichen Misston,* "This is for a Christian, a virtually unbearable dissonance." This in a commentary published under Hitler in Nazi Germany in 1940, with the stench of the crematoria filling the land. Such sensitivity to unpleasant words coupled with indifference to brutal actions marks the last word in sanctimoniousness and moral obtuseness. Haller would have done well to remember *Job* 13:5 and *Mat.* 7:4.

4:1 The verb *yū'am* has been emended to *yizzā'em,* "is hated" (Ehr.), or to *yū'abh,* "is abominated," from a presumed Hebrew root (cf. the Comm. on 2:1; so Hillers), on the ground that (a) gold does not tarnish or lose its luster; and (b) that elsewhere gold is always mentioned for its value and not for its brightness. On the legitimacy of a poet's striking out for an original figure of speech, see the Comm. on 2:1. The power of the metaphor derives precisely from the fact that gold, unusally impervious to tarnishing, here loses its luster. In stich b, the verb *yišneh* is changed to *yissānē'* (Ehr., Hillers), but the emendation is inferior to MT—conceivably gold may be despised, but it is not likely to be hated except by rare saints. For the meaning of MT, see the Translation.

For a discussion of *'abnēy qōdeš*, see J. A. Emerton, in *ZATW*, Vol. 79, 1967, pp. 233-36. The phrase "holy jewels" does not refer to the stones of the temple (so also Hillers), but to the young men, "Zion's children," v. 2. The noun *qōdeš* may here carry the connotation of "God's special property," as in Ps. 114:2.

4:3 On the emphatic *Lamed* of *l^e'akhzar* (Arabic *la;* Akkadian *lu*), cf. Isa. 32:1b; Ps. 32:6; Ecc. 9:4; II Chr. 7:21; and see I. Eitan, in *AJSL*, vol. 45, 1928, p. 202; *KMW*, pp. 294 f.

4:5 Stich a, which consists of two longer words, הָאֹכְלִים לְמַעֲדַנִּים receives three beats because of the exigencies of the *kinah* meter (3:2), thus parallelling stichs c and d.

4:6 As was noted above, on 3:39, עָוֹן and חַטָּאת mean "punishment", (so Kimhi); not "sin" (ag. Meek). *Ez.* 16:47-50 which he adduces, contains a catalog of Sodom's specific sins (vv. 47-50). Here it is the calamity and not the offense with which the poet is concerned.

In the closing stich, Thenius interprets "no one wrung his hands over her." Haller emends to read, לֹא חָלוּ בָהּ יְלָדִים, which he translates "though children did not suffer there." The verb חָלוּ is generally associated with the familiar Hebrew root *ḥūl*, "dance, whirl." The root in our passage is probably an independent homonym and means "fall, descend." It occurs in יָחֻלוּ עַל רֹאשׁ יוֹאָב *II Sam.* 3:29; cf. also *Jer.* 23:19 = 30:23. It is common in rabbinic usage in the meaning "fall on, take effect" as e.g. *Meg.* 1:1 חָל לִהְיוֹת; *B. Shebuot* 25a. The distich means "no human hands descended upon her." Unlike Jerusalem, Sodom was destroyed directly by God without human intervention. Cf. "a house not built by hands."

4:7 The noun *gizrāthām*, which cannot be associated with the use of the word in Ezek. 41:12 ff.; 42:1 f., has no satisfactory etymology in Hebrew or in the cognate languages. It is generally rendered "cutting or polishing (of the form)". On the basis of the comparison in the v. with *sappir*, "lapis lazuli," and on the basis of various Sumerian, Akkadian, and Egyptian pass-

ages, Hillers suggests that either "beard" or "eyebrows" would
be an appropriate meaning for the noun.

However, the passage speaks of the physique as a whole
rather than of any specific organ. Indeed, one would expect
a hyperbolic praise of the beauty of the young men in general, rather than a comparison with the color of one bodily
feature. Thus, in Song of Songs 5:11, the lover is dark-haired,
but his beard is compared to fine gold. It would, therefore, seem
preferable to interpret our noun from the root "cut, carve," and
to give it the general meaning "carved shape, form"; cf. the
noun *tō'ar* in v. 8.

4:9   The second stich שֶׁהֵם יָזֻבוּ מְדֻקָּרִים מִתְּנוּבוֹת שָׂדָי is
very difficult. It is generally rendered, "for they pine away
stricken, for want of the fruits of the field." However, זוב
can scarcely mean "pine away." Meek, following Ehrlich,
emends יָזֻבוּ to יְזוֹנוּ and renders, "for they can feed, though
wounded, on the fruits of the field." The emendation is
uncalled for. It is necessary to recognize here a special feature
of Biblical poetry. In exceptional cases, a phrase will be
violently contracted in order to maintain the meter pattern.
An instance occurs in *Isa.* 66:3c מַעֲלֵה מִנְחָה דַּם חֲזִיר, Here
the prophet is arraigning those who go through the forms of
traditional piety, while committing every religious and
moral offence, and compares them to transgressors of the law.
Stichs a, b and d are clear:

a. He who slaughters an ox is like one who kills a man,

b. He who sacrifices a lamb is like one who breaks a dog's
neck . . .

d. He who offers up frankincense is like one who blesses
an idol.

Obviously, stich c must correspond in form to the others,
but it has no verb in the second half. It is clear that we have
an elipsis. A verb, which was omitted for metric reasons here,
must be understood: "He who offers a cereal offering is
like one who offers swine's blood."

A similar elipsis occurs in the closing stich of our verse.
מִתְּנוּבוֹת שָׂדָי means "he *who dies for lack* of the fruits of the

field." As in *Isa.* 66:3, the meaning is clear because of the earlier distich to which it is parallel. זוב is the regular term for "blood flow" (Lev. 15:2, 19, 25). The particle שֶׁ is the relative pronoun "who" like *'ašer, cf. Job* 29:25, כַּאֲשֶׁר אֲבֵלִים יְנַחֵם "like one who leads a camel-train," [44] *Ecc.* 9:2 כַּאֲשֶׁר שְׁבוּעָה יָרֵא "he who swears is like one who fears an oath."

Our passage is therefore to be rendered:

> Happier were the victims of the sword
>> than the victims of hunger;
> they whose blood flowed, being stabbed,
>> than those who perished for lack of the fruits of
>> the field.

In the Hebrew, the *kinah* rhythm, which it is impossible to recapture in translation here, is perfect 3:2 // 3:2, thanks to the elipsis.

Dāqar "stab," is always associated with the sword.

4:10   הָיוּ לְבָרוֹת לָמוֹ is generally rendered "they (i.e., the children) became their food," on the basis of *bārāh* (*II Sam.* 12:17, *Ps.* 69:22). A far better view is to see in *lebhārōt* the name of a demon or vampire known from Akkadian folk-lore.[45] It occurs in the Akkadian text "I Will Praise the Lord of Wisdom" (Column III reverse, 11.7.8):

> "The countless demons he sent back to Ekur (i.e., the underworld)
> The demon Labartu he knocked down, he drove her straight
> to the mountain (of the underworld)." [46]

Our passage is therefore to be rendered, "They (i.e., the compassionate women) became vampires to them (their own children)."

[44] The evidence for this translation will be found in our projected *Commentary on Job.* Provisionally, see our rendering in *The Book of God and Man: A Study of Job* (Chicago, 1965), p. 281.

[45] This suggestion was advanced by Perles and M. L. Margolis, but has unaccountably been ignored or dismissed.

[46] The text is available in a translation by R. H. Pfeiffer in J. B. Pritchard, *Ancient Near Eastern Texts Relating to the O.T.* (Princeton. 1950), p. 436 b.

Since the Akkadian noun is now correctly read *lamaštu,* the identification with our vocable has been generally surrendered and the older interpretation reinstated. For the emphatic Lamed which this rendering presupposes, see the Comm. on 4:3.

4:14 This verse and the preceding are in alternate parallelism, a, b // a¹b¹:

v. 13   Because of the sins of her prophets
        the transgressions of her priests,
    who pour out in her midst
        the blood of the righteous,

v. 14   they (the prophets) now wander blind through the
                          streets;
        they (the priests) are defiled by blood,
      So that no one can touch
        their garments.

The closing distich is to be scanned 3:2 as follows:

בְּלֹא יוּכְלוּ יִגָּעוּ // בִּלְבוּשֵׁיהֶם

As we have noted several times, the poetic caesura does not coincide with the logical pause. בלבושיהם, as a long word, receives two beats. The finite verb יגעו, after the auxiliary יוכלו represents one characteristic Hebrew mode of expressing the complementary infinitive, by using a finite verb instead of the infinitive construct: *Cf. Deut.* 1:5 הוֹאִיל מֹשֶׁה בֵּאֵר אֶת הַתּוֹרָה הַזֹּאת; *Hos.* 5:11 הוֹאִיל הָלַךְ אַחֲרֵי צָו, as against *I Sam.* 12:22, נִגְאָלוּ—הוֹאִיל ה' לַעֲשׂוֹת אֶתְכֶמְלוּ לָעָם is a conflate of the *Pual* גֹּאֲלוּ and the *Niph'al* נִגְאֲלוּ See note on 3:22.

4:15 This v. offers problems both with regard to its meaning and its form. The verb *naṣū* in MT, if correct, is a hapax legomenon. It is generally given the meaning "fly," both because of its proximity to *nāʿū,* "wander," and the noun *nōṣāh,* "plumage." In view of the difficulty of the verse, it is uncertain whether the two words *'ām^erū baggōyim* are to be read together or are to be assigned to stichs c and d respectively. In favor of reading *baggōyim* with stich d and rendering "they shall dwell among the nations no longer," are such passages as 1:3 and

4:20, "in his shadow we shall live among the nations." The verb *'ām^eru* in the 3rd person plural is impersonal: "men said" as, e. g., Gen. 29:8 and often. Metric considerations also favor this stichometry. The verse is not in the usual 3:2 pattern, but in an acceptable variation of the *Qinah* meter (see the Introduction); it may be scanned as 4:4 ‖ 3:3:

> *sūrū tāmē' qār^e'u lāmō   sūrū sūrū 'al tiggā'ū*
> *kī nāsū gam nā'ū 'ām^erū   baggōyim lō' yōsīphū lāgur.*

The verse is to be rendered:

> "Turn away, you are unclean," men called to them,
> "Turn away, turn away, do not touch us!
> Indeed, they have wandered far away," men said,
> "Among the nations they can live no longer."

The quotation continues in v. 16a, b. For the context, see the Comm. on the next verse.

4:16 Stichs a and b, that describe God's disfavor with Judah, are completely unrelated to stichs c and d, which depict the foe's lack of deference for priests and elders. It, therefore, seems preferable to interpret stichs a and b as the conclusion of the words spoken (*'ām^erū*) by men in v. 15, who proceed to explain that the catastrophe has befallen Judah because it has lost the favor of its God. Similarly, during the siege of Jerusalem by Sennacherib, the Assyrian general Rabshakeh tells the Judahites that their God is angry with them and that it is He who has sent the Assyrians to punish them (II Ki. 18:22, 25 = Isa. 36:7, 10; cf. also 19:10 ff. = Isa. 37:10 ff.).

On *pānīm* "the active presence, hence, the will of God," cf. our note on 3:35, SRV translates well here, "the Lord Himself." Generally "the face of God" is used in a favorable context, as in *Ex.* 33:14, 15 and in the Priestly Benediction (*Num.* 6:24-26). It is however also used negatively, where its hostile sense is made clear by the context. *Cf. Ps.* 21:10. לְעֵת פָּנֶיךָ "in the time of your wrathful presence"; *Ps.* 34:17 פְּנֵי ה' בְּעֹשֵׂי רָע "the presence of God is against the evil-doers."

4:17 The Kethib, *'ōdenāh*, has the third person feminine plural suffix, relating to *'ēinēinū*, "our eyes are still, etc." The Qere, *'ōdēnū*, with the first person plural suffix, means "we are still, etc." The Kethib would here seem preferable. It appears in a fragment from Qumran 5Q Thr^b.

The verse pictures a desperate, hysterical hope of the people for some deliverer during the final agonies of the siege of Jerusalem, but none was forthcoming.

4:18   The verse in MT contains five stichs instead of the four characteristic of this elegy. Stich c, *qārabh qiṣṣēnū* and stich e, *ki bhā' qiṣṣēnū* are obvious doublets that have been conflated into the text. One of them is superfluous and its removal improves the sense, besides restoring the original four-stich meter pattern.

The difficult opening clause can scarcely mean "they capture our steps." Read the first word with a *Reš* instead of a *Daled*: צָרוּ צְעָדֵינוּ מִלֶּכֶת בִּרְחֹבֹתֵינוּ and *cf.   Job* 18:7 יֵצְרוּ צַעֲדֵי אוֹנוֹ, "His mighty steps become narrow." There is a talḥin in our passage between צָרוּ and רְחֹבֹתֵינוּ. The passage is to be rendered:

Our steps are narrow, so that we cannot walk
    on the broad ways.

As in 4:14, the last word receives two beats because of its length and the exigencies of the meter.

4:20   The description of the king as "the breath of our nostrils" occurs in the *Tel-el-Amarna Letters* and in an inscription at Abydos concerning the Egyptian pharaoh, Rameses II. The same monarch is described in another inscription as "the beautiful falcon who protects his subjects with his wings and spreads shade over them" (J. de Savignac, in *VT*, vol. 7, 1957, p. 82; Hillers *ad loc.*).

4:21   The historical background for this curse on Edom, occasioned by her indifference and cruelty to Judah's fate, is to be found in Obadiah. There, too, the theme of the drinking of a bitter cup is utilized in a striking figure widespread in the Bible (Jer. 13:13; 25:15 ff.; 48:26; 49:12; 51:7, 39; Ps. 60:5; 75:9; Hab. 2:15-16; Zech. 12:2; Job 21:20). The imagery may derive from the ordeal of the woman suspected of adultery who was compelled to drink "the water of bitterness that brings the curse" (Nu. 5:18). On the other hand, it may be more general in source, perhaps reflecting the use of poison, which those convicted of a crime would be compelled to drink. Socrates' drinking of the hemlock is, of course, a classic example.

5:3 כְּאַלְמָנוֹת is not "like widows", cf. stich a, but the asseverative kaph, "are indeed widows."

Following Symmachus, most moderns add the noun 'ōl, "yoke," at the beginning of the v., rendering "with a yoke on our necks, we are hard driven" (RSV). A more literal translation, "with a yoke on our shoulders we are pursued," makes it clear that this emendation creates an impossible figure of speech—one does not flee with a yoke on one's shoulders. To meet this problem, some commentators add another word to read 'ālāh 'ōl 'āl ṣavvārēnū, "a yoke has been placed upon our shoulders." However, this emended text makes stich a too long. To remedy this new difficulty, it is proposed to treat the two verbs nirdaphnū and yāgaʿnū as doublets and to delete one or the other. This is hardly likely, in view of the Biblical usage linking the roots yāgaʿ and nūaḥ together, as in Jer. 45:3; Ps. 6:7 (where the noun beʾanḥāthī is to be rendered "my couch, my resting place").

It is unnecessary to adopt these deletions and emendations that are based upon multiple errors in the text. The figure in MT is that of a pursuer closing in upon his victim; "Right upon our necks are we pursued." For another example of linguistic contraction, due primarily to metric considerations, cf. the Comm. on 4:9.

5:9 חֶרֶב הַמִּדְבָּר is to be rendered not "the sword of the wilderness" but "the heat of the wilderness" חֶרֶב may be revocalized as חֹרֶב (cf. Gen. 31:40; Isa. 4:6; Jer. 36:30) or is preferably to be recognized as a metaplastic segolate form with the same meaning. The noun ḥerebh occurs in Deut. 24:22, which details a catalog of fevers and illnesses, and in Zech. 11:17, where the parallelism makes its meaning perfectly clear as "heat":

חֶרֶב עַל זְרוֹעוֹ · · · · · זְרֹעוֹ יָבוֹשׁ תִּיבָשׁ

There is no need to rearrange the stichs (ag. Perles). The verse exhibits chiastic parallelism, a // d; b // c:

"We get our bread at the peril of our lives,
    because of the heat of the desert,
    our skin is as hot as an oven,
because of the burning heat of famine."

5:11 עֻנּוּ need not be revocalized as עֻנּוּ (ag. Perles). The *hireq* represents a sharpening of the *shureq* vowel.[47] Cf. *Job* 7:3, יְרְחֵי עָמָל מִנּוּ לִי == מִנּוּ לִי and such forms as אָמְרוּ (from בסרו. בְּסָרוּ (from בָּסָר) = בסרו and אָמְרוּ (from אָמַר).

5:13 The work of grinding grain at the millstone represented the lowest social level and was assigned to slave girls (Ex. 11:5; Isa. 47:2; Ecc. 12:3), who were also exposed to sexual violation (Job 31:10; see the Comm. *ad loc.*). That this lowest form of toil is now imposed upon highborn youth (*bāḥūr* = "chosen one") is the ultimate indignity, even worse than the physical toil involved. *Teḥōn* is best regarded not as an infinitive but as a noun, "mill, millstone." In stich b *'ēṣ* can hardly refer to "firewood, load of wood." The emendation *be'eṣebh*, "from hard labor" (Ehrlich, Hillers), is, however, unnecessary. The noun *'ēṣ* refers to the wooden bar upon which the millstone was carried and by which it was turned when in place. On the noun *'ēṣ,* "handle," of an axe, cf. Deut. 19:5; of a spear, cf. I Sam. 17:7 *Qere* = I Chr. 20:5; II Sam. 21:19; 23:7.

5:21 The verb *ve*nāšūhhāh* may sustain two interpretations in this context: (1) "We will return to You, i.e. we will repent." This is a frequent usage in Biblical Hebrew; e. g., Hos. 14:2; and (2) "we shall be restored (to our previous condition)"; cf. BDB, s.v. *šūbh* 4d (p. 997b). In view of the penitential character of the poem and the references to the nation's sin as the cause of its destruction, the first and more traditional interpretation may be preferable.

The repetition of the root gives a special nuance to the passage, "Restore us . . . and we shall truly be restored" For this "plea—and—responce" formula, see above, pp.

5:22 The closing verse, which is crucial for the meaning and spirit of the entire poem, has long been a crux, in spite of the simplicity of its style and the familiarity of its vocabulary. After

---

[47] This phenomena was first noted by S. Pinsker in his *Mābō' Laniqqūd Ha' ašuri*, p. 153 and much additional evidence has been adduced since. See e.g., A. Z. Rabinowitz-A. Obronin, *Iyyob*, (Jaffa, 5676 = 1916), p. 19.

the plea in vv. 21 and 22, the verse seems hardly appropriate, particularly as the conclusion of the prayer.

The proposed interpretations include: (1) to adopt the extreme expedient of virtually inserting a negative into the text, thus diametrically reversing its meaning: "Thou canst not have utterly rejected us, and be exceeding wroth against us" (JPSV); (2) to treat the verse as an interrogative: "Or hast Thou rejected us, art Thou exceedingly angry with us?" (RSV). There is, however, no evidence for rendering *kī 'im* as "or," whether interrogatively or otherwise. (3) To delete *'im,* which is not expressed by LXX and Pes, and is missing in 6 medieval Hebrew manuscripts. The verse is then rendered: "For Thou hast indeed rejected us, etc." However, the idea remains inappropriate at the end of the penitential prayer for forgiveness and restoration. This objection applies to virtually all the other interpretations. (4) To treat the verse as a conditional sentence: "If Thou shouldst reject us, Thou wouldst be too angry against us" (Ehr., Meed), or "If Thou hast utterly rejected us, then great has been Thine anger against us" (NEB). Actually, there is no true conditional sentence here, stich b being completely parallel to stich a, and adding nothing new to the thought. (5) To understand the *kī 'im* as "unless," on the basis of such passages as Gen. 32:27, *lō' 'ªšallēḥªrhā kī 'im bērakhtānī,* "I shall not let you go unless You bless me," and then render our passage, "Turn us unto Thee . . . unless Thou hast despised us, i.e. completely rejected us" (Rudolph). As Albrektsen points out, in all such instances *kī 'im* is used only after a clause containing or implying a negative. The syntactic difficulty aside, the problem of meaning remains: he who pleads fervently for Divine favor is not psychologically prepared to contemplate the possibility of a permanent and total rejection by God. (6) To render the verse adversatively, "But instead You have utterly rejected us, You have been very angry with us" (Hillers). He explains that the verse "merely restates the present fact: Israel does stand under God's severe judgment." However, the alleged matter-of-fact statement contradicts the cry of v. 20: "Why have you forsaken us so long?" and is totally incompatible with the plea of v. 22, "Turn us unto You, turn us back to You, etc," as noted also by Rudolph.

The clue to the structure and meaning of the passage, I believe, is to be found in Ps. 89 (vv. 51-52). Here, the psalmist's plea for God's help is expressed by the main clause in v. 51, while the grounds or circumstances behind the plea are presented in the subordinate clause in v. 52: "Remember, O Lord, the disgrace of Your servants, how I bear in my bosom the insults of the peoples, with which Your enemies taunt, O Lord, etc." Our passage exhibits the same syntactic structure, the plea being expressed by the main clause (v. 21) and the circumstances surrounding the petition being contained in a subordinate clause (v. 22).

Kī 'im is to be rendered "even if, although," a meaning which has been overlooked in several passages, e.g., Jer. 51:14, *kī 'im millētīkh 'ādām kayyeleq veʿānū ʿālaiyikh hēidad,* "Though I have filled you with men like locusts (i.e. increased your population), yet they (i.e. your assailants) lift up their shout against you" (so Ewald, Keil, Cheyne, BDB, p. 475; Rudolph, *Jeremia* (HAT series, ad loc.). So also Isa. 10:22; Am 5:22, as well as Lam. 3:33 on which see the Comm. It may be added that in medieval Hebrew *veʾim* is frequently used in the sense of "although, even if"; cf. the Passover *Piyyut Beʾrah Dodi,* for many examples.

The verbs in our verse are to be understood as pluperfects (cf. S. R. Driver, *Hebrew Tenses,* p. 22).

The last three verses of Lamentations now offer a vigorous, clear, and appropriate conclusion to the penitential prayer:

"Why do You neglect us eternally, forsake us for so long?
Turn us to Yourself, O Lord, and we shall be restored; renew our days as of old,
even though You had despised us greatly and had been very angry with us."

For a fuller discussion of this important passage, see Hillers, *op. cit.,* pp. 100 f., and our paper, "The Conclusion of the Book of Lamentations," accepted in 1973 for publication in *JBL.*

SELECTED BIBLIOGRAPHY

A. TEXTS AND VERSIONS

The Hebrew Text
BAER, S., and F. DELITZSCH. *The Books of the Old Testament.* Leipzig, 1869-95.
GINSBURG, C. D. *Masoretic Bible.* London, 1st ed., 1894; 2d ed., 1926.
KITTEL, R. *Biblia Hebraica.* 4th ed.; Stuttgart, 1937. Edited by A. Alt and O. E. Eissfeldt (Masoretic notes by P. Kahle).

The Septuagint
SWETE, H. B. *The Old Testament in Greek.* Cambridge, 1887-94.
RAHLFS, A. *Septuaginta.* 2 vols. Stuttgart, 1935.

Aquila, Symmachus, Theodotion
FIELD, F. *Origenis Hexaplorum quae Supersunt.* Oxford, 1875.

The Vulgate
STIER, R. and K. G. W. THEILE. *Polyglotten-Bibel.* 4th ed. Bielefeld-Leipzig, 1875.

The Pešita
Kethabe Kadishe. Edited by S. Lee. London, 1823.

The Targum
Mikraoth Gedoloth. Vilna, 1912, often reprinted.

English Versions
King James or Authorized Version (= A.V.)
Jewish Publication Society Version, Philadelphia, 1917 (= JPSV)
Revised Standard Version, New York, 1932 (= RSV)
The Five Megillot and Jonah, with introduction by H. L. Ginsberg, Jewish Publication Society, 1969.
The New English Bible, Oxford-Cambridge, 1970 (= NEB)
The New American Bible, New York, 1970 (= NAB)

B. MIDRASHIM

Ekhah Rabbati (Vilna, 1938)
Ekhah Zuta (ed. S. Buber, Vilna, 1895)

C. COMMENTARIES

The list is arranged chronologically in order to afford a survey of the history of interpretation of the book.

Rashi (1040-1105)

Abraham Ibn Ezra (1092-1167)

Budde, Karl. "Die Klagelieder," in *Die Fünf Megilloth,* Freiburg i. B., Leipzig, and Tübingen, 1898.

Haller, Max. *Die Klagelieder: Die Fünf Megilloth,* (HAT), Tübingen, 1940.

Meek, Theophile J., and W. P. Merrill. *The Book of Lamentations* (The Interpreter's Bible, vol. VI), New York and Nashville, 1956.

Rudolph, Wilhelm. *Das Buch Ruth—Das Hohe Lied—Die Klagelieder* (KAT), Gutersloh, 1962.

Gotttwald, Norman K., *Studies in the Book of Lamentations* (London, 1962).

Kraus, Hans-Joachim. *Klagelieder* (Threni) (BK). 3d ed., Neukirchen-Vluyn, 1968.

Hillers, Delbert R. *Lamentations* (Anchor Bible, New York, 1972).

D. GENERAL BIBLIOGRAPHY

Driver, G. R., "Hebrew Notes on 'Song of Songs' and 'Lamentations,' " in *Festschrift für Alfred Bertholet,* eds. Walter Baumgartner *et al.,* pp. 134-46. Tübingen, 1950.

―――"Notes on the Text of Lamentations," *ZAW,* 52 (1934), pp. 308-9.

Eissfeldt, O. *Der Gottesknecht bei Deuterojesaia* (Halle, 1933).

Gordis, Robert *The Biblical Text in the Making* (augmented edition, New York, 1971)

―――"The Structure of Biblical Poetry," in *PPS,* chap. 3.

―――"Quotations in Biblical, Oriental and Rabbinic Literature," in *PPS,* chap. 5.

―――*The Book of God and Man, A Study of Job* (Chicago, 1965)

————*Koheleth—The Man and His World* (3rd augmented edition, New York, 1968).

Gray, G. B. *The Forms of Hebrew Poetry* (2nd ed., Intr. by D. N. Freedman) New York 1971.

Perles, Felix. *Analekten zur Textkritik des Alten Testaments.* Neue Folge. Leipzig, 1922.

Robinson, Theodore H. "Anacrusis in Hebrew Poetry," in *Werden und Wesen des Alten Testaments. BZAW,* 66 (1936), pp. 37-40.

————"Notes on the Text of Lamentations," *ZAW,* 51 (1933), pp. 255-59.

————"Once More on the Text of Lamentations," *ZAW,* 52 (1934), pp. 309-10.

H. W. Robinson, *The Cross of the Servant—A Study in Deutero-Isaiah* (London, 1926).

————"The Hebrew Concept of Corporate Personality," in *Werden und Wesen des A. T.,* ed. J. Hempel, 1936, pp. 49 ff.

H. H. Rowley, *The Servant of the Lord and Other Essays* (London, 1952).

INDEX OF ABBREVIATIONS

AB = Anchor Bible
AJSL = American Journal of Semitic Languages
Am. = Amos
Aram. = Aramaic
AV = Authorized Version

B. = Talmud Babli
BDB = Brown-Driver-Briggs (F. Brown, S. R. Driver, and C. A. Briggs, *A Hebrew and English Lexicon of the Old Testament* (Oxford, 1907)
Ber. = Berachot
BGM = R. Gordis, The *Book of God and Man—A Study of Job*
BZAW = *Beihefte, Zeitschrift fuer die alt-testamentlliche Wissenschaft*

chap. = chapter
Comm. = the Commentary

Dan. = Daniel
Deut. = Deuteronomy

Ecc. = Ecclesiastes
ed = edition, edited by
Ehr. = Ehrlich
Erub. = Erubin
Ex. = Exodus
Ezek. = Ezekiel

Ges.-Kautzsch = W. Gesenius and E. Kautzsch, *Grammatik der Hebräischen Sprache* (28th ed.)

Hab. = Habakkuk
Heb. = Hebrew
Hos. = Hosea

Intr. = Introduction
Isa. = Isaiah

JBL = *Journal of Biblical Literature*
Jer. = Jeremiah
JPSV = Jewish Publication Society of America Version (of the Bible)
Jud. = Judges

KMW = R. Gordis, *Koheleth, the Man and His World*

Lam. = Lamentations
Lev. = Leviticus

Mic. = Micah
Mish. = Mishnah, Mishnaic

Nah. = Nahum
NAB = New American Bible (New York, 1970)
NEB = New English Bible (Oxford, 1970)
Nu. = Numbers

Pes = Pešita
PPS = *R. Gordis' Poets, Prophets and Sages*
Pr. = Proverbs
Ps. = Psalms

RSV = Revised Standard Version (of the Bible)

II Chr. = II Chronicles
II Ki. = II Kings
Syr. = Syriac

Tar. = Targum

v. = verse
VT = *Vetus Testamentum*

ZATW = *Zeitschrift fuer die Alttestamentliche Wissenschaft*
ZAW =
Zech. = Zechariah